A HISTORY OF
THE AMERICAN DRAMA

FROM THE CIVIL WAR
TO THE PRESENT DAY

BOOKS BY
ARTHUR HOBSON QUINN

A HISTORY OF THE AMERICAN DRAMA
FROM THE BEGINNING TO THE CIVIL WAR

A HISTORY OF THE AMERICAN DRAMA
FROM THE CIVIL WAR TO THE PRESENT DAY

JAMES A. HERNE

Taken in his study on Convent Avenue, New York, shortly before the production
of *Griffith Davenport*

A HISTORY OF
THE AMERICAN DRAMA

From the Civil War to the Present Day

BY

ARTHUR HOBSON QUINN

*Author of "A History of the American Drama from
the Beginning to the Civil War"*

ILLUSTRATED

———

VOLUME I

FROM AUGUSTIN DALY TO THE
DEATH OF CLYDE FITCH

———

HARPER & BROTHERS PUBLISHERS

NEW YORK AND LONDON

1927

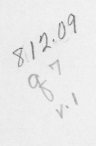

TO
BRANDER MATTHEWS

You will remember how I once suggested to you that we collaborate in this account of our drama—and then after you had declined, on the ground that your working days were over, you began to give me the invaluable assistance of your criticism and encouragement. How many errors you saved me from, you alone know. How the past moments of the stage lived for me through the vivid clutch of your memory, which never lost a fact or a friend, I wish I could record. If you ever read these pages, you will find in them many opinions and conclusions which I dared not let you see. But even when we differed, I felt the courtesy that has endeared you to four generations. You saw the beginning of this era; we saw together many of the plays of to-day. But neither time nor place could weaken the challenge of your spirit to whatever was poor or base, or dull your appreciation of the perennial beauty which survives the changing fashions of the stage.

CONTENTS

in *Arizona*—Picturesque history in *Oliver Goldsmith*—
Light comedies, *The Earl of Pawtucket*, *The Other Girl*
—The play of occult forces in *The Witching Hour* and
The Harvest Moon—Thomas's fine play of toleration,
As a Man Thinks—His sane treatment of the "double
standard"—*The Copperhead* dramatizes the patriot-
ism of the average American—Attack on prohibition
in *Still Waters*—The significance of Thomas's plays in
the struggle to preserve the liberty of the individual—
His constructive criticism of life.

The college-trained playwright—Mansfield gives him
his opportunity in *Beau Brummell*—Fitch shows in
his first play his knowledge of social values and his
ability in dialogue—Adaptations from French and
German—Vivid historical drama in *Nathan Hale* and
Barbara Frietchie—Enters on his best period with *The
Climbers* and *The Girl with the Green Eyes*—The failure
of *Major André*—Powerful melodrama of *The Woman
in the Case*—International contrasts in *Her Great Match*
—Brilliant character portrayal of *The Truth*—Its appreciation abroad—*The City*, produced after his pre-
mature death—Fitch's best characters the incarnation
of one virtue or vice—The reversal of critical opinion
in his case.

ILLUSTRATIONS

PREFACE

IN THIS survey of our native drama from the beginning of modern playwriting to the present day, I have had three objects. The first has been to paint a picture of the drama, not only in its loftiest moments, but also in those no less significant stretches of achievement in which it has been one of the most potent forces in our social history. The second has been to point out among the playwriting of the period the prevailing types and tendencies so that some coherent progress might be apparent. The third has been to indicate the relative merits of the dramatists, not only from my own point of view but also from that of the effect of their plays upon the discriminating criticism of their time. I have not indulged to any degree in quotations from that criticism; it has seemed to me my duty to absorb it and to pass it to my readers, mellowed by the judgment of time.

I have been faced by the difficulty which any historian encounters who dares to treat of the contemporary. But the great importance of recent dramatic achievements in America demands attention, and while I recognize that it is not possible to write of the playwrights of today with the same finality as those of yesterday, I have made a compromise which by a happy accident is reflected approximately in the division of the two volumes of this book.

From Augustin Daly to Clyde Fitch, I have tried to treat the dramatists historically, as well as critically, and to record completely the record of their achievement. How difficult this has been, owing to the fact that so many of the plays remain in manuscript, literally hidden by authors and managers, owing to the inadequacy of the copyright laws, I need not emphasize. From the death of Moody to the present day I have been more selective, but even here I have omitted, I trust, no important work. Sometimes the playwrights have been treated in separate chapters, sometimes they have been grouped according to the kind of play for which they have been distinguished. Usually, their work has been treated as a unit, but in some cases, it has been assigned to different chapters, when the variety of their plays demanded it. In no case have I let the dragon of uniformity keep my readers from any information which I felt should be at their service. I have laid myself open perhaps in consequence to criticism for omissions or inclusions, but I shall not defend myself in detail against it.

It is necessary, however, to explain my general principle of selection. I have treated the drama as a living thing, written for the professional theatre, and I have made no effort to consider the hundreds of dramatic poems which are for reading only, or the thousands of plays upon which the amateur practices his skill. I have tried to set the plays against the background of the stage and to explain dramatic conditions in terms of the American theatre. It seemed unnecessary, therefore, for example, to treat the dramas of Henry James, written for the English stage, and failing on it, however interesting they may be to read. On the other hand, I have written a history of the drama and not of the theatre and I have had to omit any detailed discussion of Little Theatres, Community Theatres, and kindred projects, except in so far as they contribute to establish dramatic opportunity.

I have felt it best to omit any discussion of the one-act play as a type, but rather to treat the short plays of each author under the discussion of his work as a unit. I cannot feel the distinction between the one-act play and the full length play as I do the difference between the short story and the novel. Nearly all our really significant playwrights have made use of the one-act play as a preparation for more important productions, but the condition of our professional stage holds still no great inducement to the writer of the short play. Valuable as these one-act plays are to the beginner in school or college, or to the Little Theatre group, they seem to lie outside my province. Here again, I have made one exception, in the work of Howells, for reasons which need not be repeated here.

I have had such cordial assistance in the progress of this work that it is hardly possible to record my appreciation. From the relatives and friends of the earlier playwrights I have experienced invariably courtesy and confidence, in granting me the opportunity of reading manuscripts as well as providing me with accurate information. Especially from Mrs. James A. Herne, Miss Julie Herne, Mrs. William Vaughn Moody, Miss Mildred Howells, Mr. Edward A. Daly, Dr. Anthony H. Harrigan, and Mr. R. C. Campbell have I received invaluable assistance. I can hardly estimate fully the generous interest of Miss Virginia Gerson and Mrs. J. H. Edmonds, in aiding me to make my discussion of Clyde Fitch authentic. From those in intimate touch with our dramatic past and present like Mr. and Mrs. Otis Skinner, Dr. Horace Howard Furness, Mr. Daniel Frohman, Mr. Hamlin Garland, Mr. William Seymour, Dr. John L. Haney, Mr. Barrett Clark, Mr. Arthur Hornblow, Mr. Kenneth Macgowan, Mr. T. A. Curry, and Mr. George B. Berrell, of California have come constant assistance and encouragement. To the intelligent interest of Miss Alice Kauser, Mr. T. R. Edwards and Mr. F. J. Sheil, of Samuel French, Mr. Howard Rumsey and Mr. R. J. Madden of the American Play Company and Mr. Louis Sherwin of the Charles Frohman office I owe the securing of manuscripts without which my work would have been at a stand still.

If I should thank the living playwrights who have furnished me with information it would simply be to repeat the table of contents, for I have been, I am afraid, ruthless in laying them under contribution. I must mention, however, Mr. Augustus Thomas, Mr. William Gillette, and Mr. David Belasco, who have been particularly cordial in loaning me manuscripts and permitting quotations to be made from their published and unpublished plays. And it has been an especial pleasure to be able to give my readers the benefit of the correspondence which reveals authentically the artistic purpose of Mr. Eugene O'Neill.

Among correspondents in other places, Mrs. Lillian A. Hall of the Shaw Theatre Collection, Miss Jessie L. Farnum of the Library of Congress, Professor George C. D. Odell of Columbia University, Dr. Napier Wilt of the University of Chicago have been especially helpful. My greatest debt has been, however, to my friend, Professor Brander Matthews, who read the manuscript as far as Chapter XII and whose unfaltering memory and wide knowledge of the drama made his advice invaluable.

Among my own colleagues, Professor Schelling has as always been fruitful of counsel. I am grateful for the interest of Provost Penniman, who arranged the leave of absence which permitted the completion of the work, and the help of Professor Baugh, Professor Bradley and Professor Musser has been given unsparingly. Professor Crawford, Professor Doernenburg, Professor Weigand and Professor Scholz have been cordial in helping me solve the vexed questions of foreign sources for American plays.

I wish to acknowledge here also the courtesy of Richard Badger, Walter H. Baker, Boni and Liveright, Brentano's, Dodd, Mead and Company, Samuel French, Henry Holt and Company, The Houghton Mifflin Company, A. A. Knopf, Little, Brown and Company, The MacMillan Company, and Charles Scribner's Sons, in granting permission to quote from plays published by them. I am indebted to the courtesy of Miss Virginia Gerson and Mr. Montrose J. Moses, editors of *The Letters of Clyde Fitch*, for permission to reprint certain extracts from them.

Finally I wish to record the informal but zealous assistance of my wife and children, whose interest is reflected in the play list and in countless other ways.

A. H. Q.

University of Pennsylvania, 1927.

A HISTORY OF
THE AMERICAN DRAMA

VOLUME ONE
FROM AUGUSTIN DALY TO THE
DEATH OF CLYDE FITCH

CHAPTER I

Augustin Daly, Constructive Artist of the Theatre

MODERN American drama begins with Augustin Daly. While Dion Boucicault was a greater playwright and I have elsewhere [1] paid tribute to his influence, it was individual and partially destructive. Daly was a constructive artist and through the transition decades of the sixties and seventies he laid the foundations of the days to come. He was aware, too, how through the apparently tangled skein of our dramatic history runs the clear thread of its consistent progress. He knew how firmly laid were the foundations in domestic and social comedy, in the plays of the frontier, in the drama which had revivified our great historical figures and reflected the struggles that founded and established the nation. He recognized, too, the spirit of our fine romantic tragedies and comedies. More than once he decries the general lack of knowledge of what our playwrights had already accomplished, and chooses for special mention *Brutus, Charles II, Francesca da Rimini, The Gladiator, The Broker of Bogota*, and *Jack Cade*, and suggests the revival of the plays of Mrs. Howe and Mrs. Mowatt. How he would have enjoyed the revival of *Fashion* at the Provincetown in 1924! He was hospitable to new playwrights, as we shall see. And one of his most significant criticisms, possibly aimed at Bronson Howard's *One of Our Girls*, suggests that if a contrast is desired between a "wild whooping American girl" and a conservative family, why should an American playwright lay his scene in a foreign country, when "a respectable New York, Boston or Philadelphia family would be equally amazed and distressed by such a

[1] *History of the American Drama from the Beginning to the Civil War*, Chap. XIII.

1

girl." Most important is his prophecy that "our national drama will be established without restriction as to subject or plot. The coming dramatist will be indifferent on that score. Neither Shakespeare nor any of his contemporaries, nor Corneille nor Racine, nor Schiller nor Goethe made the national drama of their native lands by the delineation of national character only. . . . We must not exact of American dramatists more than has been demanded of its dramatists by any country. The present masterpieces of the stage, in every tongue, are pictures of the passions of mankind in general, rather than attempts at national portrait painting." He recognized that notwithstanding the realistic tendency in our literature, the theatre, which by its very nature reverts to the unusual and the heroic, can never entirely lose the flavor of romance. Not all his prophecies came true, but his picture of "the silent brooding, observant boy sitting in the gallery" who is to write the play of the future, was to be fulfilled.

This is an account of our drama and not of our theatre, yet before we discuss the creative work of Augustin Daly it is necessary to portray in brief the theatrical situation in the United States during the decade from 1860 to 1870, in order that we may understand the paucity of playwriting during this transition period. It was an epoch of changing and of disturbed conditions. Before the Civil War it had been the custom for large cities and even smaller towns to have their stock companies. Stars, both native and foreign, visited these towns and were supported by the local companies. While the invention of the traveling company with one play, eventually broke down this system, the transition was gradual. In 1872 Lawrence Barrett took his company but not the scenery of his plays, but in 1876 when J. G. Stutz took out *Rose Michel*, the scenery accompanied the play. The season of 1878-79 marked the end of the stock company at the Walnut Street Theatre in Philadelphia, and Otis Skinner, who was then a member of it, attributes the change to the desire of the public to see new faces and costumes. He believes that the stock system led

2

to versatility rather than supreme excellence, but that on the whole it provided a training for the actor which the traveling company did not furnish. In New York, the situation differed from that of the rest of the country and stock companies continued until the close of the century. Obviously the effect upon the theatre would be the emphasis laid upon New York City as the origin or the goal of successful plays.

On the drama it had at first a destructive effect, as it limited the opportunity of playwrights in Philadelphia, Boston, Baltimore, Charleston, Chicago, Cincinnati, and even Mobile or New Orleans, of having their plays produced in those cities. It meant that playwrights would go to New York, as Bronson Howard did, and that for our purpose the record of the New York stage becomes, much more exclusively than in the earlier period, the background of the professional drama. The character of the New York audiences and the preferences and artistic sense of the producers becomes therefore of more and more significance. The increase in the foreign element in New York City spelled little good to the drama of American life and the attitude of such a leading manager as Lester Wallack, who though American born was much more British in his tastes and sympathies even than his English father, was unfavorable to the production of native plays. Even more striking is the fact that New York, though the producing center, did not often develop playwrights who would reveal the drama that lies inherent in its multiform civilization. Augustin Daly was born in North Carolina, Bronson Howard in Detroit, Steele MacKaye in Buffalo, William Gillette in Hartford, David Belasco in San Francisco, Clyde Fitch in Elmira, Augustus Thomas in St. Louis, Langdon Mitchell and John Luther Long in Philadelphia.

The effect of the Civil War upon the theatre was at first disturbing, but was not of long continuance. Niblo's Garden was closed from April 29 to December 23, 1861. The Bowery Theatre was dilapidated by military occupation in May, 1862. The Boston Theatre closed on April 6, 1861, after a short season of only sixteen weeks. But by 1862 the theatres in New York, Philadelphia and Boston seem to have been playing to good business, and while according to Rhodes,[1] the *Richmond Enquirer* of October 10, 1863, inveighs against the theatre, the Richmond Theatre, which had burned in 1862, was reopened in February, 1863. Of much greater importance was the shifting in the center of population in New York City which resulted in the closing of the old Broadway Theatre in 1859, the destruction of the Chatham Theatre in 1862 and the transfer of the Wallacks, father and son, from the Lyceum to the new Wallack's Theatre in 1861. "Wallack's" continued as the leading theatre in New York, but it was devoted largely to the production of British comedy except when John E. Owens played his character parts in *Self* or *Solon Shingle*. There was a competent company at Niblo's Garden, but here British plays were performed almost exclusively, except during the visits of Edwin Forrest and J. H. Hackett. Forrest kept in his repertory the romantic tragedies of the earlier days, such as Bird's *Gladiator* and *Broker of Bogota*, Stone's *Metamora* and Conrad's *Jack Cade*, while Hackett was still playing *A Kentuckian's Trip to New York* and *A Yankee in England*. Edwin Booth played Payne's *Brutus* at times, though his interest lay in other fields.

But it was not only the personal preference of a great actor that preserved the earlier drama. I notice, during the sixties, performances at the New Bowery Theatre of old favorites such as *Brutus, The Poor of New York, Paul Jones, Putnam, The Octoroon, Horse Shoe Robinson, Moll Pitcher, The New York Fireman, Nick of the Woods, A Glance at New York*, and *The Surgeon of Paris*. Noah's *She Would Be A Soldier* was played at Barnum's Museum in 1866, and J. S. Jones' *Paul Revere* was put on at the Boston Museum in 1876. Of the American plays of an earlier period, the tragedies of Robert Montgomery Bird and Robert T. Conrad and the comedies of Joseph Stevens Jones were to show the most vitality, with the

[1] *History of the United States*, V, 425.

exception of the composite *Rip van Winkle*, and the supreme creation of the early drama, Boker's *Francesca da Rimini*, which was to last until the present century.

Although no great play arose from the Civil War during the period of conflict, the theme was by no means neglected. Few of these acted dramas were printed and we can in general judge of their contents and their effect only by theatrical history. As early as January 16, 1861, an anonymous play, *Our Union Saved, or Marion's Dream* was played at the Olympic Theatre in which "the President" was played by D. J. Maguire. On February 11, 1861, George H. Miles inserted "a second act of national tableau" entitled "Uncle Sam's Magic Lantern," into a spectacle called *The Seven Sisters*, which had formerly nothing to do with the Civil War, but which filled Laura Keene's Theatre for one hundred and seventy-seven nights. The interpolated patriotic scene had a delightful mixture of characters, including Uncle Sam, Disunion, Diogenes, Massachusetts, South Carolina, Virginia, Columbia and Liberty. The older Revolutionary drama was revived at the Boston Museum, *Our Flag is Nailed to the Mast* being given on April 30, 1861, and a Civil War episode was added to *The Liberty Tree* in June.

The speedy dramatization of events during the War of 1812 was paralleled during the Civil War by the industry of Charles Gayler, the dramatist who supplied the New Bowery Theatre. Bull Run was fought on July 21, 1861, and on August 15, *Bull Run, or the Sacking of Fairfax Courthouse* was on the stage. It ran for four weeks and was afterward revived. Gayler also wrote *Hatteras Inlet, or Our Naval Victories*, put on at the New Bowery, November 2, 1861, three months after the event. His speed in dramatization was outclassed, however, by that of Harry Seymour, whose *Capture of Fort Donelson* celebrated at the New Bowery Theatre, on February 22, 1862, Grant's triumph on February 16, in what was really the first great Union victory of the war.

John T. Raymond appeared in *The National Guard* at

Niblo's Garden in 1862 and another anonymous play, *How To Avoid Drafting*, at the Bowery Theatre in the same year sounds like a comedy. There seems to have been a lull in the Civil War plays in New York during 1863, but in January, 1864, *The Unionist's Daughter, or Life in the Border States* was put on at the Bowery. At the Tremont Temple in Boston, the comic opera of *Il Recrutio*, in which seventy members of the Forty-ninth Massachusetts took part, reveals in the program of its one performance how comedy entered into the conception of the war, even in 1863.

These plays were hastily written and their disappearance is hardly to be regretted. One of the few survivals, *Off to the War* by Benjamin E. Woolf, whose *Mighty Dollar* was later to make a great popular success, was played in Boston in 1861. It is a one-act farce comedy which reflects the impatience of the public at the contradictory news from the front and satirizes the attitude of the colored contrabands. Another survival, *A Supper in Dixie*, written by William C. Reynolds under the name of James Triplet, and played in Chicago in 1865, is a farcical treatment of the situation in Richmond in February of that year. There is a ring of truth, however, in the description of the difficulties that strolling actors found in obtaining food, which makes the play appealing in spite of its farcical character.

Of much greater interest is the melodrama, *The Guerillas*, by James D. McCabe, Jr., for, according to the preface, it was the first original drama to be produced in the Southern Confederacy. It was performed for the first time at the Richmond Varieties, on December 22, 1862, and had a successful run of a week. As a drama its merits are not high, but there is a certain vigor in the intensity of the patriotic feeling which appealed to a Southern audience. The destruction of homes and other property by the guerillas or irregular troops who operated in the western portion of Virginia, forms the motive of the play. The hero is the youngest of three generations, the eldest of whom is a veteran of the Revolution, and the author dwells upon the note so often struck in Southern literature, that of the purity of their descent from the older American stock. General Frémont is one of the villains of the play, and is the center of an incident reminiscent of *Measure for Measure*. The negro character, Jerry, represents the loyalty to his master which was later to provide so appealing a motive in *Secret Service*, and in the novels of Thomas Nelson Page and Francis Hopkinson Smith.

At the end of the war the plays began to multiply. *Grant's Campaign, or Incidents of the Rebellion* by John F. Poole at the New Bowery in December, 1865; *The Union Prisoner* by Milnes Levick at Barnum's Museum in December, 1867; *British Neutrality* by T. B. De Walden at the Olympic in July, 1869; *Ulysses, or the Return of U. S. Grant* at the Union Square Theatre in September, 1871, and *The Returned Volunteer* at the Academy of Music in October, 1871, indicate perhaps sufficiently the nature of the themes treated. The Battle of Gettysburg forms the scene of the third act of Augustin Daly's *Norwood* (1867), and there is some vigor in the picture of the battle scene, even if it is conventional. Dion Boucicault's *Belle Lamar*, produced at Booth's Theatre, August 10, 1874, has been earlier described and was probably the first Civil War play that can be considered seriously. After its comparative failure, the motive was to wait until the eighties to be brought to popular approval with William Gillette's *Held by the Enemy*.

The Color Guard by Colonel Alfred R. Calhoun is said to have been popular with the Union soldiers after the war. The author, who had an interesting political career, wrote from experience, but his play has little dramatic structure. Its appeal came doubtless from the courage of the hero, Louis Ludlow, who preserved the colors of his company, in defiance of the probabilities, even in Libby Prison. To a reader of today the greatest interest lies in its reflection of the loyalty of the Tennessee mountaineers to the Union, dramatized in the words of Father Allen, who dies satisfied that "the flag has

7

come back to Tennessee." *The Color Guard* was played as far west as San Francisco, where General Grant is reported to have witnessed the performance in 1879 at the California Theatre.

But to return to the first significant figure in the record of our drama after the Civil War. Augustin Daly was born in Plymouth, North Carolina, July 20, 1838, the son of Captain Denis Daly, a sea-captain and ship owner, and of Elizabeth, daughter of Lieutenant John Duffey, of the British army. His mother, early left a widow, brought her two boys to New York City, where they soon became frequent attendants at the theatres and were members of the amateur groups, which under such names as the "Burton Association" or the "Murdoch Association" were the precursors of the Little Theatre movement of the present day. Joseph Francis Daly, in his authoritative life of his brother, tells us that Augustin rarely if ever acted. His interest from the beginning lay in the creation and production of plays, and he began his career as a manager in 1856 in Brooklyn by hiring the one available hall and boldly attempting a varied performance, including scenes from *Macbeth* and *The Toodles*, with all the artistic and financial difficulties that might have been expected. At the beginning of his career, Augustin Daly showed the unfaltering courage, the fertility of resource and the optimism under discouraging circumstances which were to carry him through years of struggle and apparent defeat to the ultimate goal of his desires. In many of his qualities and in certain of his experiences he presents a striking parallel to our first playwright and producer, William Dunlap. In their ardent love of the beautiful, in their keen sense of the theatrically effective, in their determination to improve the conditions of the playhouse, they were alike. Alike too they were in their introduction of the contemporary drama of France and Germany and their use of native themes for their own plays. But while Dunlap failed, under the intolerable burden imposed upon him by circumstances, Daly organized a company that was to become the

8

standard of artistic achievement for this country, established his own theatre in London and even invaded the Continent in 1886 and carried an English-speaking company to Germany for the first time in three centuries.[1]

At the age of twenty-one, Daly became the dramatic critic for the New York *Courier*, retaining his connection with this paper for ten years and writing also at times for the *Sun*, the *Times*, the *Express* and the *Citizen*. Among the shifting conditions in the theatre of the early sixties and the disturbed state of New York City in the days of the draft riots, Daly attentively studied plays, which he criticized honestly and with growing skill.

His career as a dramatist began with *Leah the Forsaken*, an adaptation from the German melodrama, *Deborah*, written in 1850 by Salomon Hermann von Mosenthal, a North German playwright, then living in Vienna. Daly did not translate the play himself and indeed throughout his entire career he seems to have depended upon others for the first drafts of his foreign adaptations. *Leah the Forsaken* was first produced at the Howard Athenæum in Boston, December 8, 1862, with Kate Bateman in the title role, and then in January, 1863, at Niblo's Garden. It had a great success in both places. The theme is the persecution of the Jews and the scene an Austrian village in the Eighteenth Century. The repudiation of Leah by her Christian lover, her consequent misery and her final acceptance of fate, provided a medium in which Kate Bateman starred in England and which had a long stage life. Daly's adaptation was quite a free one. The blank verse of the original, perhaps necessarily, became prose, and many of the speeches were cut. Sometimes Daly's alterations seem improvements, as in the scene in which Father Hermann protects Leah by simply holding up the Cross. At the end, however, where Daly adds a scene and brings in Nathan, a renegade Jew, to represent persecution, Mosenthal's conclusion seems

---

[1] Edwin Booth had acted in Germany in 1881, but was supported by a German company.

simpler and more artistic. Critical judgment as well as popular taste greeted *Leah* with approval in New York and Boston. George William Curtis [1] wrote enthusiastically of it.

Daly was to turn once more to Mosenthal for his inspiration. In 1873 he adapted a tragedy bordering on the melodrama, *Madeleine Morel.* It is a powerful play, somewhat after the manner of Dumas, in which a young girl who, through her loss of natural protectors, has become the mistress of an Englishman, Lord Durley, and is forced to leave her lover, Count Julian Dalberg, who has offered to marry her. The final scene, in a cathedral, in which Madeleine, who is about to take the veil, recognizes Julian, about to be married to another, and goes mad, provided Clara Morris with an opportunity for effective acting. One scene of this play, in which Lord Durley enters Madeleine's reception room from an inner apartment with his coat and hat and indicates thereby his relation to her, points forward perhaps to a similar situation, much praised for its adroitness, in Pinero's *Iris* and Walter's *The Easiest Way.*

The success of *Leah the Forsaken* led to several commissions for Daly, mainly adaptations from the French and German, which have come down only by title. With some assistance he wrote a play on a Biblical theme, *Judith,* in 1864, in which the career of the Jewish heroine is brought up to the death of Holofernes. He next turned to the field in which he was to score several popular successes, the dramatization of the British and American novel. The managers of the New York Theatre suggested to him in the fall of 1866, that he adapt Charles Reade's powerful study of jealousy, *Griffith Gaunt.* Daly constructed a play which made full use of the dramatic scenes of the novel, especially in the trial in the last act. The English law in the Eighteenth Century forbade a person accused of murder the benefit of counsel, and Kate Gaunt, who

---

[1] *Harper's Weekly*, VII (March 7, 1863), 146. Curtis drew a parallel between the persecution of the Jews in Europe and the race prejudice against the negroes which, he claimed, was the cause of the War. He said, "Go and see *Leah* and have the lesson burned in upon your mind, which may help to save the national life and honor."

is falsely accused of the murder of her husband, is compelled to defend herself. This gave Rose Eytinge, whom Daly had chosen for the part, a fine opportunity of which she seems to have taken full advantage. Daly altered the plot at this point, certainly in the interest of theatrical effectiveness, by bringing Griffith Gaunt in person to the trial scene.

Up to 1867 Daly had been experimenting in the arrangement of material already clothed in literary form by other hands. He attempted in his first original play he produced to deal with real life in New York City. So far as the setting of *Under the Gaslight* is concerned, he succeeded. The home of Laura and Pearl Courtland, with its atmosphere of comfort, the basement to which Laura flies when the secret of her birth is discovered, the police court in which she is given into the custody of the blackmailer Byke, the pier on the North River from which she is thrown, were all elements in a stage reality which goes back of course to Benjamin A. Baker's *A Glance at New York* in 1848, and perhaps more immediately to Boucicault's *The Poor of New York*. Daly developed a scene which he claimed was suggested by the railroad crossing over which he passed daily. Snorkey, the wounded soldier, who watches over the heroine, is bound to the railroad track by the villain, Byke. But Laura, who has escaped from both her captors and the North River, is in a near-by signal house where she has been locked at her own request. When the audience has been worked up sufficiently, Laura breaks out and saves Snorkey from an approaching train. This situation wa, copied almost immediately by Boucicault in *After Dark* and the court proceedings which ensued established Daly's exclusive rights in this stage property for the United States.

It has been suggested that Daly owed this scene to *The Engineer*, produced at the Victoria Theatre in London in 1865,[1] and the existence of a copy of *The Engineer* among the Daly manuscripts indicates that he knew of the play. But the circumstances are entirely different. Randall Matthews,

[1] Brown. *History of the New York Stage*, II, 384.

the villain of *The Engineer*, has taken a rail out of the track over which his rival is speeding. The engine comes on the stage and kills him instead, but without employing effectively that principle of suspense which animated the scene in *Under the Gaslight*, and which was not beneath the notice of the playwright who sounded the summons of the Scottish thanes which waked the porter in *Macbeth*.

While *Under the Gaslight* is realistic in its setting, its characters are conventional. Snorkey, probably the most enjoyable, is modeled directly on the comic servant of the French *mélodrame*, although he is used to criticize the failure of the United States Government to take care of its wounded soldiers. The account of Laura's early life is reminiscent of Sardou's *La Perle noire*, a play Daly was to use again in *A Flash of Lightning*. What remains, however, to Daly's credit is a compact structure, with interesting dialogue at times and at least an attempt at realism, even if he produced only its skeleton. The great success of the play was especially pleasing to him, for it was his first real effort as a producer. He had leased the New York Theatre for the summer season and selected his own company, which appeared for the first time on August 12, 1867. The play has often been revived, and proved to be one of the most popular melodramas written in English. It was not only played in London in 1868 under its own name, but it was also adapted as *London by Gaslight*.[1]

⌊Augustin Daly wrote, altered or adapted from British and American novels, from French or German dramas, or from earlier British plays, about ninety productions which actually saw the stage. Many of these have been known only by title for Daly published very few of his plays.⌋ Fortunately I have been able to examine the manuscripts remaining until recently in the hands of his executors, and while these are not complete, they contain the most important of his productions. The most profitable way to study his work is first, to discuss those plays which are usually referred to as his original dramas, next to examine his adaptations from English fiction and from foreign

[1] See Play List.

languages, with some reference to his alterations of earlier British drama.

Under the first group are to be included *Under the Gaslight*, *A Flash of Lightning*, *Horizon*, *Divorce* and *Pique*, *Roughing It* and probably *Judith*, *The Red Scarf*, and *The Dark City*. *A Flash of Lightning* was produced at the Broadway Theatre, June 10, 1868. It was another sensation drama of the type of *Under the Gaslight*. The main plot, concerned with the accusation of the theft of a gold chain by an innocent girl and the discovery that a flash of lightning had destroyed the chain and carried it into a coal scuttle, was based upon Sardou's *La Perle noire*, in which Christianne is accused of the theft of a locket and a necklace of pearls. The complicated relations of the Fallon family, however, have little connection with the incidents of the French drama, which is primarily a satire upon the methods of detection employed by the burgomaster, M. Tricamp. The climax of Daly's play was the burning of a Hudson River steamboat through the furnace room catching fire in the effort to race with another boat. The heroine, who has been chained to the bed in one of the staterooms, is of course saved in the nick of time. In the *Life of Daly* it is stated that the playwright had unwittingly disclosed a source of danger in the construction of furnaces that was usually overlooked. *A Flash of Lightning* was successful, running till August third and was later revived. But it is a melodrama, and marks no improvement upon Daly's earlier work. Nor was *The Red Scarf*, a story of life on the Aroostook among the New England mills, of any real significance. This play is attributed to him by Judge Daly, and the manuscript, though not autograph, is signed by him on the title-page. Yet it does not read like his work and it may be a joint product. It is a sensational play, and the principle of suspense, so well used in *Under the Gaslight*, is again employed in the final scene. Gail Barston, the hero, is trapped by his rival, Harvey Thatcher, the owner of the Dark Falls Mills, who binds him to a log that is to be sawed in two. Then he sets fire to the mill so that all trace of Gail will be lost and he will be supposed to have deserted May Hamilton, whom both men love. She arrives in time to save him, of course. *The Red Scarf* was first played at Conway's Park Theatre in Brooklyn in 1869, and was repeated at the Bowery Theatre, where it was quite at home.

The next play, however, was a great advance. *Horizon*, first produced at the Olympic Theatre on March 21, 1871, begins in New York City but is speedily transported to the West of Bret Harte. Med, the girl who has been brought west by her worthless father, and Lodor, the bad man who protects her after her father's murder, are representatives of that moral contrast which Bret Harte loved to draw. But Med is not too bright or good by any means and Lodor renounces his claim upon her affections, in favor of her Eastern lover, in a scene which for simplicity of language and restraint of passion goes far to establish Daly's claim to be the first of the modern realists in American playwriting. Sundowne Rowse, "a distinguished member of the Third House at Washington," is a vividly drawn character and the prototype of many a stage lobbyist, even if he is a bit reminiscent of Jefferson S. Batkins in J. S. Jones' *A Silver Spoon.* The Indian attacks by night on the boat [1] and later on the stockade seem to have been very effective. Competent critics like Brander Matthews and Laurence Hutton and rival managers like A. M. Palmer testify to the merit of the play on the stage, and certainly a reading of it reveals Daly's power of character drawing and his ability in writing straightforward and interesting conversation. *Horizon* ran for two months.

Horizon, though a better drama, was outdone in popular favor by *Divorce*, which began its run of two hundred nights at the Fifth Avenue Theatre, on September 5, 1871, and was later played throughout the country. In *Divorce*, Daly borrowed the idea of the lengths to which a man's unreasoning

---

[1] Daly used a panorama probably repainted from that of the *Midsummer Night's Dream* at the same theatre a few years earlier.

jealousy may lead him from Anthony Trollope's novel, *He Knew He Was Right*. The cause of the jealousy, the attentions of an older man who is a philanderer, is the same, as is also the resulting derangement of the husband, his abduction of their child, and the visit of the wife to his retreat to secure the return of the boy. But the outcome of the play is very different from that of the novel, and the character drawing is quite dissimilar. Louis Trevelyan is an English gentleman of wealth whose passion is for having his own way and his mental trouble is carried through three volumes until he dies of it. Alfred Adrianse, in *Divorce*, is not by any means so insane and yet he is placed under restraint and is cured so that the family may be reunited. His wife, Fanny Ten Eyck, is more culpable, at least of encouraging Captain Lynde's attentions, than is Emily Trevelyan, yet the natural independence of the American woman makes her handle her affairs better and Daly changed entirely the almost abject attitude which, despite her stubborn opposition, Mrs. Trevelyan was perhaps forced by the English law to assume. This difference between the position of husband and wife in England and America is only one of the aspects of life in which the play differs from its source. Trollope's novel is shot through with social and financial contrasts and he carries on several love stories, only one of which is even faintly reflected in Daly's play. There is no social contrast in the drama, and our interest lies in the study of the relations of the married couples, one serious and one almost burlesque. The detective is most like his British counterpart, but Adrianse does not employ him in the first place; Burritt is brought to the home of Mrs. Ten Eyck by Lu, Fanny's sister, who is bored by her husband and represents the silly woman who plays with the idea of divorce for the sake of excitement.

Of the twenty-four characters in Daly's play, only six are taken from the novel. Mrs. Kemp, who tries to bring Alfred and Fanny together, is perhaps suggested by Lady Milborough, but she is an entirely different person. Daly uses none of the language of Trollope and the manner in which he has sharpened the action of the episodes he has taken can be appreciated only by those who have read the leisurely pages of *He Knew He Was Right*. The play may be considered as one of his original productions, less significant than *Horizon*, but more truly his own than *Pique* and dealing with an institution that was becoming a menace to the social life of America. Daly shows truly that the only happy marriages are those based on mutual forbearance, due to the conception of the married relation as a permanent one between equals. He shows, too, the futility of divorce as a cure for the difficulties of married life. With this problem the British novel was scarcely concerned, for divorce is hardly considered as a way out and Trollope had the conventional attitude of his country that the real happiness of a wife lay in obedience to her husband. The very title of Daly's play indicated the thorough domestication of the drama.

Between the production of *Divorce* and *Pique*, Daly the producer had been very active. On January 1, 1873, the Fifth Avenue Theatre burned. Daly immediately leased the old New York Theatre and called it Daly's Fifth Avenue Theatre, which he opened on January 21, 1873.

In the same year Daly brought together a number of managers of New York City to form an association for the conduct of their business, to loan players to each other and in general to avoid the disadvantages that come from competition. Fechter, Booth, Wallack, Palmer, Jarrett and Daly were members. Perhaps the "theatrical trusts" of later days may date the beginning of their career from this apparently useful and natural alliance.

In 1873 the New Fifth Avenue Theatre was built on Twenty-eighth Street near Broadway, where once had stood the St. James Theatre in which Steele MacKaye displayed his Delsarte system of acting. On December 3, 1873, this theatre was opened. At about this time Daly gave up the Grand Opera House and the Broadway Theatre, as the old New York

Theatre had come to be called, and confined his attention to the new house. He continued in its management until the failure of *The Dark City* in 1877 forced him to relinquish it. After his trip abroad, which laid the foundations for his later associations with the foreign theatres, he transformed the old Broadway Theatre into Daly's Theatre—opening it on September 18, 1879. This theatre was long associated with his name.

It was at the New Fifth Avenue Theatre in Twenty-eighth Street that *Pique* was presented for the first time on December 14, 1875. It ran for two hundred and thirty-eight nights and was afterward played in various places and by various actors. The original part of Mabel Renfrew was created by Fanny Davenport, who with it began her career as a star. There are two main elements of interest in *Pique*,—Mabel Renfrew loves Raymond Lessing, who cares for her but cares more for money and so proposes marriage to her young stepmother, Lucille. Out of pique, Mabel accepts the hand of Captain Arthur Standish but when she is forced to live with his family she revolts and there is consequent unhappiness. This theme, which is developed throughout the first two Acts and part of the third, was taken from a British novel, *Her Lord and Master*, by Florence Marryatt. The scene is transferred to this country and some changes are made in the plot and characters. Added to the latter are Dr. Gossit, a guardian angel, and Thorsby Gill and Sammy Dymple, comedy parts, the first played by John Drew. In both stories the husband departs after a scene in which the wife tells him that she does not love him and the lover offers her his protection only to be refused. Through this scene the wife begins to realize that she does care for the man she has married. At times Daly has even borrowed the language of *Her Lord and Master*. He has omitted, however, the tiresome religious discussions of the novel and there is no social difference to add to the wife's dislike in *Pique* as there is in the British source.

The second theme is the rescue of Mabel's child who has been

17

stolen by two thugs who have taken him to "Beggars' Paradise." Here Daly left the novel entirely and created a scene which must have been as thrilling as anything of recent years. Both the den and an attic above it are shown and in the attic Thorsby and Dymple conceal themselves while the grandfather, Matthew Standish, risks his life to bring the ransom; the mother comes in disguised as old Mother Thames, one of the decoys, and the father descends through the trap door to apparently certain death to hunt for his little son. In the meantime Dymple has escaped from the attic *via* the window to call the police! The child is finally returned by Raitch, a character of Daly's creation who is a reformed if illiterate member of the gang.

This theme was probably suggested to Daly by the abduction of Charlie Ross and while it is treated melodramatically, the characters of Matthew, Mabel, and Mary, the girl whom his family wished Arthur to marry, are well drawn. The play is not as original as *Divorce* but it is better constructed. Neither, however, is of the same significance as *Horizon* for in that play we had an original theme and setting, fine construction, natural language and character drawing of indisputable veracity.

The Dark City, produced at the Fifth Avenue Theatre on September 10, 1877, was a melodrama with conventional situations, revolving around the suppression of a will which disinherited an elder daughter in favor of her stepsister. Daly had hoped for great results from the realistic effects of this play, and one of the scenes, in which the villain cuts the rope from which the hero is descending from the roof of Sybil's lodging house, seems to hold fine possibilities as a thrilling episode. But the play failed and it brought Daly's career at the Fifth Avenue Theatre to an end.

It is not easy to draw any helpful distinction between *Pique* and *Divorce* on the one hand and those more definite dramatizations of fiction which followed *Griffith Gaunt*. In November, 1867, at the request of the Worrell sisters, he dramatized *A*

18

Legend of Norwood, or Village Life in New England, by
Henry Ward Beecher. The play was not a success. It is,
however, much better reading than the novel, for the action is
quicker and the humor, provided by Peter Sawmill, whom Daly
changed from a white man to a negro, and the "boy from
Hardscrabble" who becomes a drummer boy, seems to be
largely original with the playwright. The conversation between these two on the art of war is even yet worth reading
and it secured what little success the play achieved. Daly used
the language of the novel at times, but he changed the plot
considerably in order to bring all the principal characters
together on the field of Gettysburg. While many of the characters are conventional there is in the first two Acts a realistic
picture of New England life before the war.

The last play Daly wrote for the old New York Theatre, in
January, 1868, was his dramatization of *Pickwick Papers.* He
cleverly made the most of the apparently hopeless profusion of
incident in the novel, introducing in four acts and twelve
scenes the most important elements of the comedy. In the
first scene the four Pickwickians are introduced at Wardle's
House, Tupman is shot by Winkle and Jingle persuades Rachel
to elope. Sam Weller comes on in scene two and there is
a delightful scene at Mrs. Bardell's home. Acts II and III
include the adventure of the lady in yellow curl papers and
the trial scene of Bardell *versus* Pickwick.

One of the most striking successes of Daly's early days as a
manager at the Fifth Avenue Theatre was his adaptation of
Wilkie Collins' *Man and Wife,* first produced September 13,
1870. In this effort Daly succeeded in producing a successful
dramatization where Wilkie Collins himself had failed. He
altered the order of incidents, placing first the interview between Geoffrey and Julius Delamayn, which gives Geoffrey the
alternative of deserting Anne Sylvester or being disinherited
by his father, and skillfully compressed the many complicated
scenes of *Man and Wife* into five stirring acts. Daly's sure
dramatic instinct showed not only in what he put in, but even

more clearly perhaps in what he left out. The foot race is omitted and the long interval between the flight of Anne and the conference at Lady Lundie's, in which Anne proves that she is Geoffrey's wife, is bridged over admirably. The scene of the attempted murder is also a good example of compression. Daly proved again that what carries a play is fine characterization, and the part of Anne Sylvester gave Clara Morris her first great opportunity to portray the woman who saves another woman by proving her own marriage to a man she despises. Mrs. Gilbert played the part of Hester Dethridge, the apparently dumb woman, with real distinction. Of the other dramatizations of Wilkie Collins' novels, *No Name* was a failure and *The Woman in White* seems not to have been performed.

Roughing It has been described as a dramatization of Mark Twain's novel but it is not. The first two Acts are an amusing satire on the sentimental romantic play with the scene laid in New York City but with an unmistakable French flavor. When MacDuffie, the stern father, takes the center of the stage and proclaims to Antoinetta, "I am your father—you are my daughter," the heroine looks at him naïvely and replies, "Father, you terrify me!" In the third Act the characters are sent off to Simpson's Bar and a burlesque on the Western life of Bret Harte and Mark Twain follows. We meet the "Amiable Arkansas," the "pale fire-eater, Slade," to say nothing of the chief of the Goshoots who wants to mary Antoinetta, who circumvents him by dancing the tribe into submission. It is all very amusing and seems to have been successful.

It would not be possible, even were it desirable, to compare critically all of Daly's definite adaptations from the French and German, nor is it wise to indulge in hasty generalizations concerning them. Daly varied greatly in the fidelity with which he followed his models, and actual comparison of those extant plays of which the originals are also available, is necessary to reveal his varying methods.

The earliest of the adaptations of French drama that has

Augustin Daly

survived was his version of Victorien Sardou's *Le Papillon* (1862), played as *Taming a Butterfly* at the Olympic Theatre, February 25, 1864. Among the Daly manuscripts is a printed version of this play, in which the French scene is preserved. It has, however, been altered extensively; the scene has been changed to New York City and it has been given a new title, *Delmonico's, or Larks up the Hudson,* under which it appeared in June, 1871, at the Fifth Avenue Theatre. This is the only case so far as Daly's translations of Sardou are available, in which he transferred the scene to America. Sardou remained his favorite among French playwrights. One of the most interesting of the translations from this skilful constructor of plays was *Hazardous Ground,* produced at Conway's Park Theatre in Brooklyn, March, 1867. It is based upon Sardou's comedy of *Nos Bons Villageois,* which had been performed at the Théâtre du Gymnase in Paris in 1866.[1] The adaptation is quite free. Daly preserved the central situation in which a young visitor from the city makes love to the wife of the baron and mayor of the town and, being discovered in her grounds at night, feigns that he is a thief. The characters are reduced in number and the first Act is practically omitted. The language at times follows the original closely and at other times, especially at the end, is radically changed. The result is a gain in unity and it is significant that these early scenes which Daly omitted were probably written in by Sardou to lengthen the piece and thus avoid the production of another play on the same night, with a consequent loss of receipts to the author.

When Daly leased the Grand Opera House in the fall of 1872, he opened it with a free rendering of Sardou's *Le Roi Carotte* (1872), under the title of *King Carrot.* It was a spectacle, with music by Offenbach, and dealt with the Krokodynes, a people who discarded their monarch in favor of a king from the kitchen garden, with unhappy results. Other adap-

---

[1] An adaptation of *Nos Bons Villageois* by A. W. Young, under the title of *A Dangerous Game,* had been played at Wallack's Theatre, February 4, 1867.

tations of Sardou were *Folline*, from *La Maison Neuve* (1866),[1] in 1874, a satire on the new generation in France who were breaking away from the older standards of family and commercial life, *Odette* in 1882 and *The Golden Widow* in 1889 from *La Marquise*.[2]

Next to Sardou, Alexandre Dumas was Daly's most frequent source of inspiration from the French. An example of his free treatment of French drama was his adaptation of Dumas' *Monsieur Alphonse*, played in Paris in 1873, and produced by Daly at the Fifth Avenue Theatre, April 25, 1874. In this adaptation one notices first, the loss in distinction of style, and second, the addition of characters to suit the members of the Daly Company. In one case at least this addition added to the dramatic effectiveness. Octave, who is known as Monsieur Alphonse, has deceived Madame Raymonde Montaglin some years before her marriage, and on the eve of his own brings their child to her to be brought up. Dumas gives us this information in a conversation between Octave and Raymonde. Daly introduces the plot through two peasant women, probably to provide a part for Mrs. Gilbert, but the change results in bringing the child Adrienne into the presence of Captain Montaglin without any warning to Raymonde and forces her therefore to take Adrienne, with the consequent danger of discovery. Daly provides Octave with a cynical but effective speech at the end which is not in the original, and he omits, probably wisely, certain observations about life and morals in France. Bijou Heron's performance of Adrienne seems to have been a notable one.

The American, adapted from Dumas' *L'Etrangère* in 1876, while it proved no great success on the stage, is very readable and was a comparatively free translation of the original. The

[1] *La Maison Neuve* had been adapted in 1867 by L. R. Shewell and Fred Williams, as *The Old Cockade* and played at the Boston Museum. Clyde Fitch adapted it in 1893 as *The Social Swim*.

[2] Neither *Fernande* (1870) nor *The Fast Family* (1874), from *La Famille Benoiton*, both played at the Fifth Avenue Theatre, is an autograph MS. and no claim is made that he had any share in their adaptation.

contrast of two Americans, husband and wife, with French society was the main motive of the play. In his other adaptation from Dumas, father and son, which included *The Royal Youth (The Youth of Louis XIV)* from the elder and *Denise* from the younger, he preserved the French scene.

One of his most important adaptations from the French, *Frou-Frou*, by Henri Meilhac and Ludovic Halévy, had been produced at the Théâtre du Gymnase in Paris in 1869, and on February 15, 1870, Daly placed his adaptation on the stage of the Fifth Avenue Theatre. *Frou-Frou* is a powerful drama of contrasted character. Gilberte Brigard, the apparently frivolous woman, who marries her serious husband at the advice of her sister, Louise, who herself loves him, has been interpreted by many actresses, including Sarah Bernhardt. Agnes Ethel took the part in Daly's production and made a great success of the moving scene in which Gilberte, or Frou-Frou, returns after her flight with de Valreas, to die in her husband's arms. This scene had been shortened by Daly with a gain in effectiveness and in general the changes made in the adaptation seem to be improvements, especially the omission of the last scene of Act IV, in which Baron de Cambri tells Frou-Frou that her husband has wounded her lover in a duel, for this excision concentrates the attention of the audience upon the relations of the husband and wife. The most interesting of Daly's additions are the observations upon the art of acting which he makes through a dramatic coach who is training Frou-Frou for private theatricals. According to M. Pitou's instructions, an actor should not be natural on the stage but must be in keeping with the artificial character of the scene. He tells his pupil that people will be bored if she is entirely natural. It is not clear whether Daly is quite sincere or in part sarcastic in these expressions, but they accord well with that combination of realistic stage-setting, theatrical illusion and heightened character portrayal, which makes him the transition playwright of our stage.

When Daly's adaptations from the French are considered

chronologically, two significant facts appear. He continued to adapt Sardou and Dumas throughout his career, and with one exception preserved the atmosphere of the original. With the twenty or more plays which are founded on the work of other French dramatists, a change came about 1880. Previous to that date, when he adapted *Frou-Frou; Alixe*, almost a literal translation of *La Comtesse de Somerive* by Baroness de Prevois and Théodore Barrière; *The Two Widows*, from Mallefille; *Article 47*, a dramatization of Adolphe Belot's novel of the same name, with a part augmented for Fanny Davenport; *What Should She Do?* from Edmond About's *Germaine; The Princess Royal*, from *L'Officier de Fortune*, or *Vesta*, a tragic play from Parodi's *Rome Vaincue*—he preserved the original European scene. Sometimes he changed the nationality of his characters and not always happily. Professor Brander Matthews called to my attention the fact that in *Serge Panine*, which Daly adapted in 1883 from Georges Ohnet, he ruined a strong situation. In the original, a Frenchwoman of the middle class, who has successfully conducted a business after her husband's death, finds that her son-in-law, a Polish Count, is a worthless bankrupt and hands him a pistol with which he may relieve the situation by removing his worthless self. When he declines to do so, she shoots him and calmly informs the characters who are attracted by the shot that the Count has committed suicide. Daly turned the French bourgeoise to whom, with her keen sense of commercial honor, such an action would have been possible, into an American woman of society, Mrs. Belyew, to whom the avoidance of scandal was the first consideration. She offers him a chance to escape, which he does not take, and it is really not clear, from the manuscript, whether he is shot by the officers of the law off stage or shoots himself.

Of these adaptations, one of the most attractive was *The Princess Royal*, which is a stirring romantic play with the scene laid in Germany, with good situations and with a slant toward a satire of the absurdities of the romantic drama. It was based on the love story of Baron Trenck and Princess Amalie of Prussia, and the hairbreadth escapes point forward to the moving picture of to-day.

Delmonico's, in 1871, was an early and an exceptional instance among the adaptations from the French in which the scene was changed to New York. But from 1879 when *Love's Young Dream*, a clever one-act comedy, was produced, Daly seems to have decided that with the exception of the plays of Sardou and Dumas, he could be more successful if he changed the atmosphere entirely and made as little of the original setting as possible. On the program of the first performance of *Love's Young Dream* it is stated that the play is by "Joseph Francis," a testimony to the share which Judge Daly took in the writing of the plays and which was in many cases much greater than has been usually supposed.

Whether the growing sense of the importance of American plays being laid in America caused this change in Daly's method of adaptation is a matter of speculation. Certainly it cannot be said that the change resulted in greater drama, although it led to the production of some clever plays.

Love in Harness from Albin Valabréque's *Bonheur Conjugal*, was produced in November, 1886. This domestic comedy is a study of the married relations of the three daughters of Jeremiah Joblots, and while it was a stage success, it bears evidence of being a hasty production. *Love in Tandem*, a free adaptation of *Vie à Deux* by Henri Bocage and Charles de Courcy, is a better comedy. Its motive, that of a wife who tires of her husband but insists upon selecting her successor before the separation, has obvious possibilities. This play, which was first produced in February, 1892, may have been the source for A. E. Thomas' *Her Husband's Wife*. Two clever one-act plays, *Wet Blanket* (1886) and *A Sudden Shower* (1886), were adaptations of the work of playwrights like Bilhaud, Levy and Bessier.

The production of *The Lottery of Love* in 1888, from *Les Surprises du divorce* by Bisson and Mars, afforded an opportunity to compare the Daly Company with the best of French actors in their interpretation of comedy, for Coquelin was acting in the French original at the same time in New York City. *The Lottery of Love* is a most amusing play, with complications based on a young husband being provided with a mother-in-law not only by his own action but by that of his father-in-law. The dialogue is extremely clever and the play can be read now without regard to its foreign origin.

In his adaptation of German drama, Daly also turned to the work of contemporary playwrights, and he found no one of the rank of Sardou or Dumas. Yet he provided from the comedies of Gustav von Moser, Franz and Paul von Schönthan, Julius Rosen and others, plays which delighted audiences of those days and can still be performed with success. This group of playwrights, who occupy a progressively diminishing place in the histories of German drama, differ somewhat in their material and methods and Daly also differs in the freedom with which he treats their work. In his earlier adaptations of the tragedies of Mosenthal, he had kept the foreign atmosphere, but in the comedies, with one exception, *Countess Gucki*, he transferred the scene to this country.

He began in 1875 with *The Big Bonanza*, the title given to his adaptation of *Ultimo* (1873), in which von Moser had satirized the rage for speculation that came after the Franco-Prussian war. Daly adapted the play to the somewhat similar conditions in New York City in the seventies and produced an amusing comedy, bordering at times on farce. The contrasting types, Jonathan Cadwallader, the banker and broker, and his cousin Professor Cadwallader, who thinks he is able to teach the broker how to speculate, are well established. For the young lover, Bob Ruggles, who in the original had been sent to New York to lose his money, John Drew was brought over from his mother's stock company in Philadelphia to play opposite Fanny Davenport. It was the beginning of a long association between manager and actor. While there are no vital differences in plot, Daly shortened the original from five to four acts and the drama gains in unity and construction. The play ran from February 17 until the end of the season. Von Moser next provided Daly with a rapidly moving farce-comedy in *Harun al Raschid*, which was produced in 1879, as *An Arabian Night, or Haroun al Raschid and his Mother-in-Law.* In this play, dealing with a young New York man who has a liking for adventure, John Drew scored a triumph as Alexander Spinkle. The play is fairly well naturalized.

Von Moser had begun in his *Veilchenfresser* in 1876 the drama which glorified the German officer caste. It was partly the consequence of the Franco-Prussian War, but it was also, consciously or unconsciously, a dramatic expression of the national social and political impulses, then in embryo, which were partially responsible for the War of 1914. Von Moser, born in Spandau in 1825, had been an officer from 1843 to 1856. *Krieg im Frieden,* by von Moser and Franz von Schönthan, was produced in 1880 and Daly's adaptation, *The Passing Regiment,* was first performed November 10, 1881. In adapting *Krieg im Frieden,* Daly followed his original closely. The characters correspond exactly, and the arrangement of scenes is the same. The main difference lies in the transfer of the scene to Narragansett Pier from a provincial town in Germany and the modification of the rigidly regulated relationship of a German cavalry regiment to the more comradely relations of the New York National Guard. That this is done well is due partly to Daly's skill but also perhaps to the universal feminine admiration for the military which is the ostensible motive of the play. Read to-day, *The Passing Regiment* has no foreign flavor. It is an amusing farce comedy, in which Narragansett Pier is pictured before the days of its glory. The officers of the Excelsior Regiment of the National Guard of New York, from the Colonel down, capture the hearts of the girls. The leading characters, played by John Drew and Ada Rehan, are Adjutant Paul Dexter and Telka Essoff, a Russian heiress, niece of Linthicum Winthrop, "the amiable representative

27

of one of the F. F. V.'s of Narragansett Pier." A typical change in the adaptation occurs in the second Act. In the German, Dr. Schaeffer, the regimental surgeon, who is supposed to be a bachelor, tells the General about his marrying Agnes at her father's deathbed. This scene is not badly done and it has the advantage of dramatic contrast in the positions of the two men, one all powerful and the other entirely dependent upon his superior officer's good will. This becomes in *The Passing Regiment* an interview between two men who have been friends at school, one of whom is simply better off than the other and is willing to help his friend to a hospital appointment.

Von Moser wrote a sequel to *Krieg im Frieden* under the title of *Reif von Reiflingen* which became the model of Daly's *Our English Friend*, played in November, 1882. The extent of Daly's alterations may be judged by the fact that in the printed versions there is no relation at all between *The Passing Regiment* [1] and *Our English Friend*. In the first he makes comparatively little change in the structure, though he alters the atmosphere entirely. In *Our English Friend* he makes radical changes in the structure of the play, alters the position of some scenes and rewrites others, but more important, by his substitution of Digby de Rigby, an Englishman, for Reif von Reiflingen, he turned Gustav von Moser's glorification of the German lieutenant into an international compliment. At a time when Anglomania and Anglophobia were both in the air, he represented the English gentleman as a good fellow with high standards of conduct, with unfailing courtesy, and with a certain stupidity, and yet with a promptness in action which made him a picture of at least one kind of Englishman and not a caricature. Daly thought of him as an eccentric character, however, and cast James Lewis for the part, instead of John Drew, who played Paul Spender, the husband and host at a house party at Cutty Corners in Northern New York. Daly

---

[1] In the MS. version it is indicated that Daly had intended to use Paul Dexter as the husband in *Our English Friend*, but changed his mind.

made *Our English Friend* more strictly social comedy, omitting most of the fourth and some of the second Acts, which represent the lieutenant in his relations as guardian angel to the household of the farmer and the apothecary. He thereby secured unity of scene and he made more prominent the part of Darbie Vaughn, played by Ada Rehan.

Daly next turned to the work of Franz von Schönthan, the collaborator with von Moser in *Krieg im Frieden*, and adapted two clever farces, which to-day are probably the best known of his plays. *Seven-Twenty-Eight, or Casting the Boomerang* is a close adaptation of *Der Schwabenstreich*. The scenes are the same and practically the only changes are in the conversation, especially in the last scene. "Der Schwabenstreich" in the original is the foolishness that everyone must commit at some period of his life. Daly makes this a boomerang which everyone throws at some period of his life and which returns to plague him. Launcelot Bargiss is retired and his wife Hypatia secretly sends his verses to a magazine conducted by Gasleigh, who is playing upon the vanity of unknown authors. Bargiss is delighted. She then has Gasleigh print a volume of the verses of her husband, which he had sent when courting her, but which unfortunately had been copied from Shakespeare, Jonson and others. The daughter of Bargiss, Florence, has had her portrait painted and exhibited No. 7-20-8, and this leads to her pursuit by a lover, Courtney Corliss, who finally wins her.

A Night Off, produced in March, 1885, follows its source, *Der Raub der Sabinerinnen* by Franz and Paul von Schönthan, quite closely in plot but the language is idiomatic in its American quality. The play is concerned with the efforts of Justinian Babbitt, who is a school-teacher in the original, but whom Daly promotes to a college professorship, to have his play produced. Marcus Brutus Snap, the manager of a wandering company, puts on the play with dire results.

The Railroad of Love, adapted by Daly from *Goldfische*, by Franz von Schönthan and Gustav Kadelburg, and performed in November, 1887, was, according to J. F. Daly, one of the daintiest as well as the strongest comedies that had been played at Daly's Theatre. *Goldfische* was a satire on the "Mitgiftjagerei" or hunters of money, but *The Railroad of Love* contains more characterization than is usual in the type, and Daly carries over from the original the sense of high standards of honor. In one sense he improves upon *Gold-fische*, for while he closely follows it in plot and scene, he omits some of the lines which represent that glorification of the army which was found in von Moser's plays. He therefore presents characters who secure our sympathy in their efforts to live up to standards of conduct which are imposed by themselves rather than by the traditions of a caste.

The Great Unknown, an adaptation of *Die Berühmte Frau* by von Schönthan and Kadelburg, played in October, 1889, is an example of free adaptation and was one of the most successful of the comedies. In October, 1890, came *The Last Word*, a modern comedy, received with great approval both at home and abroad, in which Daly transferred the scene to Washington and gave a fairly accurate picture of official life there. The best character was that of the Baroness Vera von Bouraneff, played by Ada Rehan. Daly changed the language of *Das Letzte Wort* radically and an example of his dramatic sense may be found in the climax of the first Act, when Faith Rutherell blocks her father's schemes by announcing her engagement to Boris Bouraneff. The long curtain speech of the original is omitted with distinct advantage.

The final adaptation from von Schönthan is interesting for two reasons. It is practically unique among Daly's adaptations from German comedy, in preserving the original scene. This change in Daly's method was due probably to the fact that the German dramatist wrote the play for Ada Rehan, providing her with a charming part in the Countess Hermance Trachau, known as "the Countess Gucki," from whom the play takes its name. Daly probably felt indisposed to alter the play radically as he had so often done with the other plays and indeed with the inspiration that von Schönthan had had, it was not necessary. *The Countess Gucki* is a clever comedy, with real characters, especially the central one, a capable, impulsive widow who directs two appealing love episodes with genuine skill.

From Julius Rosen, who in real life was Nikolaus Duffek, born in Prague in 1833, Daly adapted a lighter form of comedy verging on farce. Of these the first was *Lemons*, a bright and successful social comedy, played in 1877, having for a plot the complications caused by the guardianship of two uncles over one niece. In *Needles and Pins* he showed how the good but romantic intentions of an heiress confuse the affairs of those she tries to help. In 1886 he transferred the scenes of Rosen's *Halbe Dichter* to New York under the title of *Nancy and Company*. This is a farce in which a joint authorship of a play is complicated by disappearances into adjoining rooms and rapid changes of stage positions with consequent hilarity. Rosen's work is not up to the standard of the von Schönthan plays, but in the hands of the Daly Company it was evidently irresistible. *Nancy and Company* was very much changed in the adaptation, to the advantage of the character drawing.

Among other adaptations from the German, probably the best are *Dollars and Sense*, produced in 1883, and *Love on Crutches*, played first in 1884. *Dollars and Sense* was derived from *Die Sorglosen* (1882) by Adolph L'Arronge. It is an amusing comedy, quite well naturalized, with its scene laid in Washington. It reveals a couple who are spending too much money, in order to satisfy the wife's ambitions, another couple in which the wife rules, and a pair in which the husband is seeking an affinity. *Love on Crutches* was from Heinrich Stopitzer's *Ihre Ideale*, which itself is based in part on Sardou's *Les Pattes de Mouche*, which in its turn glances back to Poe's *Purloined Letter*. The central character, that of the woman who takes upon herself the blame of having written a compromising letter in order to shield a wife from the suspicion of her husband, suffers quite a change in the transit through three languages. It seems to have been the opportunity of Edith Kingdon, who scored a substantial success. Otis Skinner, who played Guy Roverly, the lover, tells how, when Pinero's *Lords and Commons* was failing, Daly put *Love on Crutches* in rehearsal before his adaptation was finished and describes the night rehearsals, "while succeeding acts of the new comedy came from Daly's private office, where, through the midnight hours of the deserted theatre, he worked unwearied." [1] From this and other testimony we may be assured that the adaptations of Augustin Daly were not dashed off hastily.

Toward the end of his career, Daly turned for material to the work of Oscar Blumenthal. *After Business Hours* (1886) is an amusing satire on the craze for money, dress and speculation. *Little Miss Million* (1892), in which the central character is a young widow whose husband's family resent her marriage, had a more serious note than *A Test Case* (1892), which is almost pure farce.

In 1892 he became interested in the new movement in Germany and I found among the manuscripts an adaptation of Sudermann's *Die Ehre*, by Jerome K. Jerome and himself, which, however, seems not to have been played. The scene is laid in England.

Daly's one adaptation from the Spanish was a failure from a popular standpoint, yet was so well received by competent critics and has been the subject of so much conjecture by those who have not had access to the manuscript, that it deserves attention. [2] On December 5, 1874, he produced his version of *Un Drama Nuevo* (1867) by Tamayo y Baus, one of the most significant of contemporaneous Spanish dramatists. As usual, he had the play translated and from the stiff and

---

[1] *Footlights and Spotlights*, p. 146.

[2] See *A New Drama*, translated by J. D. Fitzgerald and T. H. Guild. The Hispanic Society, New York, 1915, and "Un Drama Nuevo on the American Stage," *Hispania*, VII (1924), 171–176. In the latter the editor establishes by inductive evidence that there are probably two American versions.

literal translation he made a free and vigorous adaptation. *Un Drama Nuevo* has a special interest for us because Shakespeare is a character and it is at his theatre that the drama is partly laid. Yorick, the comedian of the theatre, aspires to play tragedy and when a new play is to be produced he begs Shakespeare to permit him to play the part of Count Octavio, whose wife is unfaithful to him and is the lover of Manfredo, his protegé. While rehearsing the play Yorick accuses his wife of being unfaithful to him and his real wife, Alicia, misunderstands him and by calling out "Mercy" raises his suspicions. Alicia and Edmundo, who is to act the part of Manfredo in the new play, are in love with each other, but not in a guilty fashion. Edmundo, however, decides that they must elope and writes a letter to her fixing the time of their departure for the next day. Walton, the tragedian of the company, who is jealous of Yorick, conceives in revenge the idea of revealing to Yorick the love affair between Alicia and Edmundo. He does this by handing to Yorick at an appropriate time in the play the letter from Edmundo to Alicia. Under the influence of his jealousy Yorick has been acting magnificently and, spurred on by the letter, he surpasses Walton as a tragedian, since he is really acting a natural part. In the original play he falls down after killing Edmundo. Shakespeare explains to the audience the death of Edmundo and also states that Walton has been killed in a duel.

Daly made certain changes in the play, whose principal result was the decreased emphasis laid upon the character of Shakespeare, with a consequently greater stress upon Yorick. At the end of the third Act, Yorick, roused to fury after the duel with Edmundo, tries to stab Alicia. She takes refuge in Shakespeare's arms. Yorick falls. The prompter brings in word that the physician gives hope of Edmundo. Yorick seems to go out of his head, saying, "It is the last call!" and dies after asking his master, Shakespeare, if he is there. Instead of making the final announcement himself, Shakespeare tells the prompter to inform the people of the tragedy and that Walton has thrown himself on his own sword.[1]

Daly's career as a director belongs to theatrical rather than to dramatic history, but at least the outlines must be sketched. In 1884 he took his company to London, opening at Toole's Theatre in *Seven-Twenty-Eight*. The most successful performance was Cibber's *She Would and She Would Not*, Daly's adaptation of the Eighteenth Century comedy being recognized as a fine interpretation. Daly visited London again in 1886, playing *A Night Off* and *Nancy and Company*, and on the 19th of August, 1886, the first English-speaking company in nearly three hundred years was seen on a German stage under his direction. Six plays were given at the Wallner Theatre, in Berlin: *A Night Off*, *Nancy and Company*, *A Woman's Wont*, *Love on Crutches*, *A Country Girl*, and *She Would and She Would Not*.

The reception was at first not enthusiastic, on the part of the German critics, but it gained in warmth with the production of the English comedies and of *Love on Crutches*. The audiences were made up of American and British residents; the Germans simply did not come. The experiment at Paris was not so fortunate, for the conservatism of the French critical mind when dealing with foreign art showed itself definitely.

The third foreign trip began in April, 1888. The most important event was the production in London of *The Taming of the Shrew* on May 29, the first performance of a Shakespearean comedy by an American company in Europe. On August 3, the comedy was produced at Stratford, probably for the first time. Daly, nothing daunted by his earlier experience in France, took *The Taming of the Shrew* to Paris, where it was only mildly praised. But the discriminating British critics recognized the significance of the restoration of the Induction and of the sub-plot of Bianca and her suitors.

The foreign triumph of *The Taming of the Shrew* was re-

[1] For an account of Howells' more successful adaptation of the same play see Chapter III.

peated when in 1890 Daly produced at the Lyceum Theatre in London *As You Like It*. Miss Rehan played Rosalind, not as the theatrical tradition pictured her, a restrained princess in disguise, but as Shakespeare drew her. The changes which Daly made in *As You Like It* are typical of his adaptations of Shakespeare's comedies. He cut some of the speeches, as at the entrance of "the clown" in Act I, Scene 2, or restored lines to a character, such as those describing Jaques, originally spoken by the first Lord, but often placed in Jaques' own mouth. He rearranged the order of the scenes, especially in the second and fifth Acts. The changes seem not to be productive of any profound alterations, but to conduce to simpler stage arrangement and unity of place. He preserved all but two of the twenty-five speaking parts.

During Daly's third visit to Paris, in August, 1891, he produced *As You Like It*, *The School for Scandal*, *A Night Off*, *The Taming of the Shrew*, and *The Lottery of Love*. The reception this time in Paris was much more cordial, due partly, no doubt, to the superior quality of the plays produced.

Encouraged by his cordial reception in London, Daly built a theatre there, the corner stone being laid in October, 1891. He also began to adapt for his use Tennyson's pastoral comedy, *The Foresters*, which was produced on March 17, 1892, at Daly's Theatre. Notwithstanding the undramatic qualities of the play, the production was a thing of beauty. *Twelfth Night* was revived in February, 1893, and practically saved the London season for Daly when he took his company to his own playhouse in that city. Daly found that he had to create a public for his theatre and it took his adaptation of Shakespeare to do it. *Twelfth Night* ran for one hundred nights.

Among the later revivals of Shakespeare, which include *Much Ado About Nothing* in 1896 and *The Merchant of Venice* in 1898, *The Tempest* in 1897 remains in my memory, at least, as the most effective. The setting was like fairyland and more important the true poetic quality of the play was brought out.

The last years of Daly's life were not altogether happy. The public was fickle; new and good plays seemed to him hard to obtain; and from the death of his two boys he never quite recovered. Difficulties with the lessor of his London Theatre made it necessary for him to go abroad in 1899 and on June 7 he died in Paris.

To one who has been privileged to examine the manuscripts of Augustin Daly, the strongest impression is that of his great knowledge of the theatre, and of his selective power. He had scores of foreign plays translated of which he apparently made no use. But by his constant study of Shakespeare, of British comedy and of these continental models he was making himself master of a technique which resulted in productions that became a standard of theatrical merit in this country at least. That his original work as a playwright belongs to the early portion of his career is to be regretted, but it was perhaps natural that his creative faculty should be checked as his critical knowledge developed. But there is much of Augustin Daly the playwright even in his foreign adaptations,— how much can be appreciated only through a comparison with his originals. When the constant dependence upon foreign inspiration which has been a characteristic of the English drama from the days of Shakespeare and his predecessors is remembered, and when the scrupulous care which Daly exercised in calling attention to his models on the title-pages of his privately printed plays is also noted, the derivative nature of his plays becomes less of moment. Much more apparent is his courageous struggle against great odds to establish the art both of the drama and of the theatre in a period when conditions of post-war days meant a general confusion of ideals, artistic and commercial. How well he succeeded, how much he encouraged other playwrights, like Bronson Howard, how inflexibly he insisted on the dignity of his profession, how he lifted the standard of good taste in this country, a reading of the fascinating biography by his brother and co-worker will reveal.

AUGUSTIN DALY, ARTIST OF THE THEATRE

Among the dramatic species that are associated with Daly's name, the one that showed most persistence dealt with low life in the large city. During the sixties and seventies, playwrights like Charles Foster, the stage manager of the Old Bowery Theatre, produced at least fifteen plays, of which two titles, *New York Burglars, or Wedded by Moonlight,* and *Bertha, the Sewing Machine Girl,* are sufficient to indicate their nature. In October, 1859, the year of the opening of the New Bowery Theatre, we find such anonymous plays as *New York and Brooklyn, or the Poor Sewing Girl,* while *New York in 1860, or a Hit at the Times* has at least an author's name, that of W. Petrie, attached to it. Charles Gayler, who dates back to an earlier period, continued to write melodramas, like *Out of the Streets* which appeared at the New York Theatre in 1868, and he has thirty plays to his credit after 1870. The status of such playwrights was probably similar to that of the Englishman, J. B. Howe, who was engaged by James Lingard, the manager of the New Bowery, as house dramatist at a salary of eight pounds a week and who on his arrival in this country found that "dollars" had been substituted for "pounds" in his contract! Certainly none of the playwrights who devoted their attention to this phase of drama during this period demand our continued attention. Their work has perished and probably justly, for they seem to have made no effort to portray life sincerely.

In his adaptation of fiction, Daly had at least one successful rival. Lester Wallack's *Rosedale,* which was first performed at Wallack's Theatre in 1863, was one of the most popular plays of its time. It is an interesting comedy, verging on melodrama, based upon a novel, *Lady Lee's Widowhood,* by Edward B. Hamley, with one of its most effective scenes, in which the hero, Elliot Grey, escapes from the clutches of Miles McKenna, taken from Bulwer's *What Will He Do With It?* *Rosedale* held the stage for more than twenty years and was revived in 1913 at the Lyric Theatre in New York. That its popularity was not due entirely to Lester Wallack's own fine

37

performance of Elliot Grey is proved by its success in other hands. It is a pity that Lester Wallack's play upon American life, *Central Park*, produced in 1861, has perished, for it also was a success on the stage and was played as late as 1886.

In the field of social comedy, Augustin Daly was to provide opportunity and probably inspiration for Bronson Howard. *Saratoga* was produced by him in 1870, to be followed by *Moorcroft* and *Wives*. It was he, too, who produced the somewhat abortive attempts of Edgar Fawcett in *Americans Abroad* and *Our Best Society* and of Olive Logan Sykes in *Newport* and *Surf* to establish a vogue of social satire in this country.

His best play, *Horizon*, was a pioneer in the frontier drama and here, too, he provided an opportunity for the work of Mark Twain and Bret Harte.

CHAPTER II

Bronson Howard and the Establishment of Professional Playwriting

THE significance of the work of Bronson Howard does not lie, as has so often been stated, in the production of *Saratoga* in 1870. That play marked no great advance over social comedies of an earlier period like W. H. Hurlbert's *Americans in Paris* (1858), but it is just because Howard so well illustrates, in the broadening of his own grasp of dramatic material and the refinement of his own skill, the development of American playwriting during the period of his creative achievement from 1870 to 1906, that his work becomes of such significance. He represents also the establishment of the profession of the dramatist in this country. He was not, of course, our first professional playwright. William Dunlap, John Howard Payne, Joseph Stevens Jones, Augustin Daly and others were professionals in the sense that they were not amateurs, and remembering Shakespeare and Molière, their association with the theatre as actors or managers does not prevent the inclusion of the American playwrights in the professional class. Even in a stricter sense, Robert Montgomery Bird and George Henry Boker had preceded Howard. Both were eager to devote their lives to the production of plays and Bird actually did attempt to make a living by this means until the untoward circumstances of the time drove him into other fields of writing. But the great difference lies in the fact that where they had failed Howard succeeded. When he had established the possibility of a playwright in the United States making a good living by his art, a new era began in the history of the drama in America.

Bronson Crocker Howard was born in Detroit, Michigan,

October 7, 1842, the son of Charles Howard, a merchant and afterward Mayor of the city. His family had long been native, his great-grandfather, Seabury Howard, having fought both in the French and Indian War for Great Britain and in the Revolution for his adopted country, falling at the Battle of Monmouth. After Bronson Howard's schooling in Detroit was completed, he prepared for Yale, but owing to an affection of the sight he was prevented from entering college, and returning to Detroit, began his preparation for playwriting in a school from which many dramatists have graduated, that of the newspaper. His first writing seems to have consisted of humorous sketches for the *Detroit Free Press* and it was in Detroit that his first play was produced in 1864. This was *Fantine*, a dramatization of the tragic episode of Cosette, in *Les Misérables*.[1]

Realizing that the first essential to success as a playwright was contact with the theatre, Howard came to New York in 1865 and supported himself, while writing more than one play which never saw the stage, by reading exchanges and doing other work for the *Tribune* and the *Evening Post*. Finally success came with *Saratoga*, which was produced by Augustin Daly at the Fifth Avenue Theatre on December 21, 1870. It ran for one hundred and one nights and was later revived. *Saratoga* is a farce comedy, with clever situations but with no significance of plot and with characters that are types rather than real people. Bob Sackett, a New York man, has become engaged to Effie Remington, Olivia Alston, Lucy Carter and Virginia Vanderpool. As all four women go to Saratoga, where Bob also arrives, many complications ensue, including several abortive duels. Bob Sackett is a likeable fellow and the audience is in sympathy with him in his efforts to triumph over the circumstances. Howard succeeded in being amusing without being vulgar and even the scene in Sackett's bedroom, where all the women come at the same time

---

[1]Mawson, H. P., "A Brief Biography, " in *In Memoriam, Bronson Howard*. N. Y. 1910, p. 51.

to save either him or their lovers, avoids the easy possibilities of the indecent. This reticence, which has remained a characteristic of a certain portion of our playwriting, makes all the more unfair such criticism as that leveled at *Saratoga* by the late William Archer in his *English Dramatists of To-day* (1886). In speaking of the feminine characters, he says, "Ordinary modesty, not to say delicacy of feeling, is apparently a thing unknown and undreamt of among them" and then quotes a passage which is certainly vulgar enough but which is not to be found either in the printed copies of *Saratoga* or in the original manuscript. The explanation lies in the fact that *Saratoga* was "adapted" for the English stage by Frank Marshall under the title of *Brighton*, Charles Wyndham appearing in the part of Bob Sackett, which James Lewis had played so successfully at Daly's Theatre; and Archer was solemnly criticizing an American for vulgarity which had been inserted by the British adaptor. Wyndham produced *Brighton* at the Court Theatre in 1874 and it was put on for a long run afterward at the Criterion. Wyndham also produced the play in Germany under the title of *Seine Erste und Einzige Liebe* and Howard witnessed the performance although he was not able to understand his own work. It was probably the first American play performed in translation in Germany.

With all its imperfections, *Saratoga* showed Howard's skill in the handling of situations and the writing of dialogue.[1]

Diamonds, which was a comedy of manners, laid in New York City and in a villa on Staten Island, was written definitely for the company of Augustin Daly, who produced it at the Fifth Avenue Theatre on the opening night of the season, September 3, 1872. While it ran until October 28, it was not considered by Howard as one of his important plays, but it revealed again a skill in the technical handling of situation. *Moorcroft*, produced also by Daly, on October 17, 1874, ran

---

[1] In several places the suggestion has been made that it was based on *Les Eaux* [?], by Scribe. There is certainly no resemblance between the play and Scribe's *Les Eaux du Mont-Dor*, and there is no Gallic flavor about *Saratoga*.

only until November 3. It exists now only in the autograph manuscript. The play begins in 1840 at the Moorcroft mansion near Savannah. Russell Moorcroft, who is in financial difficulties, decides to sell his half brother, Cyril, into slavery. Katherine Mordaunt, a neighbor who loves Cyril, buys him for $15,000, but he elopes with Virginia St. John. After an interval of eighteen years the brothers meet at Newport. Russell's son, John, and Cyril's daughter, Marie, fall in love. Katherine Mordaunt, who has nursed her hatred for Cyril, tells him she owns him and can demand his return as a fugitive slave. A reading of the scene between these two, with its exaggerated expression of emotion, shows clearly how Howard grew in power through experience and failure. The love scenes are not bad and the confident belief of Marie that her father will give her a husband just as he has given her everything else she wanted, is even charming. But the final act, in which Russell calmly tells Cyril that he has really no stain of negro blood and is not his half brother since the will which stated that fact is a forgery, and in which the two men shake hands and pair off their children, is absurd.

Moorcroft is interesting as an illustration of Howard's literary honesty. On the program he states, "As the author of *Moorcroft* I wish to acknowledge my obligation to Colonel John Hay for a strikingly dramatic idea, of which I made use. An admirable short sketch by that gentleman, entitled 'The Foster Brothers,' originally published in *Harper's Magazine*, March, 1859 [September 1869], was brought to my attention about three years ago. In that sketch may be found in outline the relations existing between four of the sixteen characters of the play, namely, Cyril Moorcroft, his half brother Russell and their two children, who fall in love with each other. With the exception of the peculiar relation in which these four characters stand to each other, there is nothing in common between the play and the story referred to. . . . I cheerfully acknowledge the very great obligation under which I am placed."

BRONSON HOWARD
[From the portrait in possession of Mr. Thomas R. Edwards]

BRONSON HOWARD

Brander Matthews is authority for the statement that John Hay would never have suspected his own share in the work if Bronson Howard had not called attention to it.[1] Howard turned the tragedy of *The Foster Brothers* into melodrama. In Hay's story, the scene is the city of Moscow, on the Mississippi River, in Illinois, and the main interest is centered in the love story of Clarence Brydges of New Orleans and Marie Des Ponts, the daughter of a French Creole, who corresponds to Cyril Moorcroft but who is really a negro and an escaped slave and is not connected by any ties, real or supposed, to his master, Victor Brydges. The latter comes to the wedding in ignorance of the facts and is saved from drowning after his steamer has caught fire, by his former slave. After a powerful scene in the open boat between the two men, Des Ponts drowns Brydges in order to save his own daughter from disgrace and dies with his former master at the bottom of the river.

Howard's next play, *The Banker's Daughter*, has a singular interest for students of the drama since the playwright has given an account of its development in his *Autobiography of a Play*, delivered first as a lecture at Harvard University in 1886 and published in the Bronson Howard Memorial Volume in 1910. *The Banker's Daughter* was first produced in 1873 at Chicago as *Lillian's Last Love*. In the original form, Lillian Westbrook has married John Strebelow, a man older than he, partly to save her father from financial ruin and partly because of a quarrel with her lover, Harold Routledge. Five years later, in Paris, Routledge returns and Lillian's love is revived, but she remains true to her husband on account of the passionate devotion she feels for their child. Count de Carojac also loves her and a duel occurs between Routledge and the Count in which Routledge is supposedly killed and at which Lillian reveals to her husband by her outcry that she has never loved him. He takes their child away, and in the final scene, in

---

[1] "An Appreciation," reprinted from the *North American Review* in the Memorial Volume, p. 37.

America, she dies heartbroken, although the child really has been returned to her, too late.

Howard offered the play to A. M. Palmer and it was put on, September 30, 1878, at the Union Square Theatre, and became one of the most appealing plays of the time. The account of the changes made in the meantime is given so admirably by Howard that a paraphrase would be an impertinence, but it can be reproduced, of course, only in part:

A dramatist should deal, so far as possible, with subjects of universal interest, instead of with such as appeal strongly to a part of the public only. I do not mean that he may not appeal to certain classes of people, and depend upon those classes for success; but, just so far as he does this, he limits the possibilities of that success. I have said that the love of offspring in woman has shown itself the strongest of all human passions; and it is the most nearly allied to the boundless love of Deity. But the one absolutely universal passion of the race—which underlies all other passions—on which, indeed, the very existence of the race depends —the very fountain of maternal love itself, is the love of the sexes. The dramatist must remember that his work cannot, like that of the novelist or the poet, pick out the hearts, here and there, that happen to be in sympathy with its subject. He appeals to a thousand hearts at the same moment; he has no choice in the matter he must do this; and it is only when he deals with the love of the sexes that his work is most interesting to that aggregation of human hearts we call the audience. This very play was successful in Chicago; but, as soon as that part of the public had been exhausted which could weep with pleasure, if I may use the expression, over the tenderness of a mother's love, its success would have been at an end. Furthermore—and here comes in another law of dramatic construction—a play must be, in one way or another, "satisfactory" to the audience. This word has a meaning which varies in different countries, and even in different parts of the same country; but whatever audience you are writing for, you work must be "satisfactory" to it. In England and America, the death of a pure woman on the stage is not "satisfactory," except when the play rises to the dignity of tragedy. The death, in an ordinary play, of a woman who is not pure, as in the case of *Frou Frou*, is perfectly satisfactory, for the reason that it is inevitable. Human nature always bows gracefully to the inevitable. Th

only griefs in our own lives to which we can never reconcile ourselves are those which might have been averted. The wife who
has once taken the step from purity to impurity can never rein-
state herself in the world of art on this side of the grave; and so
an audience looks with complacent tears on the death of an erring
woman. But Lillian had not taken the one fatal step which would
have reconciled an audience to her death. She was still pure, and
every one left the theatre wishing she had lived. I yielded, therefore, to the sound logic, based on sound dramatic principle, of my
New York manager, Mr. A. M. Palmer, and the piece was altered.

I have called the play, as produced in New York and afterward
in London, the "same play" as the one produced in Chicago. . . .

[But] the play which finally takes its place on the stage usually
bears very little resemblance to the play which first suggested
itself to [the author's] mind. . . . The first duty of a dramatist
is to put upon the stage the very best work he can, in the light of
whatever advice and assistance may come to him. Fair acknowl-
edgment afterward is a matter of mere ordinary personal honesty.
It is not a question of dramatic art.

So Lillian is to live, and not to die, in the last act. The first
question for us to decide—I say "us"—the New York manager,
the literary attaché of the theatre, and myself—the first practical
question before us was: As Lillian is to live, which of the two
men who love her is to die? There are axioms among the laws
of dramatic construction, as in mathematics. One of them is
this—three hearts cannot beat as one. The world is not large
enough, from an artistic point of view, for three good human
hearts to continue to exist, if two of them love the third. If one
of the two hearts is a bad one, art assigns it to the hell on earth
of disappointed love; but if it is good and tender and gentle, art
is merciful to it, and puts it out of its misery by death. Routledge was wounded in a duel. Strebelow was supposed to be lost
in the wreck of a steamer. It was easy enough to kill either of
them, but which? We argued this question for three weeks. Mere
romance was on the side of the young artist. But to have had
him live would have robbed the play of all its meaning. Its moral,
in the original form, is this: It is a dangerous thing to marry, for
any reason, without the safeguard of love, even when the person
one marries is worthy of one's love in every possible way. If we
had decided in favor of Routledge, the play would have had no
moral at all, or rather a very bad one. If a girl marries the wrong
man, she need only wait for him to die; and if her lover waits, too,

it'll be all right. If, on the other hand, we so reconstruct the whole play that the husband and wife may at last come together with true affection, we shall have the moral: Even if a young girl makes the worst of all mistakes, and accepts the hand of one man when her heart belongs to another, fidelity to the duty of a wife on her side, and a manly, generous confidence on the part of her husband, may, in the end, correct even such a mistake. The dignity of this moral saved John Strebelow's life, and Harold Routledge was killed in the duel with the Count de Carojac.

All that was needed to effect this first change in the play was to instruct the actor who played Routledge to lie still when the curtain fell at the end of the third Act, and to go home afterward. But there are a number of problems under the laws of dramatic construction which we must solve before the play can now be made to reach the hearts of an audience as it did before. Let us see what they are.

The love of Lillian for Harold Routledge cannot now be the one grand passion of her life. It must be the love of a young girl, however, sincere and intense, which yields, afterward, to the stronger and deeper love of a woman for her husband. The next great change, therefore, which the laws of dramatic construction forced upon us was this: Lillian must now control her own passion, and when she meets her lover in the second Act she must not depend for her moral safety on the awakening of a mother's love by the appearance of her child. Her love for Harold is no longer such an all-controlling force as will justify a woman— justify her dramatically, I mean—yielding to it. For her to depend on an outside influence would be to show a weakness of character that would make her uninteresting. Instead, therefore, of receiving her former lover with dangerous pent-up fires, Lillian now feels pity for him. She hardly yet knows her own feelings toward her husband; but his manhood and kindness are gradually forcing their way to her heart. Routledge, in his own passion, forgets himself, and she now repels him. She even threatens to strike the bell, when the Count de Carojac appears, and warns his rival to desist. This is now the end of the second Act, a very different end, you see, from the other version, where the little girl runs in, and, in her innocence, saves the mother from herself.

Here let me tell a curious experience, which illustrates how stubbornly persistent the dramatic laws are, in having their own way. We were all three of us—manager, literary attaché, and author— so pleased with the original ending of the second Act (the picture of the little girl in her mother's arms, and the lover bowing his head in its presence of innocence) that we retained it. The little girl ran on the stage at every rehearsal at the usual place. But no one knew what to do with her. The actress who played the part of Lillian caught her in her arms in various attitudes; but none of them seemed right. The actor who played Routledge tried to drop his head, according to instructions, but he looked uncomfortable, not reverential. The next day we had the little girl run on from another entrance. She stopped in the center of the stage. Lillian stared at her a moment and then exclaimed: "Mr. Howard, what shall I do with this child?" Routledge, who had put his hands in his pockets, called out, "What's the girl doing here, anyway, Howard?" I could only answer, "She used to be all right; I don't know what's the matter with her now." And I remember seeing an anxious look on the face of the child's mother, standing at the side of the stage. She feared there was something wrong about her own little darling who played the part of Natalie. I reassured her on this point; for the fact that I was in error was forcing itself on my mind, in spite of my desire to retain the scene. You will hardly believe that I am speaking literally, when I tell you that it was not until the nineteenth rehearsal that we yielded to the inevitable and decided not to have the child come on at all at that point. The truth was this: now that Lillian saved herself in her own strength, the child had no dramatic function to fulfill. So strongly did we all feel the force of a dramatic law which we could not, and would not, see. Our own natural human instinct—the instinct which the humblest member of an audience feels, without knowing anything of dramatic law—got the better of three men, trained in dramatic work, only by sheer force, and against our own determined opposition.

The third step, in the changes forced upon us by the laws of dramatic construction, was a very great one; and it was made necessary by the fact, just mentioned, that the child, Natalie, had no dramatic function to fulfill in the protection of her mother's virtue. In other words, there is no point in the play now where sexual love is, or can be, replaced by maternal love, as the controlling passion of the play. Consequently, the last two Acts in their entirety, so far as the serious parts are concerned, disappear, one new scene and a new act taking their place. The sad mother, playing with a little shoe or toy, passes out of our view. The dying woman, kissing the hand of the man she has wronged; the husband, awe-stricken in the presence of a mother's love; the child clasped in Lillian's arms; her last look on earth, a smile, and her last breath, the final expression of maternal tenderness—these scenes belong only to the original version of the play, as it lies in its author's desk. With an author's sensitive interest in his own work, I wasted many hours in trying to save these scenes. But I was working directly against the laws of dramatic truth, and I gave up the impossible task.

The fourth great change—forced on us, as the others were—concerns the character of John Strebelow. As he is now to become the object of a wife's mature affection, he must not merely be a noble and generous man; he must be something worthy of the love which is to be bestowed on him. He must command a woman's love. When, therefore, he hears his wife, kneeling over her wounded lover, use words which tell him of their former relations, he does not what most of us would do, but what an occasional hero among us would do. Of course, the words of Lillian cannot be such as to close the gates to all hopes of love, as they were before. She still utters a wild cry, but her words merely show the awakened tenderness and pity of a woman for a man she had once loved. They are uttered, however, in the presence of others, and they compromise her husband's honor. At that moment he takes her gently in his arms and becomes her protector, warning the French *roué* and duelist that he will call him to account for the insults which the arm of the dead man had failed to avenge. He afterwards does this, killing the count—not in the action of the play; this is only told. John Strebelow thus becomes the hero of the play, and it is only necessary to follow the workings of Lillian's heart and his a little further, until they come together at last, loving each other truly, the early love of the wife for another man being only a sad memory in her mind. There is a tender scene of explanation and a parting, until Lillian's heart shall recall her husband. This scene, in my opinion, is one of the most beautiful scenes ever written for the stage. At the risk of breaking the tenth commandment myself, I do not hesitate to say, I wish I had written it. As I did not, however, I can express the hope that the name of Mr. A. R. Cazauran, who did write it, will never be forgotten in connection with this play as long as the play itself may be remembered. I wrote the scene myself first; but when he wrote it according to his own ideas, it was so much more beautiful than my own that I would have broken a law of dramatic art if I had not accepted it. I should not have been giving the public the best play I could, under the circumstances. Imbued as my own mind

Lilian ~~Let Love~~

A Drama in Five Acts,
by
Bronson Howard.

Characters

Archibald Streblow — An American Gentleman
~~Le~~ Le Comte de Carojac — A French Gentleman
Owen Routledge — Successful in Art; — unfortunate in love. —
Lawrence Westbrook — A victim of prosperity.
G. Washington Phipps. N.Y. U.S.A.
Babbage; Mr Westbrook's senior partner.
Montvillars; or Nothing, although critical
Brown — Millionaire. Winter mistakes itself for Summer.
M. le Docteur Beaumarchais; — ~~strictly impartial to both parties.~~
Dr. Mildwinter — a family physician.
Thomas
Lilian Westbrook
Florence St Vincent — Brown. Very Aristocratic in taste. accepts Widowhood with Christian cheerfulness.
Aunt Fanny — Gentle in nature and subdued by Sorrow.
~~...ette. — A .... of le Bsl ....~~
~~...lie — A.B.C — X.Y.Z ....~~

THE ORIGINAL TITLE PAGE OF
"THE BANKER'S DAUGHTER"
IN THE HANDWRITING OF BRONSON HOWARD

was, with all the original motives of the piece, it would have been impossible for me to have made changes within a few weeks without the assistance Mr. Cazauran could give me; this assistance was invaluable to me in all parts of the revised piece. In the fifth Act the husband and wife come together again, the little child acting as the immediate cause of their reconciliation; the real cause lies in their own true hearts.

The scene for which Howard thanks Cazauran probably owed its original inspiration to the interview between Rodolphe and Armande in Boucicault's *Led Astray*, but the tone was altered. *The Banker's Daughter*, revised by Howard with the aid of James Albery, was played with success in London as *The Old Love and the New*. It was played in stock as late as 1914 in this country.

Howard's careful workmanship is revealed also in a comparison of his *Baron Rudolph* with its earlier form, *Only A Tramp*, which was copyrighted in 1877 and belongs distinctly to his earlier manner. Written originally for Mr. and Mrs. W. J. Florence but not played by them, it became the property of Mr. and Mrs. George S. Knight, who seem to have performed it first at Hull, England, August 1, 1881. It was a moderate success in this country for a few seasons, but when revived at the Fourteenth Street Theatre in 1887 after some revision by David Belasco, it met with failure,[1] attributed by Belasco to Knight's acting as the tramp.

Only a Tramp is a melodrama, in which we are invited to sympathize with a weak but amiable man, Tom Goddfroy, who has squandered his fortune and who is unable to support his wife and child, both in danger of starvation through the strike of the employees of Whitworth Lawrence, the president of an iron manufacturing concern. Rhoda Goddfroy leaves Tom, drunken and hopeless, and divorces him, to marry Lawrence. Years later Tom returns, a tramp, debonair if still

[1] For detailed reports, with obvious contradictions, see Brown II, 362, 622, and 496, and Winter, *Life of Belasco*, I, 321-6. Both state that it was purchased by Knight from Howard in 1886, yet Knight played in *Baron Rudolph* at the Grand Opera House in New York, September 12, 1881, and at the Windsor Theatre on October 17.

willing to drink, joins apparently in a robbery of Lawrence's home in order to protect his daughter, and kills Lawrence in the consequent struggle. He is convicted of murder and sentenced to be hanged, then pardoned by the governor, who as one of the characters has provided the comedy element, which centers around a young widow. In the revised form,[1] Howard changed his hero from an American to a German baron, who passes through the same decline and misery, but there is no murder or trial scene, and Lawrence commits suicide on account of his own defalcations. Instead of being tried for his life, Baron Rudolph inherits a large estate and returns from Europe to bless his daughter's love affair, which is stressed much more than in *Only a Tramp*. *Baron Rudolph* is less sentimental, the comedy is much more sure in tone, and both characters and situations are more natural in their conception and arrangement. Howard recognized apparently that his forte lay not in melodrama but in comedy.

Hurricanes, a three-act farce comedy, played first in Chicago in 1878, has not survived. The scene was laid in New Rochelle, near New York, and it belonged to the type of *Saratoga*. When it was brought to the Park Theatre, New York, on August 31, Howard wrote as a curtain raiser a charming one-act play, *Old Love Letters*, in which Agnes Booth and Joseph Whiting scored a distinct success. Edward Warburton, a diplomat of forty, calls upon Florence Brownlee, a widow of thirty-two, to return a packet of love letters which she had written him during their engagement, broken after a quarrel thirteen years before. The revival of old memories brings about a renewal of their earlier love. Howard showed his skill in the way he used the rainy day outside to sharpen the contrast with the cozy interior of Mrs. Brownlee's apartment, in which the reunited pair begin to feel the unquenched fire of their early passion. His deftness is apparent also in the natural way in which Mrs. Brownlee sends her maid for

---

[1] First revision, autograph MS. in possession of Samuel French. A later revision is indicated in an autograph manuscript memorandum dated March 2, 1882.

Warburton's letters while she really has them in her bosom at the time. Howard knew well one secret of the skillful playwright—to take the audience into his confidence and by imparting to them information which has been withheld from some of the characters, identify them with the progress of the play.

In *Wives*, produced at Daly's Theatre in October, 1879, Howard cleverly combined Molière's *L'Ecole des maris* and *L'Ecole des femmes* into a bright comedy whose success is described entertainingly by one of the cast.[1] Howard took from *L'Ecole des maris* the story of two brothers, Sganarelle, who has brought up his ward, Isabelle, in the strictest manner, intending her to be his wife, while his brother, Ariste, has allowed her sister, Léonor, many liberties. Isabelle in consequence deceives Sganarelle and marries Valère, while Léonor is content to wed the man who trusted her. With this plot he interwove the story of *L'Ecole des femmes*, in which Agnes, who is being reared by Arnolphe as an innocent fool, in order that she may be a perfect wife, deceives him completely by carrying on an affair with Horace. Howard saw clearly what indeed the criticism of Molière's own day had indicated, that the plot of *L'Ecole des femmes* is too slight for an entire play. In his hands it amplifies admirably the earlier comedy and by making the leading characters friends the combination was easily achieved. Howard treated his material freely. The verse of Molière is translated into effective prose and the speeches are cut judiciously to make room for the added situations and dialogue. The most important change was the substitution for Valère of Captain Fièremonté, who is made a bit stupid in his love-making in order to heighten the comic effect and to strengthen the character of his valet, Dorival, who takes the place of Ergaste in the original. In the third Act, Horace informs the group of male characters of his intention to carry off Agnes that night. Arnolphe departs to prevent it but the remainder agree to help Horace, Ariste pledg-

[1] *Diary of a Daly Débutante*, pp. 38–45 and 49–54.

ing himself to obtain an order from Mazarin to transfer the person of Agnes to the King's protection. The scene in which this is later accomplished by the King's troops under Captain Fièremonté, notwithstanding the arrest of Horace by the city guard, forms the striking climax of the fourth Act and effectively welds the two plots together through the introduction of material of Howard's own creation. The incident in which the innocent Agnes, having been directed by Arnolphe to throw a stone at her lover, wraps a love note around it, is only described by Molière but is brought on the stage in an amusing scene in *Wives*. Indeed, so effective did it prove that an addition in the prompt copy indicates that Agnes, in her anxiety to carry out her guardian's instructions completely, returns to her window and precipitates her flower pot, intended for the lover, on Arnolphe's own devoted head. It is worth noting that this addition, which is farcical, is not in Howard's own handwriting.

Fun in a Green Room, a farce comedy with music, dealing with a broken-down tragic actor and providing a vehicle for the Saulsbury Troubadours in 1882, has not survived.

Up to this time, Howard had been ornamenting clever situations by amusing dialogue and in one play, *The Banker's Daughter*, had drawn two human beings whose happiness was frustrated for a time by the operation of human weakness. In *Young Mrs. Winthrop* he placed on the stage for the first time in America a group of characters whose actions are determined by the power of social laws and the interruption of social distractions without making the prevailing note one of satire. There had been native gentlemen and gentlewomen on our stage before this, as early, in fact, as our first comedy, *The Contrast*, but that play was written to satirize our affectation of foreign customs, and so was *Fashion* in 1845. *Young Mrs. Winthrop* is shot through with a consciousness of social values, but there is no effort made to establish the security of the positions of the characters; it is taken for granted. Douglas Winthrop and his wife Constance are drifting apart. He is immersed in business and she in social affairs. On the night of their little daughter's birthday he asks her not to go to a ball at the house of a Mrs. Warrington of whose standards he does not approve. She has decided to stay at home, when Mrs. Dick Chetwyn, who represents concretely the power of rumor in shaping our destinies, comes to take her to the ball and casually mentions the fact that Douglas has been seen calling at the home of Mrs. Dunbar, one of the set who frequent Mrs. Warrington's house. He has gone there on business but the circumstances lend color to his wife's suspicion of his fidelity. She goes to the ball and while both of them are away the child is taken ill and Constance comes home too late to see her alive. Husband and wife separate but are reunited through the efforts of a fatherly old lawyer, who makes a rather sentimental appeal to them in the last Act. Howard relieved the tension of his main situation by clever comedy, expressed chiefly by Mrs. Chetwyn, who confuses her husbands, past, present and to come, in an amusing manner. But after all, it is the real significance of the main theme, the growing complication of social and professional life in America, which interferes in the happiness of a man and a woman who really love each other, that carried the play to success. It was first performed at the Madison Square Theatre, October 9, 1882, and after its run there was played for years in stock.

Another indication that Howard was broadening in the selection and treatment of his material lies in the fact that while his earlier plays had been "adapted" for the British stage and he had himself altered *Hurricanes*, under the title of *Truth*, before its presentation in London, *Young Mrs. Winthrop* was played there without any modification. Farcical treatment, unless it be strongly marked burlesque, like our earlier Yankee plays, is often unintelligible to a foreign audience, but the gentleman and gentlewoman of one race appeal immediately to those of another and Douglas and Constance Winthrop needed no interpretation to British audiences.

It was perhaps Howard's recognition of this development which prompted him to write his first international contrast, *One of Our Girls*, which ran for two hundred nights, beginning November 10, 1885, at the Lyceum Theatre. The scene is laid in Paris and its suburbs and against the background of the Fonblanque family, who are "mentioned in Froissart," and who are arranging a marriage between their daughter Julie and the Comte de Crebillon, a roué and an accomplished duelist, Howard sets the figure of Kate Shipley, the daughter of an American millionaire, whose frank and self-respecting nature brushes aside the French standards which have wrecked her cousin's life and under which a marriage has been planned between her and the Duc de Fouché-Fonblanque. Captain John Gregory, of the British army, wins Kate and becomes her protector in the complications that follow Julie's flight to her lover, Henri Saint-Hilaire. In this climax of the play, at Henri's rooms, where Kate has followed Julie to prevent her eloping with her cousin, the essential conservatism of the American girl reveals itself. Of course, the model for this scene lay in a similar situation in Sardou's *Les Pattes de Mouche* (1860) in which Suzanne tells Vanhove that she is concerned in an affair with Prosper in order that she may save Clarisse, who has taken refuge in Prosper's room. But a comparison of the scenes will show how well Howard adapted the situation to the character of Kate, just as still later Wilde used it in a British setting in *Lady Windermere's Fan*. Helen Dauvray made an appealing Kate and the lines undoubtedly presented her with many opportunities. But it is capacity rather than charm which is the most definite impression and that innate refinement of imagination which has carried so many of her compatriots through much more trying situations on the Continent. The French characters are frankly conventional stage types, but Howard has represented quite accurately their utter inability to comprehend the essential decency of the relations of American young men and women, and Kate Shipley is like a breath of fresh air in a hothouse. She is much more real than Daisy Miller, in whom Henry James had confused two different types of American girl, and in the Englishman, Captain John Gregory, Howard created a character in which E. H. Sothern made a distinct hit.

The uncertainties of the theatre were strikingly illustrated in the failure of Howard's next play, *Met by Chance*, although Miss Dauvray and Mr. Sothern were again the leading members of the cast. It was a social comedy with an international contrast laid partly in the Adirondacks. According to Daniel Frohman, the difficulty lay in the fact that the subsidiary characters usurped interest to the exclusion of the principal motive. This failure, however, was atoned for by the success of *The Henrietta*, which began its career at the Union Square Theatre on September 26, 1887. It was written for Stuart Robson and William H. Crane and in their hands it achieved one of the greatest popular triumphs of its day. In sixty-eight weeks it drew the sum of $497,852, an object lesson to the managers as to what could be accomplished by the union of a skillful playwright and capable actors, in a play dealing with native conditions. It is a study of a strong, grasping, yet singularly human capitalist, Nicholas Vanalstyne, who is opposed in his domination of Wall Street by his son, Nicholas, Junior, who has ambitions of his own. The younger son, "Bertie, the lamb," played by Robson, is looked upon by his father as a fool. He is a satire on the club man of the period and yet he has won the love of Agnes Lockwood, the sister of Rose, the wife of Nicholas, Junior, and in his quiet but complete contempt for the feverish life which his father and brother live he wins the sympathy of the audience from the start. In the climax of the second Act, a packet of letters written by Nicholas, Junior, to a woman he has betrayed and abandoned, is about to fall into Rose's hands, when Bertie quietly puts them in the fire and assumes the blame in order to save Rose from knowing of her husband's guilt.

The most vivid scene on the stage was that in the broker's

office. Vanalstyne, Senior, is absent and his son attempts to wrest the control of the market from him, even robbing the safe of the securities upon which his father is depending. When the "Old Bull" returns and finds that his fortune is swept away he meets the event with courage, but on learning who it is that has ruined him he attacks his son and then leaves brokenhearted. Bertie arrives just about this time and, with a happy chance that comes as a turn to melodrama, saves the day with the four hundred thousand dollars which his father had given him as his share of the huge fortune he was expecting to leave in its entirety to his elder son. Nicholas, Junior, dies of heart failure while the inexorable stock ticker grinds out its monotonous message as the curtain falls. Bertie wins Agnes in the end, of course, and continues his successful operations on the stock exchange by buying and selling on the toss of a coin. This last is not by any means the only farcical touch in the play. Lady Mary, Nicholas' daughter, and her husband, Lord Arthur Trelawney, while amusing are burlesque, and when the play is read in cold type absurdities appear which pass unnoticed in the rapid action and clever dialogue of the performance.

Howard acknowledged, with his usual scrupulous care, that for one episode in the play, he was indebted to a chapter in *Vanity Fair*.[1] He probably referred to the self sacrifice of Dr. Parke Wainwright, who has loved Rose silently and has concealed his knowledge of her husband's relations with the other woman. Even after his death, Wainwright allows her to preserve her illusions, but Mrs. Cornelia Opdyke, a widow whom Nicholas, Senior, is pursuing, finally tells Rose the true state of affairs. The long service of Major Dobbin to Amelia in *Vanity Fair* and the way in which Becky Sharp finally reveals George Osborne's perfidy, may have suggested this portion of the plot of *The Henrietta*, but the theme is treated so differently that Howard might safely have left the debt unacknowledged. Bertie's placing of the letters in the fire is indeed much

[1] Matthews, Brander. "An Appreciation." *In Memoriam*, p. 37.

more definitely reminiscent of Henry Esmond's sacrifice of his birthright to save Lady Castlewood pain.

The Henrietta is definitely a satire upon the rush and the heartlessness of financial and social life, and being a satire it does not rise to the significance of *Young Mrs. Winthrop* or *Shenandoah*, yet it has a heartiness of humor, a rapidity of action and a prodigality of interesting situations and characters which put many a more sophisticated play to shame. It was played for years by Robson to whom it went after the separation of the partners in 1889, and in 1913 it was revised by Winchell Smith and Victor Bates, and William H. Crane resumed his role of Nicholas Vanalstyne. The changes, which included the turning of Vanalstyne's son into his son-in-law and the omission of Lady Mary and her husband, seemed to mark no improvement on the original. But to at least one auditor the play still compared favorably with its modern rivals. It shines still more in comparison with *Knave and Queen*, which Howard wrote in collaboration with Sir Charles Young about 1887 but which was never played. It is a melodrama, laid in the English countryside, with a conventional plot and little characterization.

It may have been the success of William Gillette's *Held by the Enemy* or it may have been Howard's recognition of the essentially native quality of his art which prompted him to take a comedy of his early days, produced at Macauley's Theatre in Louisville about twenty years before and laid during the Civil War, and build upon it the most successful play of his career. Brander Matthews has called attention to a characteristic action of Howard in his early days of struggle in New York. He took *Drum-taps* to Lester Wallack but that manager was distrustful of a play on an American theme, and inquired of Howard whether he could not lay the scene in the Crimea. But Howard declined to ruin the play and waited for the right occasion. It came in 1888 when *Shenandoah* was produced at the Boston Museum by Montgomery Field.

At first the play was received with little favor,[1] either by the critics or by Field himself, and it was withdrawn. But a young producer who had been among the New York managers who had witnessed the Boston production had faith in the play and Charles Frohman produced it, after certain changes had been made, on September 9, 1889, at the Star Theatre in New York. The ensuing success established Charles Frohman and brought fortune to Bronson Howard. Nor was the success due fundamentally to the fine cast, which included Wilton Lackaye as General Haverill, Henry Miller as Colonel Kerchival West, Viola Allen as Gertrude Ellingham and Effie Shannon as Jenny Buckthorn. After its first long season, it went on tour and has been played by many different companies, and it could be produced to-day with little revision. For while it has no one outstanding character of the vigor of Nicholas Vanalstyne, the main motives, those of love, of patriotism and of self-preservation, are the most universal in their appeal and lift the play to a dignity of sincerity to which no satire can reach. All the leading characters are individualized with Howard's constantly growing skill, and the balance of sympathy between the North and the South is artfully kept without in any way weakening the appeal of patriotism to a generation long enough removed from the Civil War to view it with interest as a theme for artistic treatment.

From the moment when the play opens in Charleston, on the night of the firing on Fort Sumter, the note of conflict is struck. The two friends, Kerchival West and Robert Ellingham, make concrete at once the different points of view of the North and the South. When Ellingham says, "Every loyal son of Virginia will follow her flag. It is our religion," West replies, "My state is New York. If New York should go against the old flag, New York might go to the devil. That is my religion." But Howard never for a moment loses sight

---

[1] H. P. Mawson. *Bronson Howard*, p. 56. But see enthusiastic letter from Boston by Henry Whitby, *Theatre*, IV (1888), pp. 465-7. "*Shenandoah* has captured the town."

of the personal relations of his characters in the discussion of
points of view. Kerchival West and Gertrude Ellingham are
separated by the fortunes of war, but at the end of each act
the action centers upon their love story. In fact Howard carries four love stories through *Shenandoah,* three of them closely
intertwined. The love of General Haverill for his young wife
and his suspicion of her relations with Kerchival are woven
skillfully into the second Act, in the valley of the Shenandoah,
with the war drawing nearer every instant. The natural way
in which the letter from Mrs. Haverill and her portrait come
into West's possession through the capture of the spy who has
in turn taken the portrait from the son of General Haverill,
the finding of them on Colonel West when he lies wounded, and
the proper transfer of the apparently incriminating evidence
to his commanding officer, pass on the stage as the art that
conceals the art. But in a closer study of the play they reveal
the deftness with which Howard makes use of the functions of
war to advance the plot. He understood too that when Gertrude Ellingham is brought face to face with the inevitable
choice between her lover and her country she will choose the
former and it was a sure dramatic instinct which made Howard build the climax of his play on the scene in which she
cheers on her wounded lover to fight for his cause and urges
on her own horse as he dashes by with Sheridan upon him.
For deeper than patriotism and deeper than loyalty is the instinct to which she is responding, the instinct that keeps the
race alive.

But it was not only the stirring quality of *Shenandoah*
which carried it into success. It is, to use Howard's own
phrase, employed in his analysis of *The Banker's Daughter,*
a "satisfactory" play. The audience is keenly interested in
the central motive, the love of Kerchival and Gertrude, and
the author never lets them doubt for a moment the importance
of that motive. But with a prodigality which has before been
mentioned, he brings in a touching scene of tragedy in which
General Haverill pays mutely the last tribute to his dead son,

who goes unrecognized and unforgiven to his grave, and he created that scene of beauty upon which the curtain rises in the third Act, in which Jenny Buckthorn, in her suit of army blue, sounded the trumpet signal to her father's battalion. It is many years since I saw that curtain rise but the scene still lives in my memory with a charm that defies both analysis and time.

Howard never wrote hastily. Augustus Thomas tells us that in his workshop in New Rochelle he would be satisfied if a day's labor produced a dozen lines with which he could be satisfied. His next play, *Aristocracy*, was first performed at Palmer's Theatre, November 14, 1892. It is a deliberate contrast of the rich American from California, the New York family of long-established position and the European patrician. It is evident that Howard's sympathy lies with the first group. He created in Jefferson Stockton a Western capitalist who has real power and self-respect, who has already seen the East and Europe and is under no illusions concerning them. His young wife, Diana, is socially ambitious and he explains to her carefully that the way to conquer New York is *via* London. So he rents a London house, including its titled owner, and everything proceeds according to schedule. His daughter, Virginia, has been engaged to Stuyvesant Laurence of New York but the latter's father has crossed the continent to explain to Stockton the undesirability of the alliance from the point of view of New York, so the engagement is left in abeyance. This conversation is absurd and the entire Laurence family are simply caricatures. We see the Stocktons next in London and when Howard begins to develop the personal relations of his characters he is on surer ground. Mrs. Laurence has succeeded in separating Stuyvesant and Virginia and it is not unnatural that upon the day when she believes her faithless lover is to be married to another girl, Virginia should accept out of pique the urgent suit of the Prince Emil von Haldenwald, of Vienna. The Prince is a caricature also but at least he is more real than the Laurences or than the other examples of European nobility who appear in the drama. He is in pursuit of Diana Stockton and the most natural scene in the play is the one in which the power of his fascination for her, even against her own will, brings about a deadly struggle between Stockton and his son-in-law. The play ends in a weak fashion with the Stocktons established in New York City and with the news of the Prince's death in a duel with his friend the Duc de Vigny-Volante, who has been converted to a startling state of virtuous indignation at his friend's vices by the chastening influence of Virginia. *Aristocracy* was moderately popular but has not held the stage, although it was seen recently in the moving pictures, where it was turned into a sordid and suggestive picture of depravity which would have made its author turn in his grave. It is certainly one of the weakest of his plays.

Peter Stuyvesant, the last of Bronson Howard's plays to be produced, was written in collaboration with Brander Matthews, who contributed the main plot, and in particular the central character, that of the choleric old governor of New Amsterdam. This character was created for William H. Crane and portrayed the governor as a lovable but tyrannical matchmaker, who fails in his attempt at ordering the lives of two young couples, who insist upon arranging them to suit themselves. This love interest had as a background the attempt of the English to capture New Amsterdam with the help of Connecticut. The sense of the period was well established and the play was distinctly better as a piece of literature than *Aristocracy*. It had only a moderate appeal, however, and was withdrawn four weeks after its production at Wallack's Theatre, October 2, 1899.

Howard wrote but one more play, *Kate*, which has not been performed, probably because the nice adjustment of parts, which would have been rendered necessary by the even distribution of interest among the characters, called for a stock company which was not then available. It was published in 1906 in a form midway between the drama and the novel, so that we do not have it as it was originally written for the stage. It is a comedy of social life in England, with the last scene in New York. While it is an international contrast, and the heroine, Kate Hardenbeck, who is the daughter of a rich American, becomes engaged to be married to Earl Catherst without love on either side, the play is not primarily a satire and the tone is more sincere and the treatment firmer than in *Aristocracy*. Lord John Vernor, who has become a rector to keep the living in the family, his *fiancée*, the saintly Dorothea Catherst, and the other English characters are much better drawn than Howard's French or Viennese noblemen; and there are strong scenes in the play such as that between Lord John and Kate in the second Act, in which their growing interest in each other is shown and in which he tells her that he despises her for marrying a man whom she does not love.

From *Saratoga* in 1870 to *Kate* in 1906 Bronson Howard's progress was steady if not entirely constant. The strongly marked caricatures in black and white which disport themselves through the conventional situations in the earlier plays bear little resemblance to the subtler studies of a more settled social order in which the characters take their rightful places as the dominating forces of the drama. Just as Augustin Daly was a transitional force in the theatre of his time so Howard, watching and profiting by the lessons which the deepening art of the drama of his day both at home and abroad could teach him, himself led that transition with a liberal conservatism which was never too old to learn. It was in the expression of his art rather than in the choice of his material that his development came, once the farce of *Saratoga* and the melodrama of *Moorcroft* had been put aside. One must not be confused by the fact that the summit of his success as a dramatist was reached with *The Henrietta*, a play of business and *Shenandoah*, a war play. From first to last, Howard was interested in men and women moving in social relations and he never let his background of finance or war obscure the personal relations of his characters. On the contrary he made that background bring out in sharper relief the great power of social laws and conventions in shaping the lives of human beings. His realism shows perhaps at its best in the restraint which the pursuit or the possession of good form imposes upon a character. It is the inarticulate quality of Bertie Vanalstyne's self-sacrifice which made the instant appeal to an audience and it is the chivalry rather than the personal courage of Kerchival West that made him a hero. Bronson Howard left to others the depiction of the proletariat; he was concerned with the gentleman and gentlewoman. When he wrote of a Western type, he did not select a bad man or a card sharp, and his portrait of Jefferson Stockton is much more true to life than many a more famous character in our fiction or drama. It is the reticence of good breeding which makes even the Prince von Haldenwald almost endurable as a stage creation and this ability of Howard to draw a patrician, by birth or instinct, makes all the more surprising his failure with the Laurence family in *Aristocracy*. That it was the playwright rather than the social observer who erred is proved sufficiently by the existence of *Young Mrs. Winthrop* and *Kate*.

It was not only as an artist but also as a leader of his craft that Bronson Howard assisted in the establishment of the profession of playwriting in the United States. In 1891 he founded the American Dramatists Club with the purpose of giving a sense of solidarity to those who were writing for the stage. Eventually they were to take steps for their professional advancement and protection. He made the initial occasion a luncheon to Charles Gayler, a now forgotten playwright who antedated the Civil War in his efforts in melodrama, and it is interesting to note that among the thirty-five guests, only seven, Clyde Fitch, David Belasco, Franklin Fyles, Paul M. Potter, Henry C. de Mille, Maurice Barrymore, and Sydney Rosenfeld, are remembered to-day. As president of the club, which later became the Society of American Dramatists and Composers, Howard took the leading part in amending the copyright laws to make the piracy of a play a misdemeanor and punish, for the first time, the theft of a playwright's labor by imprisonment.[1] During the close of his career he was fully recognized as the representative dramatist of his time. He met the gradual approach of death through an affection of the heart with the dignity that was his strongest personal characteristic, and during his inactive later years he encouraged and sustained the efforts of younger writers with unfailing generosity. He died on August 4, 1908, at Avon-by-the-Sea, New Jersey, bequeathing his dramatic library to the society he had founded.

Howard, of course, was not alone in his treatment of social contrasts upon the stage. One of the most successful international contrasts of social types came from Howard's collaborator in *Peter Stuyvesant*. Brander Matthews, assisted by George H. Jessop, wrote *A Gold Mine* for John T. Raymond, who produced it in Cincinnati in 1887. Raymond's death did not prevent its further performance, for the part created for him, Silas K. Woolcott, of Grass Valley, California, was afterward played with great effect by Nat C. Goodwin. Woolcott, who has a gold mine to sell, is contrasted with a group of British characters at Sir Everard Foxwood's house at Kew. His sacrifice of his mine to save young George Foxwood is made without heroics, and his wooing of the Honorable Mrs. Meredith is as convincing as it is brief. Sir Everard is the combination of snob and shrewd business man not unknown in the British gentry, and the young Irish barrister, contributed by Jessop, himself an Irishman, is real. The acting of Goodwin when he realized his mine was gone and he must begin the world again, justified his claim to be more than a comedian.[2] *On Probation* (1890), also the joint product of Matthews and Jessop, is a cosmopolitan comedy in which the central character, Jonathan Silsbee, played by William H. Crane, is traveling through Europe with his sister, his niece and her governess, Mary Marlowe, to whom he is secretly engaged. Due to his philan-

[1] *In Memoriam, Bronson Howard*, p. 66
[2] See review of play, *Theatre Magazine*, V, 245.

64

dering, Mary has placed him on probation, and he has lapses
with Lady Frank Brock and Señora Oliveria y Duarez, which
are amusing and are deftly woven into a plot that carries the
somewhat brittle characters successfully.

Matthews' one-act plays, among which *This Picture and
That* (1887) and *The Decision of the Court* (1893) are the
best, belong to the same species as Howells' comedies. The first
is a clever depiction of the second wooing of a widow, with
the background of the Civil War. The second, in which a husband who is about to be divorced calls on his wife to apologize
for the conduct of his attorney in the divorce suit, is sharpened in its contrast by making the husband an Englishman.
Their reconciliation, after the receipt of the telegram announcing the verdict in her favor, is swift and telling. At a
recent production in Philadelphia, the comedy seemed as fresh
as ever. Brander Matthews, however, passed from creative
work to criticism and interpretation of the drama, native and
foreign. For many years he has been the inspiration of students who have learned not only the history but also the principles of play writing from one whose wide knowledge has made
him aware of what is permanent and what is passing in the laws
of the art.

CHAPTER III

WILLIAM DEAN HOWELLS AND THE APPROACH TO REALISM

ONE of the common errors in the discussion of American drama is to assume its divorce from the main currents of our literature. I have shown in my survey of the playwriting before the Civil War how Irving, Willis, Bird, Boker, Longfellow, Mrs. Howe and others were associated with the rise of the romantic drama at a time when the literature in general was following the romantic fashion. It was the untoward circumstances that surrounded the production of plays by native playwrights that prevented or cut short their connection with the theatre. The slow improvement in these conditions which began in the seventies led to the attempts of Mark Twain, Bret Harte, William Dean Howells, Thomas Bailey Aldrich and others to write plays, and while their success in most cases lay rather in the providing of dramatic material than in the shaping of it, this was due to no disregard of the drama, for which indeed all had a profound attachment. Their contributions will be discussed in the appropriate places, but among them Howells demands special treatment, on account both of his achievement and of his influence upon others. The leader in the realistic treatment of familiar life, his example and his critical judgments and inspiration, guided and encouraged Harrigan, Herne, Thomas and Fitch, who have expressed their obligation to him directly and implicitly.[1] From his editorial chair on the *Atlantic Monthly* and from his "Editor's Study" and "Easy Chair" in *Harper's Magazine*, during a period extending with but a few intermissions from 1866 to 1920, he

---

[1] Thomas, *The Print of My Remembrance*, p. 78; *Clyde Fitch and His Letters*, 47, 257, 258; see also chapter on Herne in this volume.

preached the doctrine of truth to life in all art, and when he touched the drama his judgment was sane and discriminating.[1]

But his creative work, of course, surpasses his critical articles in permanent importance. To have done one thing extremely well is enough to justify any dramatist, and Howells is surpassed by no one who has written in English in the creation of the farce comedy, which depends for its effect upon the delicate contrast of domestic and social values. The fact that the one-act plays of Howells were acted chiefly by amateurs has obscured their significance. They were written by a master playwright, whose longer plays were successful on the professional stage, and the fact that there was almost no market for the one-act play unless it were distinctly written for the variety stage restricted their vogue to the amateur. In every sense of the word they are professional plays, as is proved by the performance of *The Mouse Trap* by Mrs. Kendal in London [2] and of *The Garroters*, played under the title of *A Dangerous Ruffian* at the Avenue Theatre, London, in November, 1895. William Archer speaks appreciatively of this performance, noting especially the opportunity which the character of Mrs. Roberts gave to a competent actress.[3] Bernard Shaw also paid tribute to the merits of this performance.[4]

Howells published his farces first in the *Atlantic Monthly,* then in *Harper's Weekly* and finally in *Harper's Magazine,*

[1] See especially "The Recent Dramatic Season," *North American Review,* CXXLII (1901), 468-80.

[2] Howells states definitely in a letter to J. Henry Harper, printed in *The House of Harper,* p. 320, "One of them enjoyed a most noble distinction in London, where *The Mouse Trap* was twice played with an all-star cast for a charity which naturally and rightly did not include the author; he thought it riches to have his play done by Miss Ellen Terry and Mrs. Kendal." No record of the performance by Miss Terry can be found and in a letter from Mrs. Kendal to Miss Howells (August 10, 1926) she states that her own performance was given at Queen's Hall, "many years ago" and that "Miss Ellen Terry did not appear in your father's farce of *The Mouse Trap.*" That Howells was in receipt of some return from the professional performances of his farces is evidenced also in a letter to Mark Twain (April 26, 1903) in which he speaks of his agent arranging for the production of "one of my farces on the London stage" and transmitting to him "22 pounds on account of farce."

[3] *Theatrical World,* Nov. 30, 1895, p. 373.

[4] *Dramatic Opinions and Essays,* I, 265-6.

where they became one of the attractions of the Christmas number, advance sheets being in demand months before their publication.[1]

In *The Parlor Car* (1876) the qualities that make these comedies fresh and vital even to-day are at once apparent. First of all comes naturalness. Beginning with the choice of scene, a place in which people may easily meet, we meet probability everywhere, from the catching of the heroine's polonaise in the window to the jar that throws her into the hero's arms at the proper moment. The dialogue is never "literary"—it is just that compromise between actual conversation and perfect English which is suitable for the stage. Next we notice the rigid economy of the reader's attention. Not a word is wasted, and if retort follows retort with a cleverness that no rival has surpassed, there is no oversubtlety to confuse. Finally, the situation, even when it dominates, never overshadows the characters. These qualities are not so vivid in *The Parlor Car* as they became later, but they are real and Howells' knowledge of the feminine nature in its ability to escape the consequences of its inconsistencies is already apparent.

Howells' first dramatic effort to be produced professionally was, curiously enough, in the field of the heroic play. It was a translation of *Sansone* by Ippolito d'Aste, made for Charles P. Pope, who produced it first at the Olympic Theatre in St. Louis on October 5, 1874, apparently with success.[2] Howells seems to have followed the structure of the Italian play closely but his blank-verse rendering of the Italian is free and shows his intuitive sense of the distinction between dramatic and epic blank verse. He was able too to enter into the spirit of a play based upon passion, revenge and the fate of a great soul who pulls down his enemy's temple, content to be crushed himself within the ruins. Howells' version was used in 1889 by Alexander Salvini.

In 1877 Howells wrote two longer comedies, *Out of the*

[1] Harper, J. H., *The House of Harper*, p. 320.
[2] Letter from Pope to Howells, October 9, 1874.

Question and *A Counterfeit Presentment*. The latter was produced by Lawrence Barrett at the Grand Opera House in Cincinnati, October 11, 1877. It is to be regretted that *Out of the Question*, the first of these to be written, should not have had an opportunity upon the professional stage, although there can be no doubt that of the two it is less suited for the theatre. In this play Howells had a theme that he loved to treat, the contrast of the natural gentleman with the girl who is the product of generations of breeding, and who is held back by her traditions, made concrete by her family, but who triumphs over them. It was a theme which Bret Harte also treated, but from a sentimental point of view. Howells approached the situation from the satiric angle, and some of his best shafts at the artificial standards of human conduct are contained in this almost forgotten comedy.

A Counterfeit Presentment departs from the normal in the central situation. Bartlett, an artist who is painting at the Ponkwasset Hotel, is naturally disconcerted when three new arrivals, General Wyatt, his wife and his daughter Constance, betray the greatest abhorrence upon meeting him. This is explained by the extraordinary resemblance Bartlett bears to a scoundrel who had been engaged to Constance and who has been forced by General Wyatt, upon the discovery of his crimes, to break the engagement. General Wyatt prefers to conceal the real nature of his daughter's lover from her, hoping that her pride will bring her through the ordeal. But she drops instead into nervous collapse, which is naturally not improved by her meeting with Bartlett. This situation is presented to us by the most uncompromising realist of his day without apology, and his defense might well be that he provides a dramatic situation which, once the initial difficulty is surmounted, is developed logically enough. Of course Bartlett falls in love with Constance, and the attraction and repulsion of the man with his temperamental nature and the woman struggling out of a nervous breakdown caused by disappointed love provide some scenes which give opportunities for clever acting. *A Counterfeit Presentment* is not farce. The characters carry the main interest, and the dialogue reveals Howells' powers of implication. When Mrs. Wyatt assures Constance that Bartlett does not know of her earlier engagement, the scene proceeds:

Mrs. Wyatt: But what made you think he knows?
Constance: (*Solemnly*) He behaved just as if he didn't.
Mrs. Wyatt: Ah, you can't judge from that, my dear. (*Impressively*) Men are very different.
Constance: (*Doubtfully*) Do you think so, mamma?
Mrs. Wyatt: I'm certain of it.

According to Barrett's letter to Howells, October 13, 1877, *The Counterfeit Presentment* was a genuine and pronounced triumph. Barrett asked, however, for certain changes, and a new first Act was written by Howells and performed in December to Barrett's satisfaction. Howells in consequence began the adaptation of *Un Drama Nuevo* by the well-known Spanish playwright, Tamayo y Baus, and while Daly's adaptation had failed, that of Howells succeeded.[1] In a letter written January 14, 1916, in response to an inquiry of mine, Howells said:

Yorick's Love is not my play, though I tampered with a masterpiece in making some slight additions to it. . . . I translated it for Lawrence Barrett, who, against my entreaties, called it mine in his advertisements.

Howells was too modest in speaking of his changes. In the first Act he introduced the author and the prompter to explain the situation and he cut the longer speeches occasionally. He also changed the prose at times to blank verse. The most serious change was the substitution of Heywood for Shakespeare. This change was made by Barrett probably in order that the part taken by Shakespeare should be reduced in importance in favor of the star part of Yorick. Howells seems to have acquiesced in this alteration, however, for among the manu-

[1] See for plot of *Un Drama Nuevo* and discussion of the Daly version, pp. 32-4.

scripts of the play are found later revisions in his hand, in which the word "Heywood" appears.

But the changes in the final scene of the play are most important. Yorick kills Edmund, who is defending Alice, and Yorick goes out of his head and begins to babble tragically over Edmund's body. For this scene, Howells provided, in flexible and moving blank verse, a picture of the love of an older man for the boy he had cherished. As Howells' version remains unpublished, the beginning of the scene is quoted:

Yorick: My boy, my boy, my boy! Why! Look you, Master,
   He was a little lad when first I saw him,
   Tattered, and wan with hunger, with such eyes,
   Full of such silent histories of sorrow,
   Of orphanage, and all the world's unkindness,
   They went straight to my heart. I took him home
   And there I have kept him ever since; nor love
   Nor hate, nor even murder, could
   Dislodge him. There he lieth dead, within
   My heart. O I could tell you things, of how
   I used to watch him in the night, and rise
   And creep and kneel beside his little bed
   Where we had prayed together ere he slept
   And listen to his breathing, feel his pulse,
   To know if any sickness threatened him.
   If he were hurt, I suffered worse than he;
   His childish joys made me a happy child.
   You all can bear me witness how I loved him:
   My love has made me many a time the laugh
   Of all of you.
    . . . .
   (*After a pause*)
   And when he grew a man, he grew a man
   After my heart, so generous, true and bold,
   So faithful and so loving—
    . . . .
   (*to Shakespeare*)
   Master, how ill a thing it is to be
   Revenged! Ay, vengeance is too much
   For us weak mortals—the blood makes us drunk,
   It makes us mad! Ay, vengeance is the Lord's:

"Vengeance is mine; I will repay," He said.
He will repay; He will repay, He said.
Canst thou imagine how I could kill my boy?
It must have been an accident, methinks;
A slip o' the foot, an error of the hand,
That did so often bless him. I would fain
Know how it chanced. Lend me thy sword good master.
Since he hath worn my point within his heart,
   I—cannot touch it.
   (*Shakespeare shrinks back but Yorick snatches his
sword from its sheath*)
               Why, be not afraid!
You are thinking of that blackamoor of Venice,
And surely not of this poor, merry Yorick,
That never yet was apt for tragedy.
I shall not harm myself: I am past all harm!
It must have happened thus.
(*As he turns the point on his breast, they start toward
him; he laughs and uncovers it.*)
               Nay, do not fear:
If I should pass this rapier through my breast,
It would not hurt me; I am dead within.

Yorick's Love was first performed at the Euclid Opera
House in Cleveland, Ohio, October 25, 1878, and it retained a
regular place in Barrett's répertoire as late as 1891, the year
of his death, when he produced it at the Broadway Theatre. The
effect on a competent judge may be seen in the letters of John
Hay to Whitelaw Reid and to Howells. "It was a very different play," he said, "from the one I saw at the Fifth Avenue
Theatre some years ago, improved almost beyond recognition."
He also approved of "keeping Shakespeare behind the flies,"
saying that "he was almost grotesque in the original." [1] In
the opinion of other critics, *Yorick's Love* gave Barrett an
opportunity to show real ability in characterization, and to
advance from theatricality to adequate power in interpreting
dramatic action. *Yorick's Love* was played at the Lyceum
Theatre in London, April 14, 1884. It was revived by Lewis
Morrison in 1895 in Boston.

[1] Thayer, W. R. *The Life of John Hay*, I, 398–402.

WILLIAM DEAN HOWELLS

Howells' professional attitude is evidenced by his dramatization of *Miles Standish* for Barrett in 1879, with which the actor planned to open his season, though it apparently was not produced.

His versatility as well as his inventive ability is shown in the delightful libretto for *A Sea Change or Love's Stowaway.* It was to have been produced at the Bijou Theatre in Boston, November, 1884, with musical accompaniment by George Henchel, but owing to the death of the manager it never saw the stage. Howells calls the published version a "lyricated farce," and indeed the supple and varied lyrics rival Gilbert, from whom the general inspiration came. But *A Sea Change* is not directed at any current craze or foible; it satirizes the capricious, inconsequent type of American girl who rejects a lover for no reason, finds him on the steamer, "a Retarder," on which they each have taken refuge, and promptly demands that he go ashore. The captain solemnly suggests his transfer to a floating iceberg, and Howells then introduced a dream scene of ingenious incongruity in which nearly all the passengers decamp on to the iceberg to join the Ice Princess and her maidens. It is fooling of a priceless quality—the absurdities of comic opera are woven into the plot with a skill that causes us to wonder again why Howells made only one attempt in this field. For example, when Muriel first comes on board this conversation follows:

Captain: And what can I do for you, miss?

Muriel: Nothing. But the man at the wheel makes me giddy, turning it round so.

Captain: (*Through his trumpet to the man at the wheel*) Lash your wheel!

Man at the wheel: (*Obeying*) Ay, ay, sir! (*Attempting to sing*) I am the—

Captain: (*Sternly*) Belay that! (*To Muriel*) Anything more, miss?

Muriel: No,—only the ship seems to tremble a good deal.

Captain: (*To the man at the wheel*) Tell the officer on duty to send me the engineer.

Man at the wheel: Ay, ay, sir! (*Down speaking tube*) Engineer!
Engineer: (*Appearing instantly, and attempting to sing*) I am
    the—
Chorus: Oh, stow it!
    We know it.
Captain: We've had enough of explanation and we'll show it.

Of the lyric that ensues one stanza will illustrate his capacity:

> If you are a statesman or ward politician,
> A man with a grievance, a maid with a grief,
> An agent, a dentist, a soul with a mission,
> Beware how you turn to your friends for relief.
> I'll be frank with you all:
> The right way for you is to hire a hall!
> Yes, hire a hall!

Howells also dramatized his novel of *A Foregone Conclusion* and it was produced at a matinée performance at the Madison Square Theatre on November 18, 1886. Alexander Salvini played the part of Don Ippolito, the priest who falls in love with an American girl. The theme is at best an unpleasant one and the novel is hardly one of Howells' best efforts. The drama did not secure a place upon the stage, although it was played in Boston in November, 1889, at the Tremont Theatre.

It was, however, in 1883, when Howells was at the height of his creative power, that he introduced in *The Sleeping Car* the characters which were to delight two generations. Mrs. Agnes Roberts is incomparable. From the moment she begins her tireless communion with the world, giving expression to every thought as it rises to the surface of her mind, she is a perfect fountain of humor. With a skill that is positively uncanny, Howells never allows her to become merely a caricature; she is a living woman whom we have all known and heard, thinking aloud in private and public. Her husband, the absent-minded Edward Roberts, and her brother, Willis Campbell, whose advent from California provides her with conversa-

tion through the enlivening hours while she scatters relentlessly
the silence of the sleeping car, are merely introduced in this
opening farce. But in *The Elevator* (1885) Willis Campbell
reveals his practical nature in saving the guests of the Roberts, who are imprisoned in the elevator which has come to rest
between the fourth and fifth floors. The gathering of the
guests, the wonder at the lateness of the missing ones, is carried just to the point when one actually feels the nervous tension
of Mrs. Roberts, then we are transferred to the elevator in
which all the prisoners, from Aunt Mary to the elevator boy,
reveal themselves by their reaction to supposed danger. The
device of making this second scene contemporaneous with the
first brings the next action on at just the right moment, for
the anxiety of the prisoners makes them react to the well-
meaning but stupid inquiries of Roberts, Mrs. Roberts, Dr.
Lawton and the others, which are spoken through the grating
of the elevator shaft. Then Campbell arrives and inquires
why they do not try running it *down* since it will not go *up*.
The art with which Howells has kept the reader or hearer from
making the same suggestion can be appreciated only when he
carefully studies the subtle suggestions by which the conversation in the elevator directs his thoughts away from the obvious
solution.

The Elevator requires two changes of scene and *The Garroters* (1886) one, but after all it is not as one-act plays that
these farces are important. Every sentence in *The Garroters*
tells, from the moment Roberts arrives in his drawing room
dishevelled and worn out after his supposed encounter with a
robber on the Common, to be met with a torrent of sympathy
and admiration from his wife for his courage in recapturing
his property. The sickening moment when he realizes that
his watch has never left his dressing table and that the tousled
Mr. Bemis has been his victim is matched only by the futile
effort of Roberts, at Campbell's suggestion, to carry the matter off as a joke. Archer rightly selected Mrs. Roberts as the
most promising character when the play was produced at the

Avenue Theatre, for her amplitude of conversational vibration envelops the action.

To this group Howells next added Mrs. Amy Somers, a young widow, the heroine of *Five O'Clock Tea* (1889) and *The Mouse Trap* (1889). She is more clever than Agnes Roberts, yet just as feminine, and Howells never confuses their functions. The sophisticated skirmish between Campbell and Amy Somers which takes place in the intervals of a tea-party is masterly in its revelation of deeper feeling beneath. There is finer art here than in *The Mouse Trap*, but the picture of the ladies perched upon the furniture in dread of the mouse that exists only in Campbell's imagination is unforgettable. It leads up also to a climax that must have given Mrs. Kendal a fine opportunity, for the dialogue between Mrs. Somers and Campbell after the rest have fled contains in epitome the eternal masculine and feminine, until she guides the action by declaring:

Mrs. Somers: Nothing. But if I were a man—
Campbell: Well?
Mrs. Somers: Well, in the first place, I wouldn't have got you wrought up so.
Campbell: Well, but if you had! Suppose you had done all that I've done, and that I was up there in your place standing on a chair, and wouldn't let you leave the room, and wouldn't get down and walk out, and wouldn't allow myself to be carried, what should you do?
Mrs. Somers: (*Who has been regarding him attentively over the top of her fan, which she holds pressed against her face*) Why, I suppose if you wouldn't let me help you willingly—*I should use violence.*
Campbell: You witch!
   (*As he makes a wild rush upon her, the curtain which in the plays of this author has a strict regard for the covenances, abruptly descends.*)

In *A Likely Story* (1889) the conversation between Mr. and Mrs. Willis Campbell reaches almost the high-water mark of

Howells' effortless ease. The incidents here, however, are not so capably handled and the ending is therefore weaker. *The Albany Depot* is amusing, if a bit more obvious, for there is a distinction in social values which seems to come in and go out with Amy Somers, and she is absent except as the impelling motive of Mrs. Roberts' urgent necessity for a cook. The social cleavage which separates Mrs. McIlheny from her cousin Maggie, the cook, is, however, a subtle hit at the artificialities of all social rifts.

The perfection of Howells' art in the farce came with *A Letter of Introduction* (1892) and in the comedy with *The Unexpected Guests* (1893). In the first, Edward Roberts, longing to be rid of a traveling Englishman, has given him a letter of introduction to his uncle in New York and has written to his uncle privately, telling him his opinion of the visitor. He asks the Englishman to mail the latter missive and returns to his writing, to be interrupted by Mrs. Roberts' verbal flow of sympathy for his wasted time and by the visit of Willis and Amy Campbell. Of course Willis suggests that Roberts has misplaced the letters in their respective envelopes, and when the Englishman returns with an inquiry as to a possible mistake, the conversation in which they all try to placate him before he mildly reveals his envelope with nothing in it, is delightful.

In *The Unexpected Guests* the same group assemble for dinner, as in *The Elevator*, but this time they are at the home of Amy Campbell. Again they come late, but Mrs. Campbell meets the delay with much more ease than Mrs. Roberts did and she rises to the supreme necessity for social falsehood on the arrival of the Belforts, whom she believes have declined her invitation. Despite her skill, the guests one by one become aware of the situation, while as a chorus to their fibs the phonograph in the next room chants "Truth crushed to earth shall rise again." Finally the Belforts re-enter and then the stentorian voice of the man below calling the Iroquois Club to send a dozen more quails for the unexpected guests ends her attempts at concealment. But she meets the blow with her flag flying, and even the disclosure that her hasty misreading of Mrs. Belfort's note of acceptance has been the cause of all the difficulty only brings out her reserves, which leave her mistress of the situation as the curtain falls.

In *The Unexpected Guests* Howells passes out of the category of farce into the comedy of manners, but in *Evening Dress* (1893) he once more allows us to revel in the domestic difficulties of Roberts, left by his wife to dress and follow her to a musicale. Her conversation, as she floats out of the apartment while she urges him to think of something else she should remember to tell him, is a little classic of married life, but the search for his dress suit is pure farce and never rises above it. *A Masterpiece of Diplomacy* (1894) and *The Smoking Car* (1900) are amusing, but somehow we wish we had said good-by to the inimitable quartet in one of their great moments. With the disappearance of the Campbells and the Roberts the best period of comedy was over. It corresponds naturally to the greatest period of Howells in the novel, which began with *A Modern Instance* and ended with *The World of Chance*, but just as it was with his fiction, an occasional effort of his later period almost rivals his finest work. In fact, *Bride Roses* (1893), his one serious prose play, belongs to the great creative moments, and its poignant tragedy is intensified by the contrast between the typical indecision of the First Lady, who is selecting flowers for her tea at which a young girl is to pour, and the swift choice of the Second Lady, who selects the same roses for the funeral of the girl, who has suddenly died. Social consciousness is here in its real sense, but *Bride Roses* is allied more closely to such a dramatic sketch in verse as *The Mother and the Father* (1909) than it is to the other prose plays. These become lighter through *A Previous Engagement* (1897) and *Room Forty-Five* (1900), *An Indian Giver* (1900), and *Parting Friends* (1911). We remember the situations but not the characters, and indeed in certain of the farces which have had only magazine publication, Howells passes from satire of life to a satire on the stock figures of melodrama. *Saved; an Emotional Drama* (1908) brings on the stage at night the burglar, the child who finds him, the wife who is about to elope with her lover, the lover, the wife's sister who takes him away from her, and the husband and father who desires above everything a cup of coffee. In *A True Born Hero* (1909) Howells presents us with the conventional situation of the youthful hero who is planning to sacrifice himself to save a worthless woman who is trying to use him as a screen for her intrigue. But Howells makes him take the sensible course of declining to be a sacrifice, and expresses through one of the other characters the hope that some day such a hero will be present in plays and novels. Further than this, satire could hardly go, though Howells, in *The Impossible; a Mystery Play* (1910), made a not very successful attempt to preach a moral with the aid of a supernatural telephone.

It is only by a consideration of his work historically as well as critically that its importance and its variety become apparent. We have seen how the great realist was one of the prime movers in the revival of romantic plays on the stage, and it must not be forgotten that *A Counterfeit Presentment* was played by Lawrence Barrett before Bronson Howard had passed out of melodrama into comedy. How much more permanent is Howells' work in its essential quality of timelessness can be appreciated most quickly by comparing this play with *The Banker's Daughter, Old Lavender* or *The Danites*. His sense for the permanent is shown in his choice of those modern improvements, many new in his day, for the scene or the mechanics of his plays. He chooses the elevator, the sleeping car, the phonograph, the telephone, never the bicycle or any passing fad. Consequently they can be played or read to-day with little sense of outworn fashion. Of course they are based on eternal motives, love, marriage, the insistent clutch of the feminine upon the direction of personal affairs, the masculine carelessness or absentmindedness in Roberts, the masculine love of teasing in Campbell. Dwelling upon similar motives so often, it is surprising how little he repeats himself.

It is indeed this variety in his material and method which is usually disregarded. He began in *The Parlor Car, The Sleeping Car* and *The Register* with domestic farce. With *The Garroters* and *The Elevator* the social scene becomes a background but the complications are still external. In *The Mouse Trap* Amy Somers takes her place as the central figure, and with her entrance the rules and inhibitions of social life begin to be the directing forces of the plays. They remain so in *Five O'Clock Tea, A Likely Story, A Letter of Introduction* and *The Unexpected Guests*, and the progress of Howells' social consciousness cannot better be exemplified than in a comparison between *The Elevator* and *The Unexpected Guests*. Both have a dinner party as their setting, but in the first, laid at Mrs. Roberts' apartment, social laws have no bearing upon the plot, while in *The Unexpected Guests*, which takes place in Mrs. Campbell's drawing room, the whole significance of the play depends upon her maintenance of a social illusion. In *The Elevator* the danger is physical and is sufficiently serious; in *The Unexpected Guests* there is no danger except to the social susceptibilities of the hostess, and yet the art of the playwright holds our attention more closely and with more real interest. For Howells has drawn deftly characters who determine the action and are living beings. It is therefore comedy of manners and not farce at all. That is why *Five O'Clock Tea*, which is also comedy, rises with *The Unexpected Guests* above the level of the farces. For in *Five O'Clock Tea* there is also the interplay of character rather than the precipitation of action by accident.

The form of both comedies and farces reflects the exterior arrangement into scenes which Howells learned from his study of French drama. But there is little that is foreign in his atmosphere or form. Usually, outside of his definitely longer plays, the form is that of the one-act play. But the scene changes in several, and Howells was satisfied with the higher unity of action. In his earlier plays he introduces his characters by delightful touches of description in which he anticipated both Barrie and Shaw, to mention only two of his many successors. For as Clyde Fitch well said, the eighties and nineties were "the Howells age," and many who do not acknowledge it were affected by his unending struggle for truth in art. His plays taught manners and social values to thousands who played in them or saw them on the amateur stage. That they were played professionally so seldom was a loss to our stage which can hardly be estimated.

CHAPTER IV

HARRIGAN, HOYT, AND THE COMEDY OF TYPES

WHILE Bronson Howard was placing on our stage his studies of men and women moving in social relations, there was developing a drama wrought out of the lower life of the larger Eastern cities, written by a playwright native to New York, and significant because of the fidelity with which the types of character are portrayed.

Edward Harrigan was born in New York City, October 26, 1845. His family came to Canada in the Eighteenth Century and Cape Harrigan, on the northern coast of Labrador, was named for an ancestor of the playwright. William Harrigan, his father, a native of Newfoundland, was a sea captain and shipbuilder. This relation to the sea is reflected in several of Edward Harrigan's plays.

His connection with the theatre began about 1867. He had run away from home, on account of his father's second marriage, and gone as far as Panama by sea. Reaching San Francisco, he joined the company of the well-known comédienne, Lotta, and remained in San Francisco, playing in comedies, melodramas and farces, mainly at the Bella Union Theatre. Forming a partnership with Sam Rickey, a comedian, he made his way East, playing in Chicago and appearing first in New York at the Globe Theatre, November 21, 1870, where the partners produced a sketch entitled *A Little Fraud*. But his marked success came with his union with Anthony Cannon, whose stage name was Tony Hart, and whom he met during a later trip to Chicago. They varied their road tours with occasional appearances at the Union Square and Bowery Theatres, and became established in New York, when on December 2, 1872, they appeared at the Theatre Comique at 514

82

Edmund Hausge

Broadway in *The Day We Went West* and *The Big and Little
of It*. They withdrew in July, 1875, but became managers
in August, 1876, and made the house one of the best known
in New York City. Here were produced some of their most
successful plays, like *The Mulligan Guard Ball*. In April
1881, the house was torn down. They then refitted the old
Globe Theatre, at 728 Broadway, as the New Theatre Comique, and it was opened August 29, 1881, with Harrigan's
play, *The Major*. Here *Squatter Sovereignty* and *Cordelia's
Aspirations* first saw the stage. This theatre was destroyed
by fire December 28, 1884. Not daunted by this misfortune,
for the insurance had lapsed, Harrigan leased the Park Theatre at Thirty-fifth Street and Broadway, which he conducted
with slight interruptions as Harrigan's Park Theatre, until
April 13, 1891. In the meantime he and Hart had parted
company. In 1890 he built a new theatre on Thirty-fifth
Street near Sixth Avenue, which he leased to Richard Mansfield in March, 1895, and which is now the Garrick Theatre.
Harrigan continued to act, especially in his own characters,
such as *Old Lavender*, his last appearance in regular drama
being in *His Wife's Family* at Wallack's Theatre, October
6, 1908, although he took part in a public Gambol of the
Lambs, at the Metropolitan Opera House in 1909. He died
June 6, 1911.[1]

Harrigan's plays grew out of the vaudeville sketches in
which he as the male character and Hart as the female, impersonated the types of city life which delighted the audience
of the Theatre Comique with their humor and fidelity to life.
But fortunately, no question as to joint authorship disturbs
the historian of the drama, for after the separation of the
partners in 1885, the plays went on and Hart made no attempt
at drama. Record can be found of over eighty vaudeville
sketches composed by Edward Harrigan between 1870 and
1879, and while these are duplications in some cases, the va-

---

[1] The details of Harrigan's life, which differ from printed accounts in several instances, have been furnished by his son, Dr. Anthony Hart Harrigan.

riety of treatment is indicated by the titles, which take in politics, baseball, life insurance, the army, the militia, and deal with the negro and the Irish, German, Italian and other immigrant types. In their first stages, these sketches returned, curiously enough, to the primary conception of French *vaudeville:* a popular song composed and sung by the Provençal troubadours to ridicule some well-known personage.

The development from this song to the articulated play is a significant one for the history of the theatre in America. The song led to the duet, the duet to a dialogue. In the early sixties, the Theatre Comique presented a variety show with a more or less permanent company. F. S. Chanfrau was still appearing in *A Glance at New York* (1848), which reveals the continuity of our dramatic history. In 1872 Josh Hart, the manager, engaged Harrigan and Hart to give their songs and dialogues as part of a variety show. The programs of the Theatre Comique show how gradually the share of Harrigan and Hart in the entertainment grew from one number to several, and how even before they assumed the management of the theatre in 1876, a short play of from one to seven scenes like *The Blue and the Gray*, a Civil War sketch, and *Down Broadway*, a local burlesque, won their right to the coveted position at the end of the program. Harrigan's success was not confined to this country. A program of the variety theatre, the St. James Hall in Piccadilly, London, for November 7, 1877, reveals "an entirely new musical sketch, . . . by Edward Harrigan, Esq., entitled 'Walking for dat Cake,' " which is made a feature of the evening.

Another phase of Harrigan's development is illustrated by the various forms of *The Doyle Brothers.* As early as August, 1874, a three-act play by that name was produced at the Theatre Comique. This was probably the anonymous melodrama which, according to the manuscript, was "written for Harrigan and Hart," and which is simply an old-fashioned murder and arson play, laid in New Orleans. During its progress two actors, Darby and Lanty Doyle, rescue the hero,

Jerold, from prison. It is evident from the changes made in Harrigan's autograph manuscript of *The Doyle Brothers* how cleverly he used older material and adapted it to his own needs and talents. In its new form it is still a play in three acts, but Darby and Lanty have become the heroes, and in the court scene in which they rescue Jerold they occupy the center of the stage. Indeed, the old melodrama has become a vehicle for the character acting of the two partners. Harrigan took three parts, Darby Doyle, an Irish actor, old Pete, a loyal negro, and Italian Joe, a peanut vender. Hart played in three also, Lanty Doyle, Luke, a minor character, and Johanna, the heroine, who is beloved by Jerold. The old murder and arson play had become simply a means of giving Harrigan and Hart time to change their make-up for the new character part. The play reappears in their répertoire for several years, either as *Darby and Lanty* or under its original name.

Obviously it is difficult to assign a beginning to the original full-length play by Harrigan. One of the earliest, which also showed the longest vitality, was *Old Lavender*, first produced at the Theatre Comique, September 3, 1877, and growing out of a vaudeville sketch, *Old Lavender Water or Round the Docks*, played earlier in the year. Old Lavender is the genial drunkard, the descendant of Rip Van Winkle and the ancestor of "Lightnin' " Bill Jones. As the cashier of a bank he takes the blame for the misdeeds of others, and his degradation brings us to the docks of the river and to the lower form of sailors' boarding houses in New York. It held the stage for many years and was a favorite part of its creator, who undoubtedly filled its traditional outlines with life. But it did not reveal any original characterization.

While the Mulligan cycle was slowly maturing, Harrigan was also experimenting in the Irish play of the school of Boucicault. Possibly the earliest of these was *Iascaire*, a play in nine scenes, produced November 20, 1876, at the Theatre Comique. It is called a romantic play by its author, and it has certain elements of romance. Harrigan played the character of Michael Delany, a misshapen foundling whose father, Cornelius Lynch, is the villain of the piece—the stock figure of the lawyer who grinds the poor. The conception of Michael is not bad, however. He turns at last on his father and persecutor and after saving Jerold Sullivan, the Irish rebel, kills Lynch in a desperate struggle. Hart played Shaun O'Kelly "the best fisherman in Galway." Another imitation of Boucicault came in 1878, in *The Lorgaire*. It was first a vaudeville sketch, then a three-act play, an interesting drama of the older fashion, laid in a fishing village on the west coast of Ireland. The Lorgaire is a detective from Scotland Yard and he solves the traditional situations, which involve the missing heir, a murder and a false accusation.

That Harrigan was influenced by Boucicault's dramas of Irish life cannot be doubted, for we find him playing in a sketch called *Arrah-na-Brogue* in 1873. But his conception of Irish character, while it vied in reality with that of Boucicault, was of a different nature. Boucicault's contribution, as I have indicated,[1] lay in his treatment of the Irish villager and the Irish gentry, on their native soil. With equal insight, Harrigan treated the Irish immigrant who had come to this country after the famine of 1848, and who had remained in the cities of the East. He did not touch the generation that had come before that time, the younger sons of the gentry, or of the commercial class, who had become assimilated into our national life. For the purposes of vivid contrast, he chose the keeper of the corner grocery, Dan Mulligan, who had fought in the Civil War with "the Sixty-ninth," and who is a leader of his clan. He is honest, courageous, loyal, impulsive, irrational, likely to become drunk and disorderly at slight provocation, and while irascible and quarrelsome, is forgiving and generous even to his enemies. His mate, Cordelia, is his counterpart, and yet she is individualized. She is at the beginning of the cycle his prudent and frugal helpmeet, she looks up to him and is at once a wife and a mother to him. But

---

[1] *History of the American Drama from the Beginning to the Civil War*, pp. 373–86.

later she becomes affected by the itch for social distinction and one of the best of the plays, *Cordelia's Aspirations*, tells the story of her rise and his fall, to his financial ruin. The quiet courage with which he returns to his corner grocery and she takes boarders to pay their debts, and the stoicism of both, are most appealing.

But the Irish characters are not Harrigan's only creations. As a contrast to the Celtic temperament of Dan Mulligan, he drew Gustave Lochmuller, the German butcher, his arch enemy and rival; and the instinctive antipathy of Celt and Teuton flourishes in comedy on American soil. They dislike each other for their very virtues; and their utter inability to comprehend each other's point of view makes for real comedy.

Even more vividly drawn than the German were the negro types, Rebecca Allup, the widow who cooks for the Mulligans; the Reverend Palestine Puter, who disappears with the treasury of the Full Moons, "a secret order formed to keep the Irish off the street cars"; Captain Primrose, the barber; and the rest. They are almost perfect pictures of the guerillas of life, hanging on the skirts of the other races and in their reckless gayety, improvidence, impudence and superstition, adding almost unlimited possibilities to the human comedy.

The name of Mulligan first appears in the sketch and song of *The Mulligan Guard*, produced at the Academy of Music in Chicago, July 15, 1873, and later, September 8, at the Theatre Comique in New York. It was a burlesque upon the target excursions of the military organizations, named after local politicians, which sprang up in the wards of New York City. After paying their respects to the ward leader, these companies marched to the depot or steamer landing, en route to the picnic ground where the target, carried in the rear by a negro, was to be placed. These excursions sometimes concluded with a small riot, in which people were killed or wounded. In a letter written in 1874, Harrigan states that he wrote the sketch as a burlesque upon this "nuisance." In 1875 the contrast between the Irish and negro races appeared in *The Mul-*

ligan Guards and the Skidmores. The slow development by which a song with casual dialogue slowly grew into a coherent play, with occasional songs, is illustrated by the two forms of *The Mulligan Guard Picnic.*[1]

The first form, which took about forty minutes to play, appeared on the stage of the Theatre Comique, September 23, 1878. Harrigan describes it on the manuscript as "an outrageous sketch," and with the instinct of a playwright he took it off after a short run, because he wished to give more body to it. It is little more than the amplification of the picnic in *The Mulligan Guard,* although there is a slight plot concerning the disappearance of Dan Mulligan and the desire of Cordelia, his wife, to marry a dancing master. In its second form (1880), the apparent drowning of Lochmuller and the projected marriage of his widow is set against a background of the continued rivalry of the Skidmores and the Mulligans.

But it was in *The Mulligan Guard Ball,* which began January 13, 1879, at the Theatre Comique, and made a tremendous hit, running one hundred nights, that the outlines of the Mulligan cycle became established. Dan and Cordelia Mulligan are disturbed by their son Tom, who wishes to marry Katrina Lochmuller, the daughter of Gustave and Bridget Lochmuller, the latter herself an Irishwoman. The story is an old one, as old as *Romeo and Juliet,* but in the hands of a capable playwright it is of perennial interest. It is mingled in a medley that at times becomes uproarious, with a contest between the Mulligan Guards and the Skidmore Guards, a negro organization. The theme was suggested to Harrigan by the rage for militia companies; and the lines,

> Our captain's name is Hussey,
> A military man,

were suggested by the popularity of Jack Hussey, a policeman who was also noted as a life saver. The Skidmore Guards, in

---

[1] In giving the titles of the Mulligan plays, I have followed Harrigan's spelling in the original manuscripts. This is not consistent, in the use of "Guard" or "Guards," but he evidently thought of the organization at times as individuals and at times as a unit.

their individual capacities, serve the Mulligans as waiters or barbers, but once clothed in their regalia, they admit of no inequality. In fact, they rent the same hall at the same time for their meetings, and the resultant collision becomes farce when the Skidmores, having taken the room upstairs, under protest, come through the ceiling. In the meantime Tom Mulligan and Katrina Lochmuller elope, Tom urging her not to weaken, "for many a noble family came from a marriage like this." There are other types introduced, among them Rosenfelt, the tailor, who demands his rent for the cutaways of the Mulligans, but the main theme is the contrasted race pride of the Irish and the German with the vivid background of the negro. *The Mulligan Guard Chowder* takes the Mulligans and the Skidmores over to New Jersey, for a clam bake. In the *Mulligan Guards' Christmas* appear the McFudds. Planxty McFudd is Bridget Lochmuller's brother and he has just married Diana, Cordelia Mulligan's sister, at Albany. Cordelia departs for Albany to bring them down, and Dan seizes the occasion to go off with the Mulligan braves to a shooting match. Of course all arrive, together with the Skidmore Guards, at the Mulligan home for Christmas dinner. The conflict between the German, the Irish and the negro is epitomized in the scene in which Bridget Lochmuller declines to drink with Rebecca Allup, the cook, and the latter remarks, "I admire an Irishwoman but a German woman never can lay a hand on me!" Bridget Lochmuller rolls her sleeves up, saying, "Don't you call me a German!" and proceeds to conflict. There is some clever conversation in this play and Montgomery Jangles, the crazy man who strikes attitudes representing historical characters, such as "Socrates leading Marie Antoinette to Execution" and "Pocahontas bathing at Coney Island," satirized the Felicia Hemans' vogue in verse and other forms of art that had not yet passed out of popular favor.

The Mulligan Guard Surprise (1880) is a forerunner of a better play, *Cordelia's Aspirations,* and is concerned with the moving uptown of the Mulligans and their return. Harrigan was accustomed to the reworking of his material, and his alterations invariably are improvements. *The Mulligan Guard Nominee* (1880) is an amusing satire on politics, on women's organizations, and on the British fear of American interposition in Irish affairs. When the play opens they are at the Cunard docks waiting for Bridget Lochmuller to come home. Oliver Bullwinkle, an English spy, comes on the same ship. He is trying to obtain evidence of Irish conspiracies here and in Sligo. There is a delightful meeting of the Nightingales, "a society of Irish ladies who are working for Irish freedom." Bridget Lochmuller has brought back a cipher letter and Bullwinkle is very anxious to get it. There is a contest on for Alderman-at-large, and Dan Mulligan and Lochmuller are rival candidates. Mulligan's crowd meet in Lyric Hall; there is a speech and a fight with the Lochmuller contingent, till the police come, and Rebecca tells them loftily, "I'm a member ob de Baptist church—don't push me!" It is not only farce. There is a scene appealing in its revelation of affection between Dan and Cordelia when he finds her at the negro ball and at first pretends to give her in charge, and her cry— "Oh, Dan, Dan, you're as young as ever!"—lingers in the memory. In the seventh scene, at Primrose's Barber Shop, one of Dan's men, McSweeney, raises a fight and is arrested, and the feudal organization that governs us still is reflected in this conversation:

Dan.   Raylease that man!
Officer. He's been making a disturbance at the polls.
Dan.   Raylease him! I'm 200 votes ahead of Lochmuller and
         I'll say no more.
Officer. Anything, Mr. Mulligan, to oblige *you.*

In *The Mulligans' Silver Wedding* (1881) other types are introduced, such as Washington Irving Crumbs, an author, and Edgar de Angelles, an actor, who hurl at each other epithets like "the shade of Burns" and "the fringe of John McCullough." But Cordelia and Dan remain the central characters—"twenty-five years married and wid niver an angry word, only what passed between ourselves." In the ninth scene, Cordelia, having found a letter apparently from an actress to Dan, decides to take poison. She drinks from a whiskey bottle which Dan has labeled "Rat Poison" in a praiseworthy effort to keep Rebecca Allup from drinking it. When Cordelia tells him that she is dying, he looks at the bottle and then at her lovingly, and saying, "Cordelia, we'll die together," he drinks, himself. So touched is she by his devotion, that she forgives him his apparent infidelity.

The Mulligan cycle had perhaps its best expression in *Cordelia's Aspirations* (1883) and *Dan's Tribulations* (1884). Cordelia, having saved money, decides to go to Europe and takes with her Rebecca Allup as a lady's maid. She returns with her relatives Planxty, Diana, Ellen and Rosey McFudd, some of whom had belonged to Bridget Lochmuller in *The Mulligan Guards' Christmas*. She makes Daniel sell the house in Avenue A and move to Madison Avenue, which gives rise to an affecting scene when the old furniture is sold. The second Act reveals Dan and Cordelia in their new house, at a reception, in which Dan, of course, makes blunders. There is more plot than usual, centering in Planxty's efforts to obtain control of the property and separate Dan and Cordelia. Their reconciliation is brought about by the same incident of the "rat poison," arranged even more deftly. Dan decides to move back to Avenue A and there is much comedy in consequence, some of which is built on earlier material in *The Mulligan Guard Surprise*. The main characters are well done, although the Irish relatives are intentionally burlesqued and Harrigan wisely does not individualize the supposed society at the reception. They simply furnish the room. The conversation between the negroes is as usual amusing. Rebecca tells Simpson, "Mister Mulligan's been flirting wid some other woman." Simpson replies, "You don't say!" then gives utterance to the profound truth, "You can't tell from where you sit how far it is to where you're going. Man's liable at any time ——"

91

In *Dan's Tribulations*, Dan and Cordelia have returned to Mulligan's Alley, Dan keeping his grocery once more and Cordelia teaching French to regain some portion of the savings, lost through her extravagance. Rebecca is as amusing as ever. She has married a negro, Clinton, to revenge herself for Simpson Primrose's defection, and is once more a widow. "Twice a widow, third time a ghost," she explains, and having sold the corpse to "a colored doctor" she is keeping the empty coffin in Mulligan's ice box, preparatory to burying it at night, so as to avoid discovery of her action. She passes off a bogus dollar on Bridget Lochmuller, who has also come down in the social scale. Cordelia is dunned by debtors and Dan transfers, against his better instincts, the little house he still owns to Bridget Lochmuller, to avoid his creditors. Of course, when Bridget later turns against them, the transaction is vitiated by the counterfeit dollar. The last act, laid at "Madame Mulligan's Académie Française," in which Cordelia conducts a French class and in which Tom and Kitty return to pay off the debts, is mingled comedy and hearty sentiment without burlesque. The concealment which Tom practices on his father, till he finds out the real situation, thereby saving his father's pride and self-respect, is well arranged and the revelation comes at last through Tom's taking a fall out of Dan by a trick known only to them both. Harrigan closed the Mulligan cycle with a play which leaves one with a feeling of satisfaction at the high heart and quiet philosophy of a character who was the product not only of observation but also of imagination.

Harrigan did not confine himself to the Mulligan family in his treatment of Irish life. In *Squatter Sovereignty* (1882) he dramatized the conflict between the legal owners of the rocky land lying adjacent to the East River and the "squatters" who had taken possession and who had lived there unmolested while the land had little apparent value. The play was laid, in the author's mind, in the district east of First Avenue and at the foot of East Seventy-second Street. The Widow Nolan

EDWARD HARRIGAN AS DAN MULLIGAN IN *CORDELIA'S
ASPIRATIONS*

and Felix McIntyre decide that her daughter Nellie and his son Terence shall marry, although Nellie and Fred Kline, the son of Captain Kline, the legal owner of a portion of Shantytown, have decided otherwise. The bargaining between the parents as to the contributions of the two families is richly humorous, and when the two clans, the McIntyres and the Maguires, to whom the Widow belongs, are brought into collision, the delicate shades of social distinction among the inhabitants of Shantytown are productive of real comedy. Never for a moment do the McIntyres let the Maguires forget the condescension which alone permits the alliance, and the audiences recognized the difference between the two clans. The best-drawn characters are those of Felix and the Widow, and their love-making in the last act is very amusing. *The Leather Patch* (1886), while successful on the stage, seems to be of less significance than the Mulligan plays or *Squatter Sovereignty.* It capitalized the rivalry between funeral directors and apparently led to the introduction of the "male quartet" at funeral services through the enterprise of one of the cast who represented that innovation in the play. But the finer shades of characterization are lost in a welter of fights, disguises and scenes of low life.

Much better from the point of view of characterization is *The Major,* which opened the New Theatre Comique in 1881. The central figure, Major Gilfeather, is well conceived. He lives on his wits, his vocabulary is extensive, and he emerges from situations by his cleverness in hoodwinking other people. Some of the phrases of this play, such as "You may take it and keep it forever," are still current in popular speech, and Mrs. Miranda Biggs, the keeper of a lodging house in Bleecker Street, whose father "was a Seminal Indian," revealed Harrigan's ability as a sketcher of types other than the immigrant.

The Muddy Day (1883) is a mélange of Quaker, Irish and negro types. The central character is the Widow O'Leary, who insists on remaining thirty-five years of age, and quotes as authority for her desire to be remarried the example of her father, "who lived to be eighty and had four wives, a Hogue, a Logue, a Wogue and a Brogue." She is wooed by Captain Roger McNab, owner of the schooner *Muddy Day*. *Are You Insured?* (1885) reflected a current interest. *The O'Regans* (1886) contained an attractive philosopher who is interested both in the doctrine of evolution and in Home Rule.

Of the later plays, *Reilly and the Four Hundred* (1890) was one of the most popular. It relates the love story of the son of a pawnbroker and the niece of Commodore Toby Tow, who is supposed to be among "the Four Hundred" but gives little evidence of social security and was probably intended to be simply a caricature. The knowledge of the sea which was Harrigan's inheritance is brought into the play and the lines at times are crisp and telling, but while the play had a long stage life, it seems less vital than the Mulligan cycle.

Waddy Googan (1888) introduced the Italian types; Antonio Ronzani, the clever but unscrupulous Italian lawyer, Bianca Gillano, the waif, and the lower types like Carlo Donetto, but they seem less real than the Irish or German characters. Harrigan played Waddy Googan and also Joe Cornello, a half-witted Italian, in a successful performance. Here again Harrigan's knowledge of the wharves came in, and also his acquaintance with restaurants in New York. There is evidence that toward the end of his career he was seeking for new fields, for an unproduced play, *In the North Woods*, is laid rather vaguely in the lumber regions. The heroine, Hattie Moffit, is described as being "of the M'liss type," and evidently the success of the play of the frontier made him ambitious to draw characters in another fashion. But the play is interesting only as proving that his real strength lay in a different field. Few of these later plays have the imaginative quality of *Pete* (1887), Harrigan's play of Southern life, which ran for five months at the Park Theatre. This is also a melodrama, and the main plot, concerning the abandonment of the child, May Coolidge, before the war, and her salvation afterward, is the-

EDWARD HARRIGAN AS "MAJOR GILFEATHER" IN *THE MAJOR*

atrical rather than dramatic. But Pete, the negro servant, played by Harrigan, is very appealing in his devotion to the daughter of his old master, and in his description to May of her father's death at Malvern Hill or his revelation of her identity, which he has kept from May for her own safety, can be recognized the skill which made Harrigan's plays so effective. The playwright who could put into Pete's mouth the line, "A child's memory and a very old man's belong to dreams," had a real vein of poetic feeling. Pete, as a character, goes back to the early days of *The Doyle Brothers* or *Down in Dixie*.

Harrigan's sense of discrimination remained with him to the last, and in *Under Cover* (1903) he drew characters from the lower ranks of the sporting fraternity with an accompaniment of Irish, German and negro types. His touch, while not quite so firm as in the early days, had not lost its individual quality, and the critical response was enthusiastic. His gift for song writing would need special treatment to do it justice; and the music of "Dave" Braham was set to sentiment and humor which delighted thousands.

Harrigan wrote of real people and studied his audiences closely to note the effect, sitting incognito among them. He said in 1889 [1] in an interesting statement of his dramatic principles that he had confined his work to the depiction of life among the common people, because "their trials and troubles, hopes and fears, joys and sorrows are more varied and more numerous" than those in other walks of life. The appeal is consequently greater and he was unconsciously following the example of Dickens. Human nature, he continued, was much the same the world over and he tried to portray types that were not merely accidental and local but had a touch of the universal. In the same article he added that whenever he portrayed a "type" he was applauded and so he devoted his art to the development of the New York "boy," the Irish-American and the negro. As these grew in popularity, he added

[1] *Harper's Weekly*, Feb. 2, 1889. Supplement, pp. 97–8.

other types, which were not confined to New York, but existed in the other large cities of the United States; the Englishman, the Chinaman, the German, the Italian and the Southern darky. The reason he emphasized the Irish and negro types lay in the fact that they are the two races who care most for song and dance.

After a revival of some of his plays comparatively late in his career, he remarked to a friend that the new generation knew nothing of the people depicted in *The Mulligan Guard* or *Cordelia's Aspirations*. It is true that other waves of immigration have pushed Dan and Cordelia and Gustave Lochmuller out of their habitations, and since the races they represent have risen in the economic and social scale, their types are not so easily to be recognized, while Rebecca Allup and Palestine Puter, not having progressed, are still as much alive as ever. But just because Harrigan saw the dramatic quality inherent in the foreign races that are to-day integral elements of the civilization of the United States, his plays take on a real significance as social history.

While Edward Harrigan was amusing audiences with the types which reflected the street life of New York, Charles Hoyt was delighting thousands with his farce comedies dealing with varied scenes and characters, and depicting the East and the West, the city, the country and the small town. The clergyman, the clubman, the newspaper editor and reporter, the squire, the baseball player, the politician, the railroad agent, the undertaker, the plumber, the "sporty widow," the woman's rights advocate, innumerable waiters, bartenders and tramps, jostle one another in his plays, all highly colored but with real vitality and drawn with a skill which even the manuscript reveals, but which demands actual stage performance for its proper exhibition.

Charles Hale Hoyt was born in Concord, N. H., July 26, 1860. At eighteen years of age he became associated with a newspaper at St. Albans, Vermont, and shortly after joined the staff of *The Boston Post*, acting as dramatic and musical critic as well as sports editor, and becoming one of the first "columnists" in this country. His newspaper work brought him into connection with the theatre and he studied attentively the negro minstrels who performed at the Howard Athenæum, especially the company of Rich and Harris.

Cezalia, his earliest extant play, was a comedy, put on at the Globe Theatre in Boston in 1882. The figures are conventional and the language is stilted and has none of the vigor of his farces. It was not successful. The next, *A Case of Wine*, was tried out first in the South. It was some years after revised as *A Texas Steer* and became one of the most popular of his plays.

His first substantial success was *A Bunch of Keys, or Where There's A Will, There's A Play*, although this was revised before it met with popular approval. It opened in December, 1882, at Newark, New Jersey, and came into New York at the San Francisco Music Hall, in March, 1883. The cast was headed by Willie Edouin, who seems to have collaborated, and included James T. Powers and Julian Mitchell, to become the stage manager of Hoyt and later a producer on his own account. He is authority for the statement that while Hoyt produced his own plays and made a fortune, he did not usually direct them or even attend rehearsals, but was constantly watching his audiences and making suggestions to his stage directors. *A Bunch of Keys* is farce of the broadest kind. Three sisters, Rose, Teddy and May Keys, have been made a grim jest by an uncle who has left them a hotel property on condition that it shall go to the one who is declared to be the homeliest, by a traveling salesman then staying in the hotel. They each decline to take the property under these conditions, and the consequent endeavors of their *fiancés* to persuade them to accept it, make the play.

A Parlor Match (1884), written for the comedians Evans and Hoey, is a satire on spiritualism and the search for buried treasure. While it can hardly be said to compare with the contemporary treatments of spiritualism in the novel such as

Howells' *The Undiscovered Country*, it has some very amusing
scenes, laid in a seaport village.

A Rag Baby (1884) portrays vividly the small town. Christian Berriel, a prominent undertaker, separated from his wife,
comes to place his child in Miss Pratt's school, and Tony Jay,
his brother-in-law, buys the drug store in order that he can
send the wrong medicines to Christian Berriel and keep him
ill. Tony wishes to obtain possession of his niece in order to
return her to his sister. The drug store, in which two acts are
laid, is the scene of hilarity, on account of the methods of Tony
Jay and his assistant, Old Sport, who is inspired by the fact
that in shaking hands with his employer he "can grasp the
hand that grasped Sullivan's."

A Tin Soldier (1886) is laid in New York City, apparently,
for locality meant little to Hoyt. He was concerned with types
rather than local color. Brooklyn Bridge, "a gentleman of
high position," has gone to a fancy-dress ball as a tin soldier,
and Rats, a scamp who has taken his costume, gets into difficulties with a woman who insists upon Bridge making her repa-
ration. But this plot is lost in a whirlwind of farce consequent upon the invasion of the house by Vilas Canby, a
practical plumber, who is paid four dollars an hour and who
employs Rats as his helper. The latter learns fast, for upon
being sent on his first job he says, "I might go over and see
it and shut off the water and bring away the faucets and con-
nections and the meter—that will hold the job for us till we
are ready to attend to it." Vilas Canby is a real character,
and the servant from next door, Carry Story, who comes in to
borrow supplies, has a vitality in her capacity for irritation
that is positively creepy.

Hoyt was a master in selecting situations in which a large
number of people could be brought naturally to the stage. *A
Hole in the Ground* (1887) is laid in a railroad station, and
nearly every event that happens to traveling and suffering
humanity while waiting for delayed trains is portrayed. The
agent is as thoroughly disagreeable a person as can be con-

ceived and when the Stranger, who is the leading character, asks him why he cannot be "halfway decent" he promptly replies, "Then no one would know I was the agent."

The Brass Monkey (1888) is perhaps best described in Hoyt's own words:

The Brass Monkey is a somewhat desultory reference to a variety of subjects having no particular relevancy to what little plot there may be in the play. There is an endeavor to make a little mild fun on the 1001 petty superstitions of the day which everybody derides and secretly believes in, more or less. There is an attempt to illustrate the sincerity of obtrusive grief and to show the difficulties that may beset an inexperienced man in running an auction room. In Birdie, the correspondent of *The Society Gazette*, the author has attempted to satirize the guerillas of journalism, who by their outrages upon truth and decency have managed to create more or less prejudice against an honorable profession (in which they only occupy the place of hangers-on), and have made the approach of an interviewer more terrible than the coming of a pestilence.

Hoyt describes his next play, *The Midnight Bell* (1889), as "a legitimate comedy." "It is a legitimate comedy," he continues, "because it is in four acts and farce comedies are always in three." . . . "If when the agony is over, it has been found that the characters, scenes and incidents have been presented in an amusing fashion, the author will be satisfied." Hoyt evidently felt the criticism that his work was farcical in nature and his defense is that he tried first to be amusing. That he succeeded is beyond question. The leader of the theatre orchestra in Philadelphia was often almost unable to conduct, so infectious was the humor of the plays, although he had witnessed them very many times. Perhaps it was on account of this criticism that Hoyt attempted a more serious plot in *A Midnight Bell*, dealing with the sacrifice of Ned Olcott, a young bank teller, to save Squire Olcott, his uncle, from a charge of dishonesty, and the courage of a clergyman in a rural community in defying the petty malice of the women of his congregation against a young school-teacher who, he believes, is in love with Ned. The types, however, are conventional though somewhat affected by the realism which Herne's creations were bringing to the stage. With *A Texas Steer* (1890) Hoyt's art entered into its best period. Maverick Brander, who has been made a Congressman from Texas, on account of the desire of Mrs. Brander and their daughter Bossy to visit Washington, heads a family who are real people. The adventures of the Branders in the Capital are of course exaggerated and the army officers, one of whom Bossy captures, seem less real than the Texans, for their characters, being more restrained, lend themselves less to caricature. But there have not been many more amusing scenes on our stage than the climax of the second Act when Brander is victimized by a feminine blackmailer, whose mother "had been kissed by Daniel Webster" and who leads the embryo statesman into a position where a concealed camera puts him in her power. His curtain speech—"Did it cost Daniel Webster one hundred dollars to kiss your mother?"—echoes even now in the moving pictures. In this play Caroline Miskel, afterward Mrs. Hoyt, took a leading part.

A Trip to Chinatown, opened at Hoyt's Madison Square Theatre November 9, 1891, and ran 650 times, until August 17, 1893, up to that time the longest consecutive run of any play given in the United States. It was revived February 12, 1894, and the 700th performance took place March 26, 1894. As usual, the title had little to do with the play. The scene is laid in San Francisco. Ben Gay, a wealthy bachelor, wishes to go to a masked ball, and when his niece, Tony, and her friends tell him they are going on a trip through Chinatown, he allows her to go in order to cover his own tracks. Of course they all meet at the ball with consequent comedy, in which a widow from Chicago figures largely. She is the best-drawn character, though Welland Strong, a companion of Ben Gay, who comes West for his health, is an amusing creation. This part was acted by Harry Conor, who played in it for eleven years.

Hoyt had an almost uncanny sense for human weakness and usually played upon the surface of life. But in *A Temperance Town* (1893) he seemed to be more serious in his attack upon hypocrisy and cruelty. He chose a village in Vermont in the early days when Prohibition was still a local issue, and made his central character the village drunkard, Launcelot Jones. In "Mink" Jones, Hoyt portrayed the genial vagabond who attends to anyone's business but his own, and who neglects his family to help others. He is almost a certain source of success for a playwright, for he is endowed with qualities which usually do not belong to a drunkard in real life and he appeals to that innate sympathy which is felt for the character whose mingled vices and virtues allow the sober citizen to indulge vicariously in those weaknesses he chooses for reasons of his own to forego. Mink Jones and Fred Oakhurst, who conducts a saloon, are the only honest men in a town whose leading citizens are typified by the Reverend Earnest Hardman and Kneeland Pray, the local druggist "who will sell on prescription." They persecute the honest and upright lawbreaker who is saved by the return of the son of the minister. There are many humorous scenes, but there is a serious undercurrent which makes the play of more permanent worth.

A Milk White Flag (1893) is once more pure fooling—the Ransome Guards, which consists of unlimited officers and one private, is good farcical material, but no more. *A Runaway Colt* (1895) is a defense of the professional baseball player, in which Hoyt proceeded to the unusual lengths of introducing as a central character Captain Adrian Anson of the Chicago "Colts," who is contrasted much to his advantage with clergymen and bank cashiers. *A Black Sheep* (1896), laid in Tombstone, Arizona and in New York City, is not so convincing as the farces that precede or follow it. *The Contented Woman* (1897) reveals more earnestness of purpose. It dramatizes the contest between man and woman for their respective spheres of life. Benton Holme and his wife, Grace, run against each

other for Mayor of Denver. There is some clever satire—
Grace wishes to know what to wear at a rally of her party just
as Benton wishes to know what to say, and the toast, "To
woman, once our superior, now our equal," has been revived
in recent years with effect. In fact, many of the clever sayings
of Hoyt are used to-day in ignorance of their origin.

The Stranger in New York (1897) is also of more interest
than many of the earlier plays. It is laid in New York City
and pictures the life in hotels and at a French ball with vivid
if highly colored scenes. The stranger who preserves his incognito among trying circumstances is the cool, quiet man of
resource who is always an appealing character.

In *A Day and a Night in New York* (1898), Hoyt represented theatrical life and modified the theme of *David Garrick*
by having an actress pretend that she is *not* one in order to
protect her mother, who has concealed her daughter's profession from her second husband. During the progress of the
play at the Garrick Theatre, Mrs. Hoyt died. Hoyt's mind
seems to have been affected by grief, and his next play, *A Dog
in the Manger*, already shows signs of mental deterioration,
though it is at times clever. Hoyt was committed to a sani-
tarium in July, 1900, but was released on petition of friends,
and placed under medical care until his death, November 20,
1900.

Hoyt's plays, like Harrigan's, were interspersed with songs,
not, however, always of his own creation. But also like Harrigan's, the plays were not merely musical comedies. There is
always a plot, slight though it be, and the characters, though
types, have some reality. No one rises in the memory with the
tenacity of Dan Mulligan or Cordelia or Rebecca Allup, possibly because Hoyt wrote no cycle of plays, but gave new names
to his creations, who indeed are different human beings. The
very names of Hoyt's characters, while adding by their clever
incongruity to the sum of our amusement—Rashleigh Gay,
Welland Strong, Manley Manners, Phil Graves, the undertaker, and so on forever—forbid almost at the start our se-

CHARLES H. HOYT

rious consideration of their possessors. And yet on running over the lists, one finds how few are chosen outside of the actual surnames with which we are familiar. It is only a reminder of the metaphorical processes by which these family names began.

Harrigan's art was a finer one than Hoyt's. It was based on a long study of the stage, especially of Molière. And when Brander Matthews took Coquelin back to talk to Harrigan in his dressing room, the latter conducted the conversation in French. There is an imaginative quality in his plays which came perhaps from his Celtic strain, which Hoyt's rougher and broader strokes did not reveal. With the gradual disappearance of the audiences who saw them, there likewise passes away the memory of a humor which had in it nothing sordid or debasing, but which nevertheless held thousands spellbound. The manuscripts can only faintly reflect the steady sparkle of the humor that was Harrigan's and the wit that was Hoyt's, and the best of their plays should be revived in printed form. For America is not rich enough in the records of her art to lose what they have contributed to her vanished hours of joy.

The example set by Harrigan and Hoyt was followed during the eighties and nineties by many playwrights, but few deserve mention here. Popular successes, written for actors like W. H. Crane and Nat Goodwin, were wrought out of similar material. One of the best of these was *The Senator* (1889), by David Demarest Lloyd, in which Crane made a great hit as Senator Hannibal Rivers. Even now the character of the impetuous, lovable Senator, while verging always on farce, comes out of the pages of the manuscript with a freshness that years can hardly dim. It is to be noted also that the cheapest elements, like the Chinaman, were put in by Sydney Rosenfeld. Lloyd did not live to see *The Senator* produced. He had other stage successes to his credit like *For Congress*, written for Raymond and afterward rewritten for Roland Reed by Rosenfeld under the title of *The Politician*. His political plays show, however, the essential weakness of the type play, when we compare, for example, *The Senator* with

Thomas's *The Capitol*, written five years later. We have not had many serious studies of our politics, largely because of managerial dread of controversial topics.

It was much simpler to take our politicians to a South American State, as Richard Harding Davis did in *The Dictator* (1904) and substitute for Colonel Bowie, the real consul, a young American of the romantic type Davis knew how to draw so well. Of his other long plays *The Galloper* (1906) was a clever picture of the various types of war correspondents, American and English, operating in the front during the Greco-Turkish war of 1897. Davis's dramatic work, however, while it extended into the twentieth century, began in the early nineties with one-act plays, of which *The Other Woman* (1893) was quite well done, and *The Disreputable Mr. Reagan* (1895) provided E. H. Sothern with a congenial rôle. These were dramatizations of Davis's own stories and they give one the same impression as his fiction, a sense that they come near to being first rate but just lack the element of artistic truth. But certainly his earlier one-act plays ring more truly than *The Galloper* or *The Dictator*. Perhaps this is due to the fact that Davis seems to belong to the nineteenth century, or at least he may be considered as a writer of the transition which in the case of the type play is practically a continuous process.

CHAPTER V

THE DRAMA OF THE FRONTIER

THE very essence of the frontier is its progressive nature. To the earlier playwrights Kentucky was the land of the pioneer, and when Paulding drew Nimrod Wildfire in 1831, or when Louisa Medina dramatized Bird's novel, *Nick of the Woods*, in 1838, the hero either came from that State or at least had scalped Indians within its borders. This tradition persisted perhaps because of the continued popularity of *Nick of the Woods*, and one of the best of the plays of the seventies was laid apparently in Tennessee.

The next step in the development of the frontier was the crossing of the Mississippi and a play of the transition period, *Kit the Arkansas Traveler* (1870), by T. C. DeWalden, deals with the pioneer who represented one further step westward. This play was popular for many years and the character of Kit Redding became, in the interpretation of F. S. Chanfrau, the standard pioneer. After his death Henry Chanfrau continued it in his répertoire as late as 1894. The elder Chanfrau had made a great success with his portrayal of Mose, the New York fireman, in 1848, and his power as a character actor was shown in his ability to interpret the wronged husband and father who is seeking the wife and child that had been taken from him.

A much better play, *Davy Crockett*, was the work of a nephew of the actor, James E. Murdoch, who allowed his name to be added to that of the playwright and actor, who became known as Frank Hitchcock Murdoch. He did not live to see *Davy Crockett* produced, as he died in Philadelphia shortly before the first performance, which took place in Rochester, New York, in November, 1872. Owing to an error in Hutton's *Curiosities of the American Stage*, a romantic story has grown up of Hitchcock's death on account of the unfavorable criticism of *Davy Crockett*.[1]

Frank Mayo, who created the character and produced the play, had confidence in *Davy Crockett* and, undaunted by its first cold reception, continued it successfully for many years. It was played later by his son, Edwin Mayo; and by a grim accident, Harry Hitchcock, the playwright's brother, was apparently negotiating for the purchase of the dramatic rights, when he met his tragic death at the Brooklyn Theatre fire.

Davy Crockett is based apparently on the tradition of the Tennessee trapper and hunter, who "found out what was right and went ahead," and whose autobiography is a significant document in our social history. He was certainly a less idyllic character than his stage descendant. The scene of the play is a frontier settlement, not named, but probably in Tennessee, and since Crockett died in defense of the Alamo in 1836, the action presumably takes place before that time. The character of the trapper, strong, simple, unable to read, but with a keen sense of right, is contrasted with that of the young girl, Eleanor Vaughan, whom he had known as a child, but who has been educated abroad. She returns with her guardian, Major Royston, to be married to Neil, the nephew of Oscar Crampton, a neighboring Squire, who has a hold over the Major through some notes of the usual dubious quality familiar to the finance of the stage. The plot, however, is negligible; the complications which keep Davy and Eleanor apart are brushed aside as soon as it is necessary by his simple expedient of carrying her off on the swiftest horse in the neighborhood. The literary inspiration of *Davy Crockett* is from Walter Scott and Hitchcock made no secret of that inspiration. In the second Act, which takes place in Davy's hut, Eleanor is saved from freezing by Davy's courage and decision, and while

---

[1] But see Brander Matthews, "The American on the Stage," *Scribner's Monthly*, XVIII (July, 1879), pp. 327–8. From members of Hitchcock's family I learn that his death was due to causes unconnected with his plays.

they sit by the fire she reads to him the ballad of Young Lochinvar. In Davy's vernacular, "A nod's as good as a wink to a blind horse," but just then the howl of approaching wolves is heard and the Act ends:

(Interior of Crockett's hut.)

Eleanor: What is it?

Davy: Keep still and listen. (*A howl is again heard.*)

Eleanor: I hear a long, low cry as of some animal in distress.

Davy: Ah, you hear it then. I was right, wasn't I? Thar it is again.

Eleanor: What is it?

Davy: That's wolves.

Eleanor: Wolves— (*Screams.*)

Davy: Don't be scared—

Eleanor: But—is there no danger?

Davy: Ain't I here?

Eleanor: Yes, but they are so dreadfully near.

Davy: Yes, they tracked you in the snow and smell blood.

Eleanor: Blood!

Davy: Take it easy, girl. This door is built of oak, I built it—and—blazes, the bar's gone.

Eleanor: Gone? (*Wolves howl all round cabin.*)

Davy: Yes, I split it up to warm you and your friend— Rouse him up. The pesky devils is all around the house.

Eleanor: (*Goes to Neil.*) Neil—help! help! (*The wolves throw themselves against the door and bark.*)

Davy: Quick there, I can't hold the door agin 'em—

Neil: I tell you, uncle, if the girl says no, there's an end of it—

Eleanor: My God—he is delirious—

Davy: What!

Eleanor: 'Tis true—nothing can save us.

Davy: Yes, it can.

Eleanor: What?

Davy: The strong arm of a backwoodsman.

(*Davy bars the door with his arm. The wolves attack the house. Their heads are seen through the opening in the hut and under the door.*)

CURTAIN

A HISTORY OF THE AMERICAN DRAMA

The very incident goes back to Scottish history, but the quotation will show the direct speech and the quick, if melodramatic, action. On the stage it is quite effective, for the climax grows naturally out of the situation. What makes *Davy Crockett* of significance, however, is the way in which Hitchcock created and Mayo interpreted the character of a man of few but strong traits, loving naturally a girl whose education and breeding had not blinded her to the innate nobility of his nature, and who saw him in surroundings which brought back the fragrance of a childhood's friendship. It is old-fashioned romance set in a newer stage technique and Mayo acted the part in such a quiet restrained manner that he made the romance seem possible. It is an idyll, in a way, of the pioneer life, with the crudity toned down; and the author chose wisely a contrast which from *Othello* to *The Great Divide* has never failed to appeal to human sympathy. In a way it showed progress, for there were no Indians, no tomahawking, and no shooting except of the wolves, and it may be said to mark the transition from the cult of "the natural man" to the study of the natural gentleman.

As Professor Paxson has shown, the frontier is either a line, a region, or a process.[1] For the purpose of drama, it is a region, and when the standardizing process which turns the frontier into a stable civilization has become apparent, the contrasts which are the life of drama become less vivid. What made *Davy Crockett* a success was the direct current which flowed between the opposite poles of two natures, one strong and one charming.

Davy Crockett inspired no school of play writing. But in 1871 Augustin Daly had seen the greater theatrical possibilities of another frontier, that of California, and *Horizon* is the first of a series of plays which owe their inspiration to Bret Harte. It was a different frontier, less primitive and more sophisticated, much more varied in its elements, and almost too rich in striking incidents. That it became melodrama was

[1] Paxson, F. L. *History of the American Frontier*, p. 43.

108

inevitable, for life itself was melodrama. *Horizon* has already been discussed and its directness of dialogue and vivid characterization noted. There can be no question, however, that the two most important characters, Panther John Lodor, the "bad man," who rises naturally to the greatness of self-sacrifice, and "Med" Van Dorp, the untutored product of the Western plains, are the combination of romance in conception and realism of treatment which made Bret Harte the creator of a popular school of fiction. In *Horizon* are to be found also "the Heathen Chinee" and other definite imitations of Harte, and the play, while laid ostensibly "near Fort Jackson," is really placed in that land of romance which Harte created through his observation and imagination. California objected to Harte's pictures of its life as exaggerated in their lawlessness and crudity, but the stage adopted his standards without question, for Harte's genius had seen the picturesque in the new civilization of the frontier and for his purposes the picture was more important than the photograph. His ambition was to write successful plays and he began his dramatic effort with an attempted collaboration with Dion Boucicault in a play, *Kentuck*, for Augustin Daly. But for reasons which become apparent from Boucicault's letters to Daly,[1] the two men could not work together. Bret Harte must have modified his original conception or perhaps he simply rejected Boucicault's suggestions, for the outline of the play as given in Daly's biography bears little relation to the finished product, *The Two Men of Sandy Bar*, which was produced at the Union Square Theatre, August 28, 1876. While not an absolute failure, it was hardly successful on the stage, though it went on tour after its brief run in New York. The play was based on Bret Harte's story, *Mr. Thompson's Prodigal*, which tells with mingled pathos and humor of the search of a repentant father who has driven his son from home, and who, having been converted to an emotional form of religion, seeks his son and apparently finds him. But at the dinner he gives to celebrate the prodigal's re-

[1] Daly, J. F. *The Life of Augustin Daly*, pp. 170-6.

turn the real Charles Thompson appears, hopelessly drunk, and the impostor departs. It may have been the quiet gentlemanly way in which this impostor plays his game, even at the end, which suggested to Bret Harte that he bring his favorite creation, John Oakhurst, the gambler, into the play in a similar situation. Likewise, he took the love story of Sandy Morton and Miss Mary, the central characters of *The Idyll of Red Gulch*, and made the first take the place of Charles Thompson. Finally he superimposed Colonel Starbottle, who had nothing to do with the original story, upon the plot and made him the star, to be acted by Stuart Robson. The result is a confused melodrama, with brilliant dialogue at times, but with no real coherence. Judge Daly suggests that the peculiar utterance of Stuart Robson, "which was not only not Western —but not like anything known to civilization"—killed the play.

A minor part in *Two Men of Sandy Bar*, that of Hop Sing, had been taken by C. T. Parsloe, and his performance had been so acceptable that Bret Harte and Mark Twain built a play around the character of the Chinaman, Ah Sin, who was famous as the "Heathen Chinee" of Harte's poem. It was first put on at the National Theatre, Washington, May 7, 1877, before a brilliant audience, and was sufficiently successful to induce Augustin Daly to produce it in New York, on July 31, at the Fifth Avenue Theatre. *Ah Sin* provides an interesting study of the two great exponents of Western life, working together for the first and last time. It reveals the unwholesome result of the star system. The part of the Chinaman is made prominent at the expense of probability and construction, and as a background he is provided with a conglomeration of miners, and visiting townspeople, male and female, over whose complications he presides and whom he outwits with ease. His mingled shrewdness and stupidity are not badly represented. The relative contributions of Bret Harte and Mark Twain are difficult to distinguish, for the height

ened contrasts of rough miners with the types of San Francisco
women, young and old, who are evidently intended to represent refinement and breeding, are reminiscent of both writers.
If any distinction is to be made, the men seem to be more
definitely Bret Harte's creation, while certainly Mrs. Plunkett
and her daughter are the product of Mark Twain. The former is Mrs. Malaprop translated to the West, and some of her
speeches, like, "Here we stand, two lonely, friendless, dissolute
women," or, "I cannot think of him without going into ecsta-
sies of sensibility, perfect ruptures of emotion," have earmarks
of his own. The play lasted about five weeks, then was withdrawn for lack of support. The most successful episode connected with its production was Mark Twain's curtain speech
at the first night in New York.[1] One paragraph will show its
quality:

I wish to say also that this play is didactic rather than anything else. It is intended rather for instruction than amusement.
The Chinaman is getting to be a pretty frequent figure in the
United States, and is going to be a great political problem, and
we thought it well for you to see him on the stage before you had
to deal with that problem. Then for the instruction of the young
we have introduced a game of poker. There are few things that
are so unpardonably neglected in our country as poker. The
upper class know very little about it. Now and then you find
Ambassadors who have a sort of general knowledge of the game,
but the ignorance of the people at large is fearful. Why, I have
known clergymen, good men, kind-hearted, liberal, sincere and all
that, who did not know the meaning of a "flush"; it is enough to
make one ashamed of one's species. When our play was finished,
we found it was so long, and so broad, and so deep—in places—
that it would have taken a week to play it. I thought that was
all right; we could put "To be continued" on the curtain, and run
it straight along. But the manager said no; it would get us into
trouble with the general public, and into trouble with the general
government, because the Constitution forbids the infliction of
cruel or unusual punishment; so he cut out, and cut out, and the
more he cut out the better the play got. I never saw a play that
was so much improved by being cut down; and I believe it would

[1] See *Life of Daly*, pp. 234-5.

have been one of the very best plays in the world if his strength had held out so that he could cut out the whole of it.

Harte's letters reveal how earnestly he desired to write successful plays and how he turned aside from more secure engagements to dramatize *Jeff Brigg's Love Story*, *Thankful Blossom*, *The Luck of Roaring Camp*, *Clarence*, and *A Blue Grass Penelope*, none of which saw the stage. In *The Luck* the heroine was educated by the wealthy members of the camp and brought to Paris, where, Harte hoped, "this mingling and contact of these rough men with this high-super-civilized Old World" might produce dramatic effect. Harte had undertaken this play at the suggestion of Boucicault and a version by the latter was performed at the Empire Theatre, New York, May 14, 1894, but there is no indication that Harte had any share in it.

Bret Harte's only substantial success came years later, with *Sue*, in which he collaborated with T. Edgar Pemberton, and which is a dramatization of Harte's story, *The Judgment of Bolinas Plain*. Other characters were introduced and it was first played on September 15, 1896, at Hoyt's Theatre, New York. On October 12 it started on tour, and it was produced in London at the Garrick Theatre, June 10, 1898, where Annie Russell scored a distinct personal success.[1] Sue marries Ira Beasley, the owner of Bolinas Farm, a man much older than herself. She becomes fascinated by a circus acrobat, Jim Wynd, and starts to run away with him, but is prevented from going by Parson Davies. The plot is not so important, though there is a certain cleverness in the stage management so that Jim Wynd and Ira fire at the Sheriff and each believes that he has killed him. But the character of Sue, who has never had the joys of childhood or girlhood, and who reacts instinctively to her one hope of pleasure, was a real Bret Harte figure, unmoral rather than immoral, and was drawn with the sense of the dramatic which, notwithstanding his stage failures,

[1] See *Letters of Bret Harte*, pp. 424–35 and 449–55, and *Life* by Pemberton, pp. 269–74.

Harte possessed. This gift was recognized by Clement Scott in his intelligent analysis of the play in the *Daily Telegraph* on the morning after the first performance in London. "The dramatic gift, the poetic gift, the realistic gift are seldom combined. But Bret Harte possesses them all."

It is true that his works teem with dramatic situations, but the limitations which, while allowing him to become one of the great writers of short stories, prevented him from becoming a successful novelist, also prevented him from becoming a practical playwright. If the one-act play had been at that time a profitable branch of theatrical art, Bret Harte might have succeeded in it. But his sense of construction was lacking for a broader structure, as the failure of *Gabriel Conroy*, his one full-length novel, proved. It was partly the very wealth of his material, as it was with Dickens, which stood in his way. Others could select and reject and win success as Clay Greene did with *M'liss*,[1] in which Annie Pixley starred, or as Paul Armstrong did with *Salomy Jane* (1907), played by Eleanor Robson, but the author himself could not cut out relentlessly all that was not contributory to the real essence of the plot. There is enough in *Two Men of Sandy Bar* to carry three plays, but under the star system in vogue in 1876, the very excellence of John Oakhurst, of Sandy Morton, militated against the success of a play whose star was Colonel Starbottle. More than that, Bret Harte's characters had become almost like historical personages, and even he could not take liberties with them. Playgoers who had formed their conception of John Oakhurst, of Sandy Morton, of Miss Mary, of Colonel Starbottle, from the fine art of a short story where they flashed into being through the deft description and narration of a master of the form, did not relish seeing these same characters altered by their own creator on the stage. It must be remembered, too, that Bret Harte, even at his best, is constantly

---

[1] Bret Harte's own adaptation of this story remained unacted. He was unable to prevent the unauthorized use of his material in this country, but he stopped the plays in England.

skirting the edge of danger in his treatment of the sentimental, and the touch that heightened his characters for the footlights was in some cases fatal. But if he could have worked harmoniously in collaboration with a trained playwright, he might have produced significant plays, for his great contribution to modern literature, the portrayal of moral contrasts in human beings from an objective, unmoral point of view, is in itself essentially dramatic.

Mark Twain's one success as a playwright was in a certain sense associated with the frontier, but it was the frontier of the older region. The play of *The Gilded Age* seems to have disappeared, and we have only the character as revealed in the novel and the tradition of the remarkable performance of John T. Raymond as Colonel Mulberry Sellers. The first dramatization was made by Gilbert S. Densmore, a newspaper man, in San Francisco and the play was produced by John T. Raymond at the California Theatre, April 23, 1874.[1]

Mark Twain at once challenged the right to dramatize the book and an amicable arrangement was made between him and Densmore, by which the latter relinquished any share in the play. Mark Twain wrote a version, which contained some of the elements of Densmore's plot, but the character of Colonel Sellers, which carried the play as Raymond acted it, was the creation of Mark Twain, with some contribution, including the name itself, from Charles Dudley Warner. The revised play was put on at the Park Theatre, New York, September 16, 1874, and ran for one hundred and nineteen nights. The frontier of *The Gilded Age* was, of course, a fairly stabilized region, and the play carried its hero to Washington and the lobbying of the post-war period. Yet Colonel Sellers has in him the quality of perennial youth and the spirit of adventure which have made the frontier a progressive process in our history.

[1] See Paine, A. B., *Mark Twain*, pp. 517-19, Winter, William, *The Life of David Belasco*, I, pp. 64-8, and Matthews, Brander, "Mark Twain and the Theater" in *Playwrights on Playmaking*, pp. 168-75, for discussion of the relative shares of Clemens and Densmore in the play.

THE DRAMA OF THE FRONTIER

Mark Twain's interest in the stage was keen and constant, however, and he was a capable actor. After the failure of *Ah Sin*, he made an attempt at a play dealing with a detective, but gave it up. He conceived of *The Prince and the Pauper* first as a drama, and while he wisely chose to write it in its present form, he dramatized the story later and offered it to various managers without result. The version with which many theatre goers are still familiar was made by Abby Sage Richardson in 1890, and arranged for the stage by David Belasco. *Pudd'nhead Wilson* also saw the stage through other hands. Frank Mayo, who had played *Davy Crockett* so long, dramatized Mark Twain's novel in 1895 and it was a substantial success.

A comparison of the novel with the play reveals the instinct of the trained actor for stage effects. Mayo cut the long speeches of Pudd'nhead Wilson, even in the trial scene, remorselessly. He made a climax of one act the revelation to Tom Driscoll that Roxy the slave is his mother, but he created out of "Chambers," the real heir to the Driscoll estate, who had been deprived of his birthright by Roxy when she changed the babies in their cradles, a real person instead of a mere foil to Tom. By cleverly indicating a protecting care of Chambers by Rowena, the niece of Pudd'nhead Wilson, he prepared the way for a love story when Chambers turns out to be white, and he therefore secured a wider sympathy in the audience.

Mark Twain and William Dean Howells revived Colonel Sellers in *The American Claimant, or Mulberry Sellers Ten Years Later*, in which the Colonel is represented as more wildly extravagant than ever and is also a claimant to an English earldom. This play actually saw the stage for about a week out of town and was put on at a matinée performance in New York, but it is not important. Yet it is at least an interesting circumstance that both Bret Harte and Mark Twain should have made such efforts to become practical playwrights. The successful dramatization of their fiction by other hands reveals its essentially dramatic quality. It was with Mark Twain as with Bret Harte, a lack of constructive sense and an inability to discard material which detracted from the unity of stage presentation.

The regret which Bret Harte and Mark Twain felt at their frequent failures was probably not lessened by the success of their chief rival in the delineation of Western life. Just as *Ah Sin* was withdrawn from Daly's Theatre, *The Danites in the Sierras*, by Joaquin Miller, was produced at the Broadway Theatre on August 22, 1877, and proved to be one of the most popular of the plays of the Frontier. The plot and characters are definitely based on Miller's conception of the West as a place of strong passions and emotions, of quick thinking and acting, of lurid lights and sharp shadows. The influence of Bret Harte is clear, but after all Miller knew his material. He drew vivid contrasts, not only moral but also racial and religious. The shadow of the Danite or Mormon vengeance pursuing the young girl, Nancy Williams, who is disguised as a boy and lives alone in a cabin in the Sierras to avoid their pursuit, is a dramatic theme. The character of Sandy McGee is lifted bodily from Bret Harte. He is the strong man who is animated by the desire to protect the weaker of either sex and who marries "the widow" and lives happily with her until she is murdered by the Danites, and then marries equally happily Nancy Williams, when she resumes her feminine attire. The Chinaman, the women with a past, who reform and become pillars of society, are all equally conventional stage figures. But there is a directness in the dialogue, a sense of action and a pulsing humanity felt at times in Miller's lyric poetry, which are not by any means negligible.

The play was at first the joint product of Miller and an "alert actor" in London who helped Miller put together two of his short stories, *The First Woman in the Forks* and *The Last Man of Mexican Camp*, and it was published under the name of *The First Families of the Sierras*. It was revised by Alexander Fitzgerald, an actor in Philadelphia, for Mr. and Mrs. McKee Rankin (Kitty Blanchard), and the first cast included Louis Aldrich and Fitzgerald himself. The printed version of the drama differs from the play as it was performed, but Miller has omitted some of the more melodramatic elements. *The Danites* was popular for many years,[1] being played at the California Theatre in 1878, and was the play selected by McKee Rankin when he took a complete American company to the Sadler's Wells Theatre, London, opening April 2, 1880. Rankin claimed that he was the first actor and manager to take a complete American company abroad,[2] and the venture was successful. He and Mrs. Rankin became identified with the production of the frontier play.

Forty-nine, Miller's second play, was produced by them at Haverly's Theatre, New York, on October 1, 1881. It has the theme which Miller used in his verse more than once—that of the Argonaut, the pioneer who sticks to his tunnel even after hope is gone, and who wins gold at last. The character of "Forty-nine," played by Rankin, is in a sense an epic figure, and when he takes the blame of a supposed robbery to shield his son, who is ignorant of his parentage, he achieves a certain distinction. Carrots, the girl whom he is protecting, and who turns out to be an heiress, was played by Mrs. Rankin, and is an amusing figure. The remainder of the plot is negligible, but the scene in which the old negro, Sam, identifies Carrots by the song he sang her in her infancy, is real drama.

Tally Ho! was founded according to Miller on Horace Greeley's account of his crossing the Sierras with Hank Monk, the dashing stage driver. "Joe Jefferson," he continues, "was its godfather; John Sousa wrote the music, and the present leading member of Congress from San Francisco played a part." *Tally Ho!* is another play in which the central character, Hank Monk, attempts to sacrifice himself for another, this time his wife, who is accused of murder. It is less veracious than *The Danites*, but has a certain vigor and directness of language.

---

[1] See *Plays of the Present*, pp. 80–2, and Introduction to *The Danites* in Joaquin Miller's *Poems*, Vol. 6, San Francisco, 1910.

[2] Brown. *History of the New York Stage*, II, 363.

An Oregon Idyll was his own favorite among his plays, because it dealt with the woods and the characters were known to him. It has the usual plot, with the exception that the hero, John Logan, is part Indian, and his misfortunes have a racial as well as a personal appeal. The insertion of the Boston types, Archie Shuttlebuck and Margaret Hutchinson, who are caricatures, marks Miller's one attempt at sectional contrasts.

The varying appeal of the frontier drama illustrates clearly how jealous a mistress is the art of playwriting. Bret Harte, Mark Twain, Joaquin Miller were writers of fiction and poetry who approached the stage at times, but whose main achievement lay elsewhere. The best plays of the frontier were written by either an actor like Hitchcock, a producer like Daly, or by Bartley Campbell, who represents with Bronson Howard the professional playwright, who devoted himself entirely to his craft.

Bartley Campbell was born in Pittsburgh, August 12, 1843. He began his career as a newspaper man on the Pittsburgh *Post* and, after serving on the Louisville *Courier Journal* and the Cincinnati *Enquirer*, he became founder and editor of the *Southern Monthly Magazine* in New Orleans in 1869. When he began playwriting in 1871 he retired from journalism, as he held that once a man writes a play, especially an unsuccessful one, he should never again write dramatic criticism for a newspaper. He began playwriting in 1871 with a sensational drama, *Through Fire*, and in 1872 wrote for E. L. Davenport a social comedy, *Peril, or Love at Long Branch*. In the same year he assisted R. M. Hooley to transform Hooley's Opera House, which had been the home of minstrelsy in Chicago, into Hooley's Theatre, which should produce legitimate drama in opposition to McVicker's Theatre. Bartley Campbell organized the company and directed the plays, many of which were his own. Among these were *Fate*, a domestic drama, and *Risks, or Insure Your Life*, written to give John Dillon a leading comedy part. It had for its theme a study of life insurance, which was at that time increasing in popularity. The leading character, George Washington Pembroke, was afterward played by John T. Raymond in New York and in California. Among the plays Campbell wrote while in Chicago were *The Virginian*, *Gran Uale*, *My Foolish Wife*, and *On the Rhine*, a story of the Franco-Prussian War.

In the summer of 1875, the company at Hooley's Theatre played a summer season at Maguire's Opera House in San Francisco. While there, Bartley Campbell adapted Von Moser's comedy, *Ultimo*, under the title of *Bulls and Bears*, and it was performed in San Francisco with great success on June 7 just before Daly's company arrived with his adaptation of the same play, *The Big Bonanza*, performed on July 19. For the first time Bartley Campbell came in contact with California life. He became a member of the Bohemian Club and knew Bret Harte and Joaquin Miller. It was this Western experience that was to provide him with the material for his finest play, *My Partner*. In 1876, he made his first trip to England, and in November of that year produced *The Virginian* at the St. James Theatre, with Mrs. John Wood and Sam Piercy in the cast. While in London he wrote *A Heroine in Rags* and *How Women Love*. The latter was first produced at the Arch Street Theatre in Philadelphia, May, 1877, and was afterward rewritten as *The Vigilantes, or the Heart of the Sierras*. It was a play laid in 1856 in and around San Francisco and the Yosemite Valley.

That Campbell was not unmindful of the criticism of the seventies, which urged the revival of the drama that is of permanent literary worth, is proven by his writing *Clio* in verse. It is a dramatic spectacle laid in Italy in the Twelfth Century, played first in Pittsburgh and Chicago in 1878. In 1885 he revised the play and it was produced on a great scale at Niblo's Garden with music by Operti. These early plays seem to be non-extant.

My Partner, produced at the Union Square Theatre, September 16, 1879, represents the drama of the frontier in its most impressive form. It is the dramatic treatment of the theme of the friendship of two partners broken by the love of the same woman, whose epic was written by Bret Harte. Harte's influence is seen clearly in the general atmosphere, but Campbell had been on the ground, and the play is the result of observation of actual life rather than of reading about it. Joe Saunders, the hero, is the large-hearted type of miner, rough in manner but gentle in spirit, and with a personal dignity which comes perhaps from his creator's avoidance of the tempting opportunity, which Harte seldom resisted, of providing his hero with a besetting weakness. Campbell preferred to endow Ned Singleton, Joe's partner, with that unmoral attitude which causes him to betray Mary Brandon under promise of marriage. Joe overhears their conversation and makes Ned promise to marry her. In the second Act, which is laid in the cabin of Joe and Ned, the play reaches its climax. The stage direction which indicates definitely that the cabin is *not* to be made of unplaned logs, shows how Campbell realized that the frontier of which he was writing had become stabilized. Yet even in 1869, in which year the action is supposed to occur, it remained essentially a man's country, and the dramatic value of the situation rests upon the close bond made by the friendship of two partners, and the essential sense of justice which allows them to act fairly to each other even when they are parting forever. Joe tells Ned that they must separate, "for the old confidence is gone," and they divide the gold they have held jointly. After the division, Ned turns away for a moment and Joe secretly adds a portion of his own share to his partner's stock. Yet he refuses to shake hands with Ned, for the hurt has gone too deep, and he leaves the cabin. Almost immediately Scraggs, a man who nurses a grudge against the Brandons, enters and attempts to persuade Ned that he should not marry Mary, since she had been Joe's mistress. Ned attacks him as a slanderer, and in the ensuing fight Scraggs stabs him with Joe's knife. In a few moments Joe returns and speaks to his dead partner, who is apparently sitting at the table with his back to Joe.

There he is! My partner, and he hasn't stirred yet.—Say— Ned—Ned.

Well you see, I've come back!—I couldn't go away without a feeling that we parted friends – – – When I got down thar in the canyon – – where we worked together: I set down to take a look at the old familiar spot. The dry leaves were a-dancing in the wind, the birds singing in the branches, and the creek laughing among the boulders, as if there were no such thing as pain or parting. Everything came back to me. The days we worked together, the plans we used to lay for the time we had made our pile, and could afford to let the pick grow red and rusty in the mine. All your good acts came a-crowding around me, making me ashamed of myself, that I'd refused a hand, I'd often been glad to grasp, when I warn't able to help myself – – and so – I'm here – here to offer ye my hand, and to ask yer pardon. – – Before I go away forever.

(He extends his hand.)

What, ye won't take it? All right, remember I offered it! That's all I can do.

(He goes to the door.)

Oh! darn it, Ned – – we mustn't part like this – – Look up and speak – – Ned – Ned – You ain't sick, are you, partner? Say, partner, what's the matter?

(He takes Ned's hand and comes around in front.)

What's this, Ned? Cold and rigid. Dead! No! No! – Ned – Partner – – look up! Don't sit staring there like that. Only speak to me once more – – Only say, say you forgive me – – Oh, my God, he's dead – – dead – – dead.

The remainder of the play, in which Joe is accused of the murder and is saved by Wing Lee, the Chinaman, is reminiscent of *Ah Sin*. Yet there are some very effective scenes—Joe's proposal of marriage to Mary, under the shadow of his approaching execution, is simple and sincere. Quite appealing, too, is the spectacle of Joe, practically under sentence of death, released by the Sheriff on parole, because he is "square." The apparent paradox of a supposed murderer being worthy of

trust was in fact based upon the real conditions of the frontier.
The pioneers in California developed laws and customs based
on practical necessity and the standards of right and wrong
became either confused or more clear according to the point
of view. But there is no question that *My Partner* is true to
the life it portrayed, and there is even less doubt of its dramatic excellence. It was played by Louis Aldrich for many
years. It was translated into German and was played for
about fifty nights, beginning September 15, 1884, at the Resi-
denz-Theater in Berlin, Campbell attending the rehearsals.
It had been performed in London April 10, 1884, at the Olympic Theatre. The profits of *My Partner*, in which he had only
the author's share, were so large that Campbell determined to
produce his own plays, and for a time he was successful. *The
Galley Slave*, which opened the season of 1879 at the Chestnut
Street Theatre in Philadelphia, is a melodrama, laid in Europe, well constructed and vigorous, but conventional. The
climax of the second Act, in which Sidney Norcott, being found
in Cicely Blaine's apartment at night, allows himself to be
arrested as a thief, is reminiscent of Sardou's *Nos Bons Villageois*. The subtitle is "A Reflex of American Society
Abroad," but the interest is not social but emotional. This
may have accounted for its success in Berlin, where it ran for
eighty-three nights at the Wilhelm-Theater in 1881. In fact,
wherever the scene of Campbell's plays were laid the emotional
relations were stressed. *Siberia* (1882), his other extant play
of foreign life, is an improvement on *The Galley Slave* and its
complicated plot forbids retelling. Yet at the end of each of
the six acts comes a swift and telling climax, and the sense of
peril to the exiles from Russia is ever present. *Separation*
(1884) is a melodrama, laid partly in New York and partly
in Normandy. Its theme is the puritanical prejudice against
the theatre, made concrete by the enforced separation of a
mother from her child when she refuses to obey her husband
who forbids her to sing for charity at even an amateur performance. Again the curtain descends upon emotional crises

when the mother sees her daughter after a lapse of fifteen years, or when later for the girl's own sake she declines to recognize her. If Campbell had drawn the scenes in which the latent love of mother and child come into being with the same skill with which he drew the manly affection in *My Partner*, he might have made something out of *Separation*, for the plot after all turns upon the contrasted characters of the husband and wife. Twice at least Campbell laid the scenes of his play in the South. *Fairfax* was played first in New York on December 29, 1879. It is a melodrama, in which the author has produced several effective scenes and has portrayed Southern character in its romantic aspects, but without any especially significant picture of Southern conditions. He has, however, provided an appealing heroine in Mrs. Marrigold, a young wife who is brutally treated by her husband, and who believes she has killed him in a struggle over their child. She becomes the governess of Edwin Fairfax's child, and he and she fall in love with each other. Dr. Guy Gaylord, the friend of Fairfax, who knows of her past life, believes he should prevent the marriage, but she convinces him of her rectitude. This quiet, unenthusiastic observer, who at first is suspicious but later refuses to believe even Gladys' own testimony against herself, is the best character in the play. It was written for Lester Wallack, but there was a disagreement about some proposed changes and Campbell walked out of the theatre with his play. Later, when Abbey produced it, the part was taken by Frederick Robinson with success.

The White Slave (1882) is a vivid melodrama, laid in Kentucky, near the Mississippi River. It is based definitely on *The Octoroon*, but perhaps anyone who took from Boucicault felt justified. Liza, the supposed octoroon, turns out to be white, however, and there is sufficient difference in the plot to make a striking melodrama. In the third Act occur the lines which even yet are remembered for their theatrical quality. Lacy, the brutal owner of Liza, says to her: "I can send you to the fields to work all day among the common niggers, a hoe in your hands, rags upon your back," and Liza answers, "Rags are royal raiment when worn for virtue's sake, and rather a hoe in my hands than self-contempt in my heart." Campbell deliberately planted these lines for their effect.

Paquita, produced at the Fourteenth Street Theatre, August 21, 1885, under his own management, was his last play. It is laid in the Southwest and is based on a situation in which a surgeon is called upon to perform an operation upon his wife's lover that saves the life of the latter. Campbell's end was tragic. In May, 1886, he became mentally disordered and he was committed to the State Hospital for the Insane at Middletown, New York, in November. He died there July 30, 1888. Financial difficulties, due to his effort to act as author, director and producer of plays, seem to have been the cause of his breakdown. In his incessant activity he wore himself out. In little more than ten years he had made and lost a fortune. That his plays have not gained him lasting reputation is not surprising, for none has been published, and with the exception of *My Partner,* probably none can be considered as real contributions to dramatic literature. But his plays read even in manuscript are interesting, and to have succeeded in producing a play of the frontier which shares the primary honors with *Davy Crockett* and *Horizon* is no inconsiderable claim to remembrance. For the frontier is in some respects the most significant element in American history, and to have caught and reflected its spirit is an achievement whose importance will grow rather than diminish with time.

CHAPTER VI

JAMES A. HERNE AND THE REALISM OF CHARACTER

IT WOULD be clearly an error to attribute to any one play-wright that development of our drama which gradually substituted, for the strongly accentuated type, the well-rounded natural character who dominated the situations, instead of being created for them, and whose moral, spiritual or emotional conflict provided the central motive of the play. It has become the custom to call the widespread tendency in English literature which began in the thirties and became supreme in the sixties, by the name of realism, and while much confusion has been caused by a failure to distinguish between the selection of familiar material and the realistic method of treating it, it would be idle to object to the term itself. In the late sixties and early seventies the realistic method had become well established in this country in fiction with the work of Elizabeth Barstow Stoddard, of William Dean Howells and Henry James. In their work, it was associated usually with the selection of familiar phases of life, and the influence of the novels of Howells and of Miss Wilkins upon the plays of Herne is clear. Yet Daly had used the methods of realism in dealing with romantic material in *Horizon* as early as 1871, and even at the height of the romantic impulse of the earlier period, we see in the work of Bird, of Boker, of Conrad and Willis, that sincerity of portrayal and surety of touch which produced real characters upon the stage.

The problem of tracing the development of the newer realism of the seventies and eighties is sufficiently difficult when we are dealing with a literary medium like the novel, which is entirely in the control of its creator. With the drama, the difficulty is increased by the fact that it is an art depending upon an interpreter as well as a creator. James Steele MacKaye (1842-94) was a pioneer in a sense, in bringing the quiet re-strained quality of Delsarte's method of acting to the American stage, but of MacKaye's plays unfortunately only two are available. Steele MacKaye is more significant in the history of the theatre than in the history of the drama,[1] but in the former his valiant struggles for naturalness helped in the general movement toward realism. His early plays I have not seen or read and therefore I can make no comment upon them. *Hazel Kirke*, produced first on February 4, 1880, at the Madison Square Theatre, was a revision of an older play of Mac-Kaye's, *An Iron Will* (1879). It is a domestic drama laid in England, and the plot, dealing with the expulsion from her home of Hazel Kirke by her stubborn father, who objects to her marriage with an English nobleman; the false marriage, her return to her home, and attempted suicide, belong to a species of British drama long familiar to the stage. What distinguishes *Hazel Kirke* from its dramatic ancestors is the quiet natural dialogue, and the absence of the usual stage villain. There is a fine climax, too, when Dunstan Kirke, blind, hears his daughter's voice calling for help and cannot save her. *Hazel Kirke* proved to be one of the most popular plays of its time. It had a consecutive run of about two years at the Madison Square Theatre, continuing on the stage for over thirty years and being produced in England, Australia, Japan and Hawaii.

The only other play of MacKaye's that has been published is *Paul Kauvar* (1887), a play of the French Revolution. This is a fine melodrama, intense in its situations, with a plot too complicated in its constant surprises for retelling. MacKaye skillfully kept the love story of Paul Kauvar and Diane de Beaumont the central interest, but contrasted its fidelity and purity with the clash and terror of the Revolution. As the Republic is to triumph, Paul Kauvar is made a republican,

---

[1] *Epoch*, the life of Steele MacKaye by Percy MacKaye, to my regret, appeared too late to be of service to me.

STEELE MAC KAYE

but inasmuch as the sympathy of the audience will always be with the royalists, he is made an advocate of liberal measures, rather than of anarchy. The realism of *Paul Kauvar* lay in the settings and in the acting. The characters are types and the play could have had no such effect in the direction of naturalism as *Hazel Kirke*.

MacKaye's work was frequently the adaptation of foreign or native material. That he drew pictures of life with sincerity is evidenced by the criticism of *A Fool's Errand* (1881), a dramatization of one of Judge Tourgee's novels.[1]

It is gratifying for once to see on the stage Southern people who are possessed of about the same faults and virtues as the rest of the world and no more, and to witness at the same time the usual Northern contrast without the accompaniment of suspenders and catarrh.

It is a matter of regret that MacKaye's plays are not available for study, in order that his share in the movement might be fully determined.

It is not hard, however, for one who views our dramatic progress from the historical standpoint, to see the roots of the newer realism, as far back as *The Contrast* of 1787. Jonathan, the Yankee "waiter," and Charlotte, the girl of the period, are both as real as Maria, the sentimental heroine, is unreal. But it was in the period from 1825 to 1860 that we find in the Yankee plays, like Woodworth's *Forest Rose* and Jones' *Silver Spoon*, the certain if crude ancestors of Uncle Nathaniel Berry of *Shore Acres*. Grandmother Rigglesty in *Neighborhood Jackwood* (1857),[2] by J. T. Trowbridge, is as vivid a portrait of disagreeable old age as our stage has seen, and his other play, *Coupon Bonds* (1876), places a real family, the Ducklows, in a native homely setting with a fidelity that quite matches many more widely known examples of the realistic rural drama. Both these plays were dramatizations of Trow-

---

[1] Philadelphia *North American*, October 27, 1881.
[2] For plot, see *The American Drama from the Beginning to the Civil War*, pp. 289-90.

bridge's own stories, and he was essentially a novelist, but they are of interest as showing the continuity of our dramatic impulses. Indeed, if theatrical conditions had been more favorable, Trowbridge might have made a career as a playwright, for his work is far above the usual sentimental melodrama of the time.

Before the first important play of Herne had been written, Denman Thompson (1833-1910) had developed from the most lowly of dramatic origins a real character and a play which held the stage as long as he could produce it. In the early seventies, Thompson, who was a variety actor in cheap playhouses like the Columbia Opera House in New York, or the old Club Theatre in Philadelphia, known as "wine rooms" or "free and easies," was acting in a one-act skit, *The Female Bathers*. It was a lineal descendant of *A Glance at New York* (1848), for it introduced a Yankee farmer to the seamy side of New York life. Various stories are told about the inception of *Joshua Whitcomb*,[1] but the best authenticated seems to be that J. M. Hill, of Chicago, was so much impressed by Thompson's acting that he persuaded him to write or have written by George W. Ryer, a four-act play in which the character of a farmer, Joshua Whitcomb, based on a real person, Joshua Holbrook, of Swansea, New Hampshire, became the center of a more dignified if a more sentimental drama. *Joshua Whitcomb* was apparently acted first in New York at the National Theatre on April 3, 1876, and continued in Thompson's hands to be a highly popular vehicle for ten years. In 1878, when he was playing in California, he met Herne, but that Herne was prompted toward the realistic rural drama by witnessing *Joshua Whitcomb* is unlikely. As will be seen later he had other inspiration. In 1886 *Joshua Whitcomb* had become *The Old Homestead*, with an augmented cast.[2] By this time

---

[1] A half-hour sketch under that name was acted at Harry Martin's Varieties in Pittsburgh, in February, 1875.

[2] The program of the Boston Theatre for April 5, 1886, reads, "DENMAN THOMPSON will present his new play by Denman Thompson and George W. Ryer, THE OLD HOMESTEAD, A Sequel to 'Joshua Whitcomb.' "

HERNE AND THE REALISM OF CHARACTER

Thompson had undoubtedly learned something from Herne, of whose plays he was a great admirer, and indeed it would be idle to deny the possibility of mutual influence. *The Old Homestead*, so far as plot is concerned, is negligible. What remains from the stage performance is the character of a simple, lovable old farmer. But its significance belongs to the theatre rather than to the drama. Thompson's acting made the play, and his interpretation was so natural that it is reported that one of his New England audiences demanded the return of their money, since he gave them nothing but what they could see any day. The persistence of *The Old Homestead* is perhaps, after all, its chief claim to notice, although it shares with *Hearts of Oak* and *Hazel Kirke* the credit of inspiring the great vogue of rural plays in the last decades of the century.

What makes the plays of Herne more important than those of Trowbridge on one side, or of Thompson on the other, is that he began with work of the older fashion, that he grew above it and that in him appeared the combination of the playwright and the actor. As a playwright he developed steadily, from *Hearts of Oak* to *Griffith Davenport*, in the reality of his characters and situations; as an actor he progressed also in the reality of his interpretation. Moreover, he was a conscious artist; his theories grew out of his experience and he was willing to sacrifice, for the sake of what he saw was truth, a competence, even a fortune.

James A. Herne was born February 1, 1839, at Cohoes, New York. The name was originally Ahearn, but the first letter became an initial. He never authorized the use of Alfred as a middle name, though it has been ascribed to him. His first appearance on the stage was at the Adelphi Theatre in Troy in 1859 as George Shelby in *Uncle Tom's Cabin*. After playing two seasons there he went to Baltimore and joined the company at the Holliday Street Theatre. In 1866 he married Helen Western and was a member of her company for one season, when they separated by mutual agreement. Later he became the leading man for her sister, Lucille Western, and played in a variety of parts, including Sir Archibald Levison in *East Lynne*, Bill Sykes in *Oliver Twist*, and Dan Peggotty in *Little Em'ly*. His first visit to California, in 1868, was with Miss Western's company. When he returned to California as a star he played at Maguire's Bush Street Theater in a répertoire which included Caleb Plummer, Dan'l Peggotty, Captain Cuttle and other characters of Dickens.

Herne has told us [1] how strong was the influence of Dickens upon him, how he learned from him the great significance of humanity as a motive in art. It was the humanity also in the work of Boucicault that attracted him and taught him the quickness in appeal of that art which speaks directly from the heart of the playwright to the sympathy of the audience.

During his career as stage manager at Maguire's New Theatre in San Francisco in 1874, Herne was beginning to adapt novels such as *Oliver Twist* and *Charles O'Malley*, probably reshaping older material. In the latter he played the character of Micky Free. About this time he also made a version of *Rip Van Winkle*, highly praised by David Belasco for its fidelity to the Dutch quality in the character.

When the Baldwin Theatre, first called Baldwin's Academy of Music, was opened March 6, 1876, Herne became stage manager and leading character actor. Here we find him acting in a great variety of parts, from Solon Shingle in *The People's Lawyer*, with its reflection of an earlier stage realism, to romantic characters such as the Count de Clairnot in a dramatization of Gaboriau's *Within an Inch of His Life*. This play, produced February 17, 1879, at the Grand Opera House, is of interest as the first instance of collaboration of Herne and Belasco. Herne outlined the main plan of development of the plot. With the idea of giving dignity to the play, Herne as stage director announced it simply as "Gaboriau's *Within an Inch of His Life*," and it was seriously criticized as a drama by the French writer of mystery stories. Later Belasco's name

[1] "Art for Truth's Sake in the Drama," *Arena*, February, 1897.

was attached to it, and undoubtedly his share in it was large, especially in the mechanical effects.

In 1877 there was studying with a well-known actress, Julia Melville, a girl by the name of Katharine Corcoran. Mrs. Melville, feeling sure of her pupil's talent, wished to have Herne's judgment, and a rehearsal lesson was arranged on the stage of the Baldwin Theatre. Herne became interested in Miss Corcoran's work, and shortly after offered her the part of Peg Woffington in a benefit performance of *Masks and Faces*. After this they toured the Pacific Coast in a stock starring engagement, and were married on April 2, 1878. It was only after the marriage that Mrs. Herne joined the Baldwin Theatre Stock Company.[1] It would be difficult to overestimate the importance of this marriage upon Herne's career both as a playwright and as an actor. As will be seen later, his most important plays were written definitely with her in mind as the leading woman, and her advice in the reshaping of plot and character is seen at its best, perhaps, in *Griffith Davenport* and *Margaret Fleming*.

His association with David Belasco at the Baldwin Theatre was intermittent and their relative shares in the early plays which they wrote together, such as *Marriage by Moonlight*, performed June 30, 1879, are now difficult to assign. A romantic play was needed for the company which included Rose Coghlan, James O'Neill, and "Katharine Corcoran," and Herne and Belasco took the melodrama, *Camilla's Husband*, by Watts Phillips, produced in London in 1862, and revised it to suit the company and the changing fashions of the theatre. The second Act of the manuscript of *Marriage by Moonlight* is missing, so that an exact comparison with its original is not possible. The first Act has been entirely rewritten, and the central situation, the marriage of the heroine, Lady Clarisse Calthorpe, to Lorraine, a wandering painter, in order to prevent her forced marriage to her cousin Harold, whom she dis-

---

[1] This statement, differing widely from printed accounts of their first meeting, is given on the authority of Mrs. Herne.

likes, takes place at Calthorpe Park at night instead of in the village inn. The text was probably Herne's, but in the climax with its background of the moonlight scene Belasco's touch may be recognized. It is essential to the plot that Lorraine, who has married Lady Calthorpe in a half stupor, for the money he badly needs, should not recognize her when he returns later in the play, a well-known artist. In *Camilla's Husband*, Maurice, the artist, fell in love with Lady Camilla Hailstone at first sight and married her for that reason, saved her life at a picnic and nobly renounced her and her wealth in the second Act. Herne and Belasco omitted much of this melodrama, and substituted a motive which is more appealing. Clarisse, already predisposed to favor Lorraine, sees in a picture gallery his painting, "The Innocent Convict"—described by a minor character as "A young man with strangely handsome, half-crazed, half-poetic face, bending beneath the weight of a crime never committed." It is his own portrait and reflects the effect upon him of the treachery by which Harold Calthorpe has had him convicted of the theft of the money Clarisse had given him.

This shame is made use of again quite effectively in the last Act, which takes place in his studio. A duel has been arranged between Lorraine and Harold, but Lorraine, under the stress of emotion caused by his discovery of Clarisse's love for him, has promised her he will not fight. This situation is taken from *Camilla's Husband*, but the scene is made much more powerful, indeed almost tragic, by the mingled emotions of love and shame which force Lorraine to hold himself in check under Harold's insults until Clarisse, who has been concealed in the studio, can stand them no longer and releases Lorraine from his promise. Much of the language is changed, but even when that of the earlier play has been used, there is presented the interesting case of playwrights employing exactly the same words to express much deeper feeling on account of qualities which they have written into the nature of the character earlier in the play. It is also significant that the part Herne played, "Peeping Tom," the wandering cockney-gypsy, through whom

Lorraine's real parentage is discovered, is much cut down in the revision, while that of Hazel, played by Mrs. Herne, is emphasized through a charming little love scene at the opening of the last Act.

The second joint effort of the two playwrights which has survived, has been made the subject of so much contradictory discussion that it is necessary to give a fairly detailed account of its origin and progress. In the summer of 1879, Belasco brought to Herne the second Act of a play which he called *Chums*. Apparently Belasco did not confide to Herne that the play was based upon an earlier English drama, *The Mariner's Compass*, by Henry J. Leslie, which had been acted for the first time in America at the New Bowery Theatre, May 22, 1865. Herne consented to collaborate with Belasco in building up a play out of the material offered. The first performance of *Chums* occurred on September 9, 1879, at the Baldwin Theatre, with Herne as Terry Dennison, Katharine Corcoran as Chrystal, Annie Adams as Aunt Betsy, and Maude Adams as Little Chrystal. After a run of two weeks, *Chums* was withdrawn, but although it had not met with a favorable reception both Herne and Belasco had confidence in the play, and at Mrs. Herne's suggestion it was decided to make an eastern tour. *Chums* seems to have been a failure in Salt Lake City and other western towns until it reached Chicago. The leading managers in that city, McVicker and Hooley, declined to produce the play, but when it was finally put on at Hamlin's Theatre, on November 17, 1879, it was successful. It was rechristened *Hearts of Oak*, and after a tour was brought out again in Chicago at Hooley's Theatre in March, 1880. The vagaries of law, as applied to the rights of a dramatist, are illustrated by the suit which followed Hamlin's attempt to produce *The Mariner's Compass* at his theatre under the title of *Hearts of Oak*. The courts solemnly decided that anyone could play *The Mariner's Compass*, as it was a British play, but that the title of *Hearts of Oak* belonged to Herne and Belasco. If the attorneys for Hamlin had only read *The Mariner's Com-*

pass, they would have discovered that the title "Hearts of Oak" was taken from a sailors' chorus in that play!

Hearts of Oak was played for the first time in New York, March 29, 1880, at the New Fifth Avenue Theatre. During a later engagement in Philadelphia the partners had a disagreement and Herne purchased Belasco's rights in the play. Notwithstanding its failure to meet with popular success in its early stages, *Hearts of Oak* became a valuable dramatic property and was acted by Herne and Mrs. Herne for many years. As it is the first play of Herne's that has survived in complete form, a comparison with *The Mariner's Compass* reveals certain important facts concerning Herne's methods of adaptation.

The Mariner's Compass is a domestic melodrama, first produced at Astley's Theatre, London, March 4, 1865. Silas Englehart, a coast guard, has brought up Ruby Dayrell, a sailor, and Hetty Arnold, both orphans. He loves Hetty, while she and Ruby care for each other. The play opens just before Ruby's return from sea and Silas asks Hetty to marry him. She agrees, and then comes the shipwreck of Ruby's sloop and Ruby's rescue by Silas, though he has discovered that his foster child is his rival. Silas has made up his mind to go away, but Hetty convinces Ruby it is their duty to give up their own happiness, and they persuade Silas that their love is fraternal. After a year, the married pair are shown in their happy state, and then Ruby returns. In a melodramatic scene at Margate Jetty, Hetty shows Ruby that she has determined to be true to Silas. Silas leaves for the Arctic regions, after Hetty has upbraided him roundly for leaving her and their child.

Up to this point *Hearts of Oak* follows in plot rather closely the outlines of *The Mariner's Compass*, although a comic subplot is omitted entirely, and the character of Owen Garroway, a lovable sailor, which was suggested by Dan Peggotty, was created by Herne. The relations of Terry Dennison to Ruby Darrell and Chrystal in *Hearts of Oak* are established, from a superficial point of view, in about the same way as in the earlier drama. But the difference can be appreciated only in a careful reading of both plays, for it lies partly in the closer fidelity to the natural language of human beings and partly to a deft change which deepens the tenderness of the affection existing among Terry, Chrystal and Ruby, while it lessens the theatrical intensity of its expression. The scene in *Hearts of Oak* on Whaler's Wharf, in which Chrystal and Ruby reveal their unchanged love for each other, clutches at the sympathy of the audience and is a distinct advance over the corresponding episode in *The Mariner's Compass* in which Hetty flings her unused wedding ring into the sea.

The most vital change came in the fifth and sixth Acts of *Hearts of Oak*, which replace Act IV of *The Mariner's Compass*. The violent reactions of Silas when he returns to find his wife just married to Ruby, the attempted suicide of Hetty in the mill race, her rescue from the mill wheel by Ruby, who dies in the act, and the final picture of the returned husband clasping his dripping wife in his arms, are replaced by two scenes, quiet in action and touching in their human appeal. Terry returns, blind and white-haired, to find Chrystal and Ruby married. He dies after his little daughter has called him "father"—at his request and under the impression that he has brought a message from her real father who has died in the Arctic regions, and it is only after Terry's death that Chrystal recognizes him. The scene leaves Ruby and Chrystal together, and their mutual love which they have done their best to conquer is to be rewarded. *Hearts of Oak* is by no means one of Herne's best plays, and the last scene might in incompetent hands seem sentimental, but in Herne's performance the dignity of Terry's self-sacrifice secured the sympathy of his hearers. How much of the credit for the improvement in *Hearts of Oak* is due to Herne and how much to Belasco will probably never be known. Herne was entirely responsible for the first, third and last Acts as the play now stands,[1] including the homelike scene at the supper, which is not in *The Mariner's*

[1] Statement of Mrs. Herne.

Compass, and the introduction of the baby, who is only hinted at in the British play.

The Minute Men of 1774-75, played first at the Chestnut Street Theatre, Philadelphia, April 6, 1886,[1] while not a popular success, is of interest since it is Herne's first original play that has survived. It illustrates, too, how his skill was developing, for it is uneven in merit and at times is reminiscent of a much older manner. The scenes are laid in Dorchester Heights and the neighboring forest, and the battles of Lexington, Concord and Bunker Hill are brought in as dramatic pictures after the curtain has fallen on the second and third Acts. This is, of course, poor art, for the historical episodes are thereby separated from the main action, and while in the first instance an opportunity is given for the heroine, Dorothy Foxglove, to rally the men at Lexington Common, this is the only occasion in which the characters of the drama really have any relation to historical events that is not obviously forced upon them. Herne had not learned what Bronson Howard and William Gillette were to illustrate immediately afterward in *Held by the Enemy* and *Shenandoah,* that audiences are not interested in historical episodes for their own sake. The personal relations must form the climax of the action, and in any case the scene at Lexington Common scarcely admits of the introduction of a heroine who, every schoolboy knows, was not present.

Herne speaks of the character of Dorothy Foxglove, which was written for Mrs. Herne, as "glorious," and it is indeed charming. In the same account of his work he tells us that he could not write stage comedy, but the comedy scenes in which Dorothy appears are the bright spots of the play. The plot is not remarkable. Dorothy Foxglove has been brought up by Reuben Foxglove as his daughter. She is really the child of Sir Frederick Shelton, who is commanding his Majesty's Eighteenth Grenadiers, and the discovery of her parentage

---

[1] The play was announced for April 5, but owing to extensive preparations, it was postponed. Philadelphia *Public Ledger,* April 6 and 7, 1886.

through her locket is made in the old conventional way. Her lover, Roanoke, who is supposed to be an Indian and who is really the son of Captain Winslow, a Colonial officer, is no nearer reality than Metamora, and the love story of Rachel Winslow and Ned Farnsworth, which is obstructed at every convenient point by Dyke Hampton, the villain, is carried on by stage figures rather than real people. The language at times is stilted and the sentiment exaggerated.

Yet on the other hand, whenever Dorothy Foxglove enters there seems to be blown into the action a breath of inspiration. The scenes in which she makes Lieutenant Smollet, the British officer, assist her in her cooking; the later scene in which she captures him at the point of his own pistol, when he has been sent to bring her back to Sir Frederick; her tender treatment of Reuben, her foster father, half daughterly, half maternal— all build up a picture of young womanhood that remains vivid even after a mere reading of the manuscript. What they must have been, when clothed with life and color by Mrs. Herne, it is hard to overestimate.

It was perhaps natural that the next best part to that of Dorothy should have been Reuben Foxglove, played by Herne. The simple, natural farmer is contrasted skillfully with Sir Frederick Shelton, especially in the scene in which he refuses payment for his years of care of his foster child and tells Sir Frederick, "There's some things that can't be paid for, and love's one of them." Herne made Lieutenant Smollet a likeable British gentleman, instead of the villain that so often decorated the play of the Revolution. Yet the atmosphere of the War for Independence is well caught, and the indomitable spirit that animated the women of that time is expressed not only in Dorothy but also in Ann Campbell, who handles a gun as well as her male compatriots, and is no doubt an accurate portrait of a pioneer of her type.

The next step forward in the direction of natural character drawing was *Drifting Apart*, originally called *Mary, the Fishermen's Child*, which was first produced at the People's Theatre, New York, May 7, 1888. The scene is laid in Gloucester, among the seafarers. Jack Hepburne, an attractive sailor with a weakness for drink, is married at the close of the first Act to Mary Miller, who as a foundling has been brought up by the fisher folk. In the second Act a domestic interior reveals their mutual trust and happiness. Jack goes to the village for Christmas presents and returns, to his wife's horror, in a drunken condition. In Acts III and IV the future is revealed to him in a dream which includes a powerful scene in which Mary and her child are starving. The child dies on her mother's lap, of cold and hunger, and Jack in desperation rushes out of the house with Mary in his arms. The audience is not aware that this is all a dream until the last Act, when the household is shown after Jack's return to sobriety, and the play ends upon a note of forgiveness and repentance, expressed with simplicity and with fidelity to the inarticulate quality of such natures.

The final form of *Drifting Apart* has perished and the manuscript of *Mary, the Fishermen's Child* reveals again how Herne made alterations in plots and characterization. The language of the earlier form is at times overwrought and Herne himself very truly described Silas and Hester, in whom the stagestruck girl and her lover were burlesqued, as its weakest feature. How thorough was his work in revision is revealed in his correspondence with Hamlin Garland.[1]

Drifting Apart was not very successful in popular appeal. Mrs. Herne, who acted Mary Miller, attributes the failure to the early use of what is now known as the "cut back" in the dream scenes. She feels that the audiences resented the discovery that their emotions had been harrowed by what was after all unreality, while the tragedy was too keen for it to be appreciated for its own sake. The play made a lasting impression, nevertheless, upon competent judges like Howells and Hamlin Garland, and it led to Herne's association with the group of novelists who were leading the realistic movement in

---

[1] Letter of June 4, 1889.

fiction. He was encouraged to continue his struggle to represent the lives of real people, and his work took on the color of a crusade against the meretricious in drama. He has himself expressed it [1] as "Art for Truth's Sake" in an article which is a significant document in our dramatic history. The philosophy of his playwriting is expressed in this passage:

Art for art's sake may be likened to the exquisite decoration of some noble building; while art for truth's sake might be the building itself. Art for truth's sake is serious. Its highest purpose has ever been to perpetuate the life of its time. The higher the form of expression, the greater the art. Vereschagin uses his masterly art to express truth. There is none of the "pomp and circumstance of glorious war" in his battle pictures. They reproduce war as it is. Tolstoy uses his art for truth's sake; so do Howells and Enneking and Hardy and Sudermann; and so does Whitcomb Riley. And so did Browning and Lanier and other great masters of the art. But in expressing a truth through art it should be born in mind that selection is an important principle. If a disagreeable truth is not also an essential, it should not be used in art. Mr. Howells has the art of selection in a remarkable degree. Mr. Enneking says: "The Ideal is the choicest expression of the Real." Truth is the essential of all art. I do not well see how there can be art without some truth. I hold it to be the duty of the true artist to state his truth as subtly as may be. In other words: if he has a truth to manifest and he can present it without giving offense and still retain its power, he should so present it, but if he must choose between giving offense and receding from his position, he should stand by his principle and state his truth fearlessly.

In his emphasis upon reality of portraiture Herne was not simply following the example of the novelists of his time. He was convinced of the importance of character drawing by his stage experience. In a letter to Hamlin Garland [2] he says:

Character *business*, as we call it, is *the* business of to-day in the theatrical profession. *Mansfield* is a character actor; Irving is a character actor; Wm. Warren was a character actor; Stoddart,

[1] See *The Arena*, February, 1897, pp. 361–70.
[2] Dated "Monday," written probably in 1889.

LeMoyne, Couldock, Jefferson, all these are character actors.
Character acting means the finest of all parts built upon *broad*
lines. It embraces facial expression, dialect, comedy and pathos.
You will see in *Hearts of Oak* what I mean by character acting.
Terry Dennison, Owen Garroway, Uncle Davy, in this play are
character parts,—Ned Fairweather a *straight* part. Now character acting (to be perfect) can be only acquired by *study*, with
of course as I say above a fair amount of undoubted dramatic instinct. The straight acting can be done by any person whom
nature has favored with personal qualifications.

In the same letter he suggests the dramatization by Howells
and Garland of *The Rise of Silas Lapham.*

Herne was not simply exploiting a theory. He had proved
his sincerity by sacrifice. *Hearts of Oak* had brought him a
fortune, nearly all of which he had lost in attempting to carry
his theory into practice. *Drifting Apart* ran on tour for
over two hundred and fifty performances, but it made no
money. And yet Herne, undaunted, wrote *Margaret Fleming*
which was more daring in its fidelity to truth and much less
likely to appeal to the public.

It was first tried out at Lynn, Massachusetts, for three performances beginning July 4, 1890, in which Herne acted
Philip Fleming. Herne endeavored to secure a theatre in New
York and Boston without success, and finally rented Chickering Hall, a small auditorium on Tremont Street, holding about
five hundred people, where the play was produced on May 4
1891, and ran for two weeks, creating a distinct artistic sensation. Herne was supported in his efforts by an open letter
urging him to produce the play and signed by W. D. How
ells, Hamlin Garland, Mary E. Wilkins, and other leaders o
the movement toward realism in fiction and the first perform
ance, largely through the enthusiasm of Hamlin Garland
became a confession of faith of the realistic movement in Amer
ica. The play was received with critical approval, but wa
too far ahead of its time for a popular success. On October 5
1891, it was revived for three weeks in Boston and a matine
performance took place at Palmer's Theatre, New York, o

December 9, 1891; but the critics of that city failed to appreciate the play. Herne lost several thousand dollars, but he had won recognition, no longer simply as an actor, but as an artistic pioneer and a literary craftsman. Even more pronounced was the appreciation of Mrs. Herne's acting as Margaret Fleming. *Margaret Fleming* was revived in 1894, and was performed in 1907 with Chrystal Herne in the title rôle, and again in 1915 with Julie Herne as Margaret.

Herne's experiment was one of the earliest efforts at an independent theatre and a call was issued by Thomas Bailey Aldrich, James A. Herne, Hamlin Garland, B. O. Flower, Ralph A. Cram, and others, for a meeting on May 21, at Pierce Hall, Boston, "to consider plans for the establishment of a distinctively American Theatre. In general," the notice states, "it is designed to forward the building of a theatre on the co-operative plan, and to open a Stage whereon the Drama shall be considered a Work of Art, and produced as such— independent of cheap popularity, and where Americanism and modernity shall be the prime requisites. We invite your co-operation at the meeting named above, believing that a Theatre of this general scope must have a great influence upon our literature and especially upon the development of Dramatic Art."

Margaret Fleming is the study of a woman's character. For a revelation of the nobility inherent in the cultivated American gentlewoman, it ranks with the portraits of Lina Bowen in Howells' *Indian Summer* and Isabel Archer in Henry James' *The Portrait of a Lady*. As a contrast to her there is established the character of her husband, Philip Fleming, in whose office the first Act is laid. His prompt decision is shown in the handling of the business attendant upon the conduct of his mill, and by the way in which, after the disclosure by Dr. Larkin that Lena Schmidt has had a child by Philip, he braces himself to attend to urgent matters of detail. He is drawn with great skill; he is not a mere sensualist or a weakling, but a man with a charm that is heightened, perhaps, by a light carelessness, and he has no difficulty in distinguishing his real love for his wife from the sensual passion he has had for Lena. Indeed, he has never troubled to deceive Lena into a belief that he loves her. The first scene closes upon a perfectly normal conversation between Philip and his superintendent. No attempt is made at the old-fashioned climax.

In the second scene there is a charming picture of Margaret in her home life with their baby daughter Lucy. There is no sentimentality, but the little touch by which she closes her dress as the curtain rises prepares the way for the climax of the third Act. The relation by Maria, Margaret's maid, of the serious trouble into which Lena, her sister, has fallen at the hands of some unknown lover is brought in quite simply and prepares the way for the coming disaster. Already the major relationships are established, with an economy of the personnel that reveals Herne's skill. When Philip returns from the office after some delay, there is a charming scene of wifely devotion, and the utter happiness of Margaret makes the approaching tragedy all the more poignant.

In the second Act the disclosure of the danger of blindness for Margaret through approaching glaucoma is established through the conversation of Dr. Larkin. Philip's light-heartedness and ability to forget his cares are consistently portrayed, and the comedy scenes between Maria and her husband, Joe, are used to draw Philip from the stage and permit Maria to make her request to Margaret to come with her to see Lena. The light touch of confidence and comfort with which Margaret leaves Philip is secured with the apparent ease of art.

The third Act takes place in Mrs. Burton's cottage, where in a room off the stage Lena lies dead. Dr. Larkin tries to prevent Margaret from learning the facts, but she comes first in contact with the little baby, a boy, and is attracted to him. Then the disclosure of Philip's fatherhood is made by the letter Lena has left, which Maria brings on with her. The reading of the letter by Maria serves two purposes beside the obvious one of informing the audience. It shows Margaret's growing

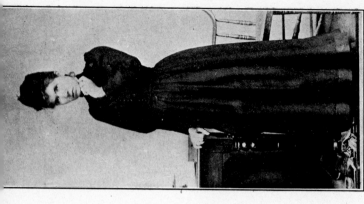

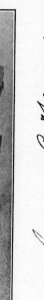

James A. Herne

Cordially Yours
Katharine C. Herne

JAMES A. HERNE AS JOE FLETCHER AND KATHARINE CORCORAN HERNE AS "MARGARET"

IN MARGARET FLEMING

dimness of vision and also proves that Philip was not the ordinary seducer, for Lena writes that she knew he never loved her, although she loved him. Margaret's reaction to the terrible truth is masterly. Instead of breaking down at once, she dominates the situation, forces Maria to give up the idea of shooting the seducer, transfers at once the sympathy of the audience from the dead girl to the injured wife:

You think I am—happy—because I am his—wife? Why, you poor fool! That girl never in all her life suffered one thousandth part what I have suffered in these past few minutes. Do you dare to compare her to me? I have not uttered one word of reproach, even against her, and yet she has done me a wrong that not all the death-bed letters that were ever written can undo. I wonder what I have ever done to deserve this! (*She loses control of herself and sinks, sobbing, in the chair; her arms upon the table; her head dropping upon them.*)

After this brief loss of control she sends for Philip without wasting a word; she parries the doctor's last desperate effort to stop her by his warning that she may endanger her sight by the shock. And then the child begins to disturb her; and the Act proceeds to its close:

Margaret: What is the matter with that child? (*Her voice seems remote. Her expression remains fixed.*) Why don't you keep it quiet?
Mrs. Burton: (*In a hushed voice*) It's hungry.
Margaret: (*In the same mood, but her voice is a little querulous*) Well, then, why don't you feed it?
Mrs. Burton: I can't get nothing for it. I've tried everything I could think of, but it's no use. (*She rises and places the child upon the sofa.*) There, be still, you poor little critter, an' I'll see what I ken get fer ye.
　　　(*As she goes out the door at the back*)
Margaret: Bring a lamp; it's getting dark here.
　　　(*There is silence, then the child's wail arouses her. She half turns her head in its direction and tries to quiet it.*) Hush, child, hush. (*Then she reaches out her hand as if to pat it.*) There, there, poor little thing. Don't fret—it's no use to

fret, child—be quiet now, there, there now. (*She turns and slowly gropes her way to the sofa; sits on the edge of it, feels for the child and gently pats it, murmuring softly*) Hush, baby, go to sleep.

(*There is silence. A pitying half smile plays across her face. She utters a faint sigh and again drifts away into that inner consciousness where she is evidently at peace. Again the child is restless—it arouses her, and hopeless of comforting it, she takes it in her arms. After a moment, she rises to her feet and stumbles towards the table. She knocks against the low chair. At the same moment, Philip Fleming dashes breathless into the room through the door at the right. He pauses in horror as Margaret raises her head, her eyes wide open, staring into his, her face calm and remote. She hushes the child softly and sits in the low chair. Philip stands in dumb amazement watching her. The child begins to fret her again. She seems hopeless of comforting it. Then scarcely conscious of what she is doing, suddenly with an impatient swift movement she unbuttons her dress to give nourishment to the child, when the picture fades away into darkness.*)

In this scene Herne revealed the strength of that dramatic action in which, while few or no words are spoken, the relations of human beings are developed or revealed with the fatal swiftness which is the essential quality of great dramatic moments. The essence of such action is quiet natural expression through word, gesture, or that repose which becomes in itself active. It is shown again in the last scene in *Shore Acres*. It differs radically from the intense brief sentences of melodrama in which the object is not revelation of character but intensification of situation.

In the first form of the play there was an interval of five years, and then in the fourth Act there were scenes on Boston Common and in a small shop at the North End. The boy had died and Maria had stolen Lucy out of revenge. There was also a certain amount of comedy here. Then came the final scene in a police station to which Philip and Margaret had gone in search of Lucy, and here she said good-by to her husband, refusing forgiveness to him. The effect of this ending,

144

in which Margaret stood alone, her figure gradually disappearing as the curtains came together noiselessly, was, according to those who witnessed the Chickering Hall performance, something new in dramatic art.

In the present form, which was acted later by Mrs. Herne, there is an entirely different close. Margaret is blind, the shock having produced the effect Dr. Larkin dreaded, but she faces the future calmly. Philip returns and she receives him with a noble reticence, with forgiveness but with an indication that she cannot again be his wife. She learns that he has attempted suicide, has been rescued and has been advised by his nurse in the hospital to return to his wife. Then the play proceeds:

Margaret: Then you must do something for your child.
Philip: Yes, our dear child.
Margaret: No, not our child—not Lucy. Your son.
Philip: My son?
Margaret: Yes.
Philip: Where is he?
Margaret: Here.
Philip: (*Resentfully*) Who brought him here?
Margaret: I did.
Philip: (*Amazed*) You brought that child here?
Margaret: Yes, where else should he go?
Philip: You have done that?
Margaret: What other thing was there for me to do? Surely if he was good enough to bring into the world, he is good enough to find a shelter under your roof.

Then after he tells her about his attempted suicide, she urges him to go to the mill and pick up his life again. He starts to do so, then says:

I'd like to see Lucy. Where is she?
Margaret: (*At table occupied with the flowers*) They are both out there. (*Indicating with a turn of the head*) In the garden.
(*Philip goes quickly to the door opening upon the garden and gazes out eagerly. Margaret pauses in her work, gives*

a long sigh of relief and contentment; her eyes looking into the darkness; a serene joy illuminates her face. The picture is slowly faded out as Philip steps buoyantly into the garden.)

Mrs. Herne believes the present form of the play is more unified and preserves the tone more securely. She is the best judge, for the changes were made through the results of her experience. Certainly the present form proceeds logically. Margaret is not drawn as unrelenting, and no artistic purpose is secured by the mere fact of unhappiness, unless that unhappiness is inevitable. Margaret and Philip represent the eternal contrast between character and personality. Her final joy rises out of the triumph of character over fate and circumstances. It comes best through sacrifice, and the mere personality through whom the sacrifice is brought about will return inevitably to the haven of character, which will just as inevitably receive it.

Herne's next play was directly inspired by his contact with the natives of Lemoine, a town on Frenchman's Bay in Maine, where he spent his summers. As early as 1889 he had had the idea of a drama based on the contrasted characters of two brothers, and after his disappointment with *Margaret Fleming*, he returned to *The Hawthornes*, as it was first called. Under the influence of the natural beauty of that region between the pine hills and the sea, Herne tells us how *The Hawthornes* "sloughed off its old skin and took on new form and color. Its stage people began by degrees to assume the character and affect the speech of the typical men and women of Maine. Stage traditions vanished. *The Hawthornes* lost its identity, and emerged a survival of the fittest, and Mrs. Herne called it *Shore Acres*." [1] Mrs. Herne played Helen Berry, Martin's daughter.

The record of *Shore Acres* is one of the many examples of the accidental happenings in stage history. One of the most successful plays of its time struggled hard for a chance of pro-

[1] *Arena*, February, 1897, p. 368.

duction. It was first performed at McVicker's Theatre, Chicago, May 17, 1892, as *Shore Acres Subdivision*, and after two weeks the title was changed to *Uncle Nat* at McVicker's suggestion. It ran for four weeks, with general critical approval, but it was not considered to be a financial success. Only an unexpected vacancy at the Boston Museum caused the manager, R. M. Field, to put on the play in February, 1893. It ran for one hundred and thirteen performances, instead of the two weeks he had arranged, but even then its fate hung on a thread. Field took the play to the Fifth Avenue Theatre in New York, where it opened on October 30, 1893. During the first two weeks it seemed about to fail and only a fortunate clause in the contract, which guaranteed the production of the play for four weeks, saved it from being taken off. By that time it had become a pronounced success both with the critics and with the public, and after transfer to Daly's Theatre, it ran for the entire season. It restored Herne's fortune, and is still being acted in stock.

Shore Acres is again a character study. Nathaniel Berry, or "Uncle Nat" as he is called, acted by Herne, is a lovable creature, who has built his life up apparently of little things, since he has let the great things pass him by on the way to others. His younger brother, Martin, has married the girl Nat loved, and even the property which they jointly own has passed into Martin's control. In order to enter into a real estate operation, Martin wishes to sell the land on the knoll, looking out to sea, where their mother is buried. How difficult it is to depict any situation in which the memory of a dead mother is made the motive can only be appreciated after a mental review of the many overwrought scenes for which it is responsible! But hoping to prevent the sale, Uncle Nat, with his quaint phraseology, draws a vivid picture of their mother's all-night vigil on the knoll when their father had been lost at sea. This is most effective on the stage.

Uncle Nat watches over the love story of his niece Helen and Dr. Sam Warren, to whom Martin objects on account of his "free-thinkin' ideas." Helen is well drawn, for the stubborn quality in Martin is revealed in her nature, mingled with the intolerance of youth, as his is deepened by the prejudice of age. Nat is the philosopher who is liberal to all opinion; perhaps because the greater joys of life have not been his, he is determined that Helen shall not lose them. The advanced opinions of Dr. Warren, which do not seem very advanced to-day, alarm Nat not a bit, nor is he unduly impressed by them. Herne brought on the stage the age-long conflict between the tory and the radical, expressed in the brief conversation between Martin and Sam:

Martin. I don't want to know nothin' and I don't want her to know nothin' that I don't want her to know.
Sam. Why, you see, Mr. Berry—you can't help—
Martin. I'm a bringin' up my family, and I don't want any interference from you, nor Darwin, nor any of the rest of the breed. What book's that yeh got there now?
Helen. One of Sam's books, Father.
Martin. Well, give it right straight back to Sam; I don't want nothin' to do with him nor his books.
Sam. It's my book, Mr. Berry, but it was written by a man—
Martin. I won't hev you a-bringin' them books here, a-learnin' my daughter a pack of lies, about me and my parents a-comin' from monkeys—

The "book" is Howells' *A Hazard of New Fortunes*, and while at first glance the whole discussion seems old-fashioned, recent developments have proved that it is not an outworn struggle and also that Herne selected for his example of Helen's reading one of the truly permanent contributions to the literature of that period. Howells must certainly have been amused to find himself quoted as an example of "advanced ideas." His philosophy more nearly approaches that of Nat, who is the eternal liberal, the force that keeps the world moving, while tory and radical both obstruct progress with recurrent fashions in morals and science.

Nat believes that life is too short for unhappiness, and he

acts promptly in helping Helen and Warren to run away upon
Captain Ben Hutchins' boat. This leads to a theatrically
effective if melodramatic struggle in the third Act, in the lighthouse, in which Martin in his desperate anger tries to prevent
Nat from igniting the beacon, hoping thereby to wreck the
Liddy Ann, in which Helen and Warren are eloping. Nat's
spirit flares up and he tells Martin his long years of self-
effacement have ended, and he drives his brother away from
the stairway leading to the light. The curtain descends upon
his apparently futile effort to reach the light in his weakened
condition, but in the next scene, on the deck of the *Liddy Ann*,
we learn that she has been saved by the sudden appearance
of the light.[1]

This act is much less artistic than the ones which precede and
follow it, in the farmhouse kitchen. In the first, the Christmas
dinner is redolent of reality, and in the last scene, after Helen
and Warren have returned with their child and everything has
been straightened out naturally, Nat puts the house to bed.
Nothing is said, but by the expression in his face, one reads his
thoughts.

*Uncle Nat has been locking up, and seeing to the fire. He
takes the candle and starts upstairs. The wind howls outside;
the stage darkens slightly as he gets to the foot of the stairs; he
looks off where the others have gone. He smiles and thinks to
himself during the remainder of the scene, without speaking:*
Uncle Nat. Well, everything's all right again. I wonder how
  long Nell 'n' Sam's going to stay. A month'r two anyway.
  By George, it's going to be pooty hard work to get the ol'
  farm inter shape again. Well, hard work never skeered me.
  I wonder if I locked that door. (*He goes and tries it.*) Gra-
  cious, what a night. (*He looks out of the window.*) Snow'll
  be ten foot deep in the morning. Ol' Berry's all right. Tim's
  there. (*As he mounts the stairs*) Bless that baby. (*Smiles
  off at it*) I wonder what the young uns'll say in the morning.
  It'll be better'n a circus here when Millie sees that baby.

[1] Winter in his *Life of Belasco* states that this scene is taken from *The Keeper of
Lighthouse Cliff*, by Frank Hitchcock (Murdoch). I have been unable to find this
play, but I am informed by Mrs. Herne that Herne acted in a play by that name in
his youth.

(*As* he disappears the stage is dark, only the firelight flickering
through the chinks of the stove. The cuckoo clock strikes
twelve and the curtain slowly descends.)

Anton Chekhov has been praised justly for the final scene in
The Cherry Orchard, in which the old servitor closes the house
after the family have left it, without a word spoken. But the
historian of the drama notes that *Shore Acres* antedates *The
Cherry Orchard* by twelve years.

This ending did not close the play in its original production
in Chicago. Here the curtain went down on the confusion
caused by the explosion of a gun with which Nat, as a veteran
of the Civil War, was going through the manual of arms,
prompted by the receipt of his arrears of pension. This bit
of fooling was put in at the request of the management. Herne
preferred the quieter ending at all times.

My Colleen, a romantic play in which the pathos and humor
of Irish character seem to have been adequately treated, was
written for Tony Farrell, a comedian, in 1891. Both Mr. and
Mrs. Herne acted in it during the season at McVicker's Theatre in which *Shore Acres* was produced.

In January, 1893, *The New South*, by J. R. Grismer and
Clay Greene, was produced. Herne acted the part of Sampson, a negro murderer, and in a powerful scene represented the
growing effect of fear in a negro's mind. It may be that this
suggested to him the motive of slavery, but the direct source of
The Reverend Griffith Davenport was the novel, *An Unof-
ficial Patriot*, by Helen H. Gardener. Herne changed the incidents and characters of this loosely constructed story into a
unified drama to which the calmest critical judgment has given
a high place among the playwriting of the time. It was first
performed at the Lafayette Square Theatre in Washington,
January 16, 1899, and later at the Herald Square Theatre,
in New York, from January 31 to February 10.

The scenes of the play are laid in Virginia and in Washington, before and during the Civil War. Griffith Davenport
is a member of an old Virginia family, who has become a

Methodist circuit rider. Naturally devout, his communings with God and nature have made him almost a mystic. To him slavery is inconsistent with Christianity, and he has vowed never to buy or sell a slave. By inheritance, however, he owns a large plantation and a number of slaves, and when he marries, his wife Katharine brings him others. To her his scruples are incomprehensible, for she represents the point of view of the patrician. In the play, their eldest son, Beverly, sides with her, while Roy shares his father's feelings. In the novel both had been strong Union men and this change adds to the dramatic element of conflict, and makes the struggle of Griffith more lonely and difficult.

The first act shows the garden of the Davenport estate; the negroes are living in a peaceful condition typical of many Virginia plantations. Into this idyllic state a personal note of tragedy is struck when Sally, Katharine's maid, enters to beg "Marse Griff" to buy her husband, John, who is to be sold by his master on the next plantation. He resists at first all appeals, even those of his wife, but finally yields to Sally's dramatic plea. This scene, which occurs in the novel, is reinforced in the play by another scene which reflects the misery of the free negro Jim and also the cruelty of a neighboring planter Nelson, who has just captured Sampson, a runaway slave. These are introduced to make clear the difficulty of the problem. If Davenport simply frees his slaves he does them an injury rather than a benefit. He must therefore leave his home if he persists in his attitude, and he can see no other solution.

In the second Act, which takes place in the stately drawing-room, Griffith frees his slaves. In a scene not in the novel, Beverly and Roy represent the family tragedy that occurred so often during the Civil War.

"Roy," the former says, "if this thing ever comes to a war between the North and the South, which side are you going to fight on?"

"On my side," replies Roy, laughing.

Beverly looks at him thoughtfully. "Roy," he continues,

151

"if I ever met you in a battle, I believe I'd kill you quicker than I would a real Yankee."

Roy takes a deep breath, and then adds, "I'm sorry, Bev, but I'm afraid I'll have to give you the chance."

The negroes, assembled in the hope of presents from the master, are stupefied at the manumission papers, which degrade them into the class of "free niggers" who belong to nobody. Suddenly Nelson's negro, Sampson, bursts into the room, a broken chain dangling from his ankle, a pruning knife in his hand. Nelson is at his heels with his dogs and men, and without an apology to Mrs. Davenport, he orders his men to take Sampson. Sampson holds up his knife.

"Ef you come neah me, I'll cut ma throat," he says quietly. Griffith, aghast, calls out, "I'll buy him, Nelson."

"I won't sell him," replies Nelson, and starts toward Sampson. But the negro plunges the knife into his throat and falls dead before them.

From this point Herne took even greater liberties with his material. A strong scene was made of the announcement of Lincoln's election, the growing hatred of his neighbors for Griffith being made concrete in Nelson's denunciation of him, and Katharine's quiet but bitter reply, "We will go." Driven from home, Griffith becomes affected by the spirit of the martyr and, gathering his family around him, he prays fervently for help and guidance in the new life which they must face, and for the safety of his country.

In the novel, Davenport went to Indiana after a brief stay in Washington. For the sake of unity Herne kept the scene of the fourth Act in Washington, in the humble home in which they are living during the war. Beverly is in the Confederate army and Roy enlists in the army of the Union. Then occurred one of the most important changes in the play. In the novel, Lincoln had sent for Davenport and asked him to guide the Union forces through Virginia. The interview, which is the best piece of writing in the novel, was at first used in the drama. Something, however, seemed to be wrong. Herne worked upon the scene for a long time and became so discouraged that he was about to give up the play. Then Mrs. Herne, who acted Katharine, saw the difficulty. It was an error in technique to bring into the most important scene in the play a character who became to the audience of more interest than the hero. Lincoln naturally dominated the scene and it was decided to indicate his influence through Governor Morton of Indiana, who had, in real life, persuaded Mrs. Gardener's father to enter the service, but who had only been mentioned in the novel. Morton shows Davenport how Lincoln has heard of him, and by displaying the map of Virginia reveals how sadly in need of guidance is the Union army. Then Morton asks him to war against his own people:

Gov. M.: He's going to send a corps of engineers down there to make a new map of that country. He wants you to lead that corps. You can go in your character of chaplain or—
Griffith: No. If Ah do this thing Ah'll do it outright. Ah've nevah seen it as yo've made me see it to-day. If Ah go Ah'll ride in the lead, not as a chaplain nor as suttlah, but as just what Ah shall be—God help me—a gov'ament guide.

While Griffith rebels at the idea of being a spy, Morton produces the telegram:

Order your man Davenport to report to me immediately.
A. LINCOLN.

Through the climax of the Act, in which is developed the conflict between Griffith and Katharine, who begs him not to betray their State, the influence of Lincoln is portrayed in a more vital manner than if he had been present, and yet the interest remains centered upon the characters upon the stage. Katharine has begged him not to leave her and he replies:

Griffith: Katharine, (*Pointing to picture*) that is Abraham Lincoln, the President of the United States, after his inauguration March 4, 1861. (*Taking cabinet photo of Lincoln from top of bookcase*) This is Abraham Lincoln March 1, 1862.

Do yo' see the change in the face? No human being has evah suffered in a lifetime what this man has suffered in one sho't yeah. Men think it is a great thing to be the president of a great nation; and so it is, in time of peace; but ah! Katharine, in time of wah! President Lincoln hasn't got a man he dare trust to map this country. (*Shows map.*) Look at that. (*Getting excited*) He turns to me, and he says, "Davenpo't, I need *you*. Ah answered when yo' all needed me. Now when I need yo'—" He points his accusing fingah at me and says, "Theah is but one way to sho'ten this wah, to lessen the awful slaughter, the carnage and suffering, on *both* sides. Theah is but one man who knows how to do this, and that man is (*Pointing to himself*) yo'. And yo' have not done yo'ah duty to yo'ah country. No sah, nor to yo'ah God, until yo' have done that." (*Falls into a chair overcome with his emotions, and buries his face in his arms.*)

Katharine: (*Almost heart-broken*) Ah know—Ah know—But ah! To think of yo', mah husband, guiding an a'my against—

Griffith: Look at that bridge. Do yo' remembah that bridge on the 22nd of last July? (*Points out of window in direction of Long Bridge*) Do yo' see young sons like yo'rs dragging bleeding limbs across it? Do yo' see terror-stricken ho'ses trampling down those wounded boys?

Katharine: (*Horrified*) Don't, Griffith! Fo' God's sake, don't!

Griffith: It is fo' God's sake—Ah pray to mah God that Ah may nevah see anothath such day in mah life. If Ah knew how to prevent a railroad accident— What would yo' think of me if Ah did not prevent it?

Katharine: Yo' have sacrificed so much already, Griffith. Yo' have impoverished yo'rself—

Griffith: Ah know, Ah know—

Katharine: The people down theah loved yo' so befo'. Ah hoped that after all pe'haps we might some day go back theah again, but now— (*Shakes her head*) Every man, woman and child in Virginia will hate—and despise yo'—

Griffith: The people down theah nevah unde'stood me. But *yo'*, yo' do—would yo' evah have loved me—had I been different?

Katharine: (*Going to him. Firmly*) No.

Griffith: Will yo' respect me now, if Ah do not respect mahself?

Katharine: No.

Griffith: Then kiss me, and tell me to go.

Katharine: Do yo' realize what yo' ask of me?

Griffith: Yes.

Katharine: Is there no othah way?

Griffith: Ah see none.

Katharine: Ah, Griffith! How can Ah say it? Suppose anything should happen to you? That yo' should be taken? (*Breaking down*) Ah'd nevah forgive mahself. Ah believe Ah'd kill mahself. (*Recovering herself*) Griffith, Ah have made sacrifice aftah sacrifice for yo'. Now yo' come to me and ask me to make the supreme sacrifice of mah life. Ah rebel; Ah cannot do it. (*Decisively*) Ah *will* not do it. (*Changing her tone*) Ah, Griffith! mah husband, yo' awe all Ah have. Ah love yo'; Ah tell yo' Ah love yo'. Ah cannot give yo' up.

Griffith: Katharine, this is not a question of yo'ah life or mah life, or of our love fo' each othah. The life of the nation is at stake. Abraham Lincoln calls out to me, "Help me to save the nation. Help me to save this nation." Ah can't shut mah ears to his pitiful cry.

Katharine: You solemnly believe it your duty to go, do you?

Griffith: Yes, Katharine. It is a duty Ah owe mah fellow men on both sides of Mason and Dixon's line. It is a duty Ah owe to the man Ah helped to make responsible for this war. It is a duty Ah owe the government undah which Ah live, and of which Ah am an infinitesimal paht.

Katharine: (*Seeing that argument is useless*) Well, then—go! (*This last with a supreme effort.*)

Griffith: (*Relieved*) Ah knew Ah could depend on you. Yo' awe the bravest little woman in the wo'ld.

In the first scene of the fifth Act, Griffith is seen leading the troops through his native mountains until they approach his own home, when he declines to go further. In the play he is then captured by the Confederates under his son Beverly and is accused of being a spy. The last scene, which is entirely different from the novel, is laid back at the old Davenport mansion. Griffith has been searched and his commission found on him, so that he becomes a prisoner of war. He is allowed to speak to Katharine before he is taken to prison, and the play ends as they are sitting together on the steps of the porch in the moonlight, renewing their vows of love and faith.

Katharine asks him to sing an old song of their courtship days, and he begins:

"Oh, if I were king of France——" as the curtain falls.

But the plot of *Griffith Davenport* cannot even suggest the sweep and color of the play, with its diversity of characters, each one a distinct portrait. That it was not a popular success remains among the unsolved problems of the stage.[1]

Sag Harbor, Herne's last play, was produced at the Park Theatre in Boston, October 24, 1899. It is a revision of *Hearts of Oak*, the main theme being the contrasted love of two brothers, Ben and Frank Turner, for the same woman, Martha Reese, who marries Ben, the older, on account of the gratitude she feels for him, while she really loves Frank. The central character, however, was not the husband, as had been the case in *Hearts of Oak*, but Captain Dan Marble, a guardian angel of everyone, played by Herne himself. The situation is a bit more keen in its sense of conflict, for the two lovers are brothers instead of foster father and son, and Frank urges Martha to run away with him, when he returns two years after her marriage to Ben. There is no Arctic voyage, although Ben threatens to go to the Klondike, and the relations are straightened out largely by the story Captain Marble tells them on Easter Sunday, of a wife who finds that after sending her husband off to war in a similar situation she has really loved him best. Curiously enough, this story follows in its main outlines the plot of Belasco's *May Blossom*, which had appeared between the productions of *Hearts of Oak* and *Sag Harbor*.

There is a certain advance in naturalness in *Sag Harbor*. Striking situations are avoided and the more insistent urge of Frank's passion for Martha, while less ideal than Ruby Darrell's sentiment, is more true to human nature. There is a

---

[1] The unique complete MS. of *Griffith Davenport* was burned. Act IV survived among the papers of the late William Archer and came into the possession of Dr. Brander Matthews, through whose courtesy the foregoing extract has been made. The analysis of the play is also based upon the scenario, furnished through the courtesy of Miss Julie Herne, who acted Emma West, the *fiancée* of Roy, and through the oral accounts of Mrs. Herne, who acted Katharine Davenport.

Addenda to Act IV

May or May not be used.

Katherine

When are you to see your President?

Griffith

"Starting as if from a reverie — Looks
at watch" Now! — Now — Jericho —
Ah'm a half hour late — "Seizes hat
and starts for door"

Katherine

Wait — one minute —. When you see
him — Tell him he must send
me our man his household through
his lines — "Pause" she goes
to him — and puts both of her hands
on his shoulders — Griffith — this
means everything to me now — You
Must help me to get back to Virginia
— promise me that you will do
nothing for him until he agrees to
do this for me —

Griffith

"After Pause" Ah. promise —

Katherine

Thank you — — Good bye —

Griffith

Won't you Kiss me

Katherine

Yes. "Kisses him warmly"

Griffith

Good bye — Katherine sometimes

A PAGE FROM THE ORIGINAL "LOST MANUSCRIPT" OF
GRIFFITH DAVENPORT

closer approach to reality, too, in the portrayal of Martha's love for Ben, and the relations between Captain Marble and his wife are delicately expressed. Several entirely new characters are introduced, especially Jane Cauldwell, a young music-teacher who comforts Frank at the end. This part was played by Chrystal Herne, and the heroine, Martha Reese, by Julie Herne.

Sag Harbor was a very substantial success. It ran until January 20, 1900, in Boston, and opened the Republic Theatre in New York on September 27, 1900, with practically the same cast, except that Lionel Barrymore played Frank Turner. After Herne's death on June 2, 1901, several changes were made in the cast.

When Herne's work is considered as a whole, it will at first seem that it represents several different species, leaving aside the early romantic melodrama, like *Marriage by Moonlight,* or the vanished Irish play, *My Colleen.* These are the domestic melodrama of *Hearts of Oak;* the domestic comedies of *Shore Acres* and *Sag Harbor;* the domestic tragedies (for no matter what the endings may be they are tragedies) of *Drifting Apart* and *Margaret Fleming;* and the historical dramas, *The Minute Men* and *Griffith Davenport.* Yet the very effort to so classify his work reveals the essential artificiality of the attempt. The significant fact which arises from the effort is that Herne's popular successes lay in the field of domestic melodrama and comedy. In *Hearts of Oak, Shore Acres* and *Sag Harbor* he was dealing with the characters of primitive people, and the motives of love, loyalty and family affection are those of most universal appeal. The reality of character and conversation is set against a background in which effective devices to secure human interest are employed. The famous supper scene, for example, which began in *Hearts of Oak,* continued to please the audiences who saw *Shore Acres* and *Sag Harbor.* Their pleasure was due to their recognition of familiar objects, and recognition is the result of an easier mental effort than any reaction which comes from a stimulus given to the imagination.

The Minute Men and *Griffith Davenport* are both historical plays, it is true, but the first relates as a piece of dramatic art much more closely to *Hearts of Oak*, as a melodrama, and the really helpful classification of Herne's play is a progressive one. He began with romantic melodrama in association with David Belasco in *Marriage by Moonlight*, and in the various forms which *Chums* and *Hearts of Oak* assumed he was working his way out of melodrama into something more assured. At first he apparently felt that the material was all important, and he turned to the Revolution for facts and atmosphere that would lend verity to his work. Yet *The Minute Men* is still tinged with the stilted language of an earlier stage epoch, though it redeems itself partly by the firmer drawing of the central characters. His own tastes led him to the study of simple natural people, and it is not strange that when he combined this selection of familiar material with the realistic treatment of it, in *Drifting Apart* and *Margaret Fleming*, that he should progress rapidly toward the summit of his creative achievement. It was at this time that his art became more conscious, under the inspiration of men like Hamlin Garland, while his reading of foreign playwrights and novelists, like Ibsen, Sudermann, Hardy and Zola, strengthened his own predilection toward realism. The result was less popularity and financial loss, but our drama gained a landmark. Howells was quite right when he called *Margaret Fleming* an epoch-marking rather than an epoch-making play. It produced no immediate effect and founded no school. But on looking back we can see that 1890 seems now the beginning of an era. One has only to compare *Men and Women*, of Belasco and De Mille, with *Margaret Fleming*, to see the difference between a play distinctly of that period and the work of Herne. The Scandinavian drama influenced him little, and the German less. He may have learned some lessons in naturalism by reading Ibsen, but he could hardly have seen any of his plays before 1890. According to Hamlin Garland, he learned from Ibsen to dispense with the "asides" and other artifices of the older stage. He mentions Sudermann in his article written in 1897, before quoted, but if any influence came to Herne from the author of *Die Sorge*, which indeed he read, it was passed through an artistic consciousness which was aware of the dignity of decency and the value of reticence in permanent art.

It was with Herne in drama as it was with Howells in the novel. He was at first subconsciously in sympathy with an impulse which was dominating Europe, and he and Mrs. Herne struggled toward an expression, in drama and on the stage, of a simpler and more sincere form of realistic art. In this they were ahead of their time, so far as America is concerned. Later, when their efforts began to receive the appreciation of Howells and Garland, they recognized their part in this movement and their efforts became more conscious. But they were authorized rather than inspired by the continental realists.

One marked difference between Herne and the European naturalistic movement lay in the humanitarian aspect of his work. He became vitally interested in social reform and, becoming convinced of the justice of Henry George's theory of the single tax, he talked in public on the subject in many of the principal cities of the Union. It became, in fact, a life work with him, and influenced his later writing, especially *Shore Acres*.

The advance in *Margaret Fleming* and in *Griffith Davenport* lies in the less obvious material and the finer subtlety of motive. Herne speaks of *Margaret Fleming* as "the epitome of a powerful but savage truth." But while its central motive, the rebellion of a wife against an action that strikes at the roots of family life, represents the most primitive impulse of our natures, it was just because Margaret Fleming was a refined and cultured woman that the climax of the third Act is so telling a piece of dramatic art. How much less effective would such a scene have been if the woman had been drawn from the personnel of *Hearts of Oak!*[1] But when a gentle-woman, whose every instinct is in open rebellion at the discovery of her husband's liaison with the sister of her servant, finds the impulses of repulsion checked and conquered by the flood of feelings that spring from the universal motherhood within her, we have that shock of conflict which comes only with great drama. Audiences of 1890, however, were not ready for the shock which arises from the relapse into the primitive.

Nor apparently did they understand the combination of patriot and mystic in *Griffith Davenport*. Perhaps the failure of that play to win popular success may have been due to a subconscious feeling that a man should remain true to his own people, as the universal hero worship of Robert E. Lee has indicated. But whatever may have been the causes which led to the failure of Herne's best plays, there can be no question that it was due to the difference of theme rather than the method of treatment. For between *Margaret Fleming* and *Griffith Davenport* had come *Shore Acres*, his greatest popular success, and the fineness of art which reflects an emotion in a glance or a movement of the hand is revealed in that play in a masterly fashion.

And finally and most important, of course, comes the revelation of character. Both from the script and the stage there emerge Margaret Fleming, Philip Fleming, Uncle Nathaniel Berry, Martin Berry, Ann Berry, Griffith Davenport, Katharine Davenport, Captain Dan Marble, Dorothy Foxglove, Mary Miller, to speak of only the leading characters among many. They are not types: they are individuals. They remain in the memory—real people—for us to speculate upon their merits and defects, to wonder whether they really did the things their creator made them do, in short to become citizens of that world which is the product of close observation and

---

[1] Winter, in his *Life of Belasco*, I, 200, says that "this incident occurs, by the way, under other circumstances, in the fourth [sic] chapter of *Hide and Seek*, by Wilkie Collins, published in 1854." The implication is unfair, since the scene in the sixth chapter of *Hide and Seek* has to do with the nursing by a circus woman of the child of a poor girl, with whom neither she nor her husband has any relation.

powerful imagination, in which they may meet the creatures
of another great human realist, Charles Dickens, whose characters Herne loved to represent upon the stage.

It is not unworthy of note that both in Herne and Mrs.
Herne that quality of imagination which is primarily Celtic
had a racial origin. Hundreds of plays upon rural life had
their rise during this period, following Herne's success, and
few remain worthy of serious consideration. They were usually simply photographic representations of eccentric types
and pleased for the moment by their obvious appeal to the faculty of recognition. But in Herne's plays there is a quality of
devotion which rises like a flame in the natures of Margaret
Fleming and Griffith Davenport, the wife and the patriot, in
their greatest hours of trial. This note of loyalty, the prevailing quality that lives in the song and story of Scotland and
Ireland, is struck in every play of Herne's from *Chums* to *Sag
Harbor*. And there is also a charm, indefinable, but present
in the domestic scenes of happiness of *Margaret Fleming* and
Griffith Davenport before the tragedy comes; throughout all
the fisher plays; in the comedy scenes in *The Minute Men*,
when Dorothy Foxglove is on the stage; which are as different
from the horseplay of the rural drama of Herne's imitators as
Conn the Shaughraun is from the average stage Irishman.
That they are often associated with the parts played by Mrs.
Herne, who was born in Ireland, raises a final problem which
the historian cannot solve—to what extent the plays as they
now exist were the joint product of the dramatist and the actress to whom Herne has frequently paid his tribute for her
inspiration.[1]

It would serve no purpose to chronicle the many imitations
and reproductions of the scenes and characters of rural life
which owed their inspiration to the popularity of *Hearts of
Oak* and *The Old Homestead*. As has been indicated, they
are not a new development in our drama, and in many cases

[1] Hamlin Garland, who was in close contact with Herne, tells me that Mrs. Herne
constantly suggested "scenes, lines, and stage business."

belong in material and treatment to the same species as *The Silver Spoon* of J. S. Jones. They rise or fall in significance as they caught the new spirit of the natural, and perhaps two examples will illustrate the difference between the real and the false notes in the rural chorus.

The County Fair, by Charles Barnard and Neil Burgess, first performed at Proctor's Twenty-third Street Theatre, March 5, 1889, was one of the great popular successes of its time, for it continued its life at the Union Square Theatre in November, 1889, and ran practically continuously until May 31, 1890. Its success was undoubtedly due to the acting of Neil Burgess as Miss Abigail Prue, the old maid who is the feminine counterpart of Joshua Whitcomb and Uncle Nat. Miss Abby has a sharp tongue, but she has a warm heart for Tags, the waif who turns out to be her own sister's child, and she is sentimental, too, over Otis Tucker, who has been courting her mildly for fourteen years. The plot is conventional where it is not negligible, but the dialogue is bright and the atmosphere is sincere.

Way Down East, by Lottie Blair Parker, on the other hand, was a "pastoral drama," which pointed backward rather than forward in the development of realism. It has all the old conventional figures, beginning with the stern father who will not let his son marry the drooping stranger who totters on the stage, having left her child in the graveyard, and not forgetting the burlesque of the college professor who makes comic love to the farmer's daughter. The lessons of simplicity and sincerity which Herne had taught were neglected, and yet the play was a great popular success, beginning at the Manhattan Theatre on February 7, 1898, a long run of three hundred and sixty-one performances in New York.

But as has been sufficiently pointed out, the rural drama was not Herne's most significant contribution; it was the establishment of character.

CHAPTER VII

DAVID BELASCO AND HIS ASSOCIATES

OF ALL the playwrights who form the subject of this study, David Belasco presents the most difficult problem. He has written so often in collaboration with others, the plays bearing his name present apparently so many different aspects both as to selection of material and method of treatment, and his career has been so long and fruitful as playwright, producer and director, that generalizations become at first glance almost impossible. It will be best to consider his work as a series of stages, in which, often with the aid of others, he has passed through various phases of dramatic fashion, sometimes determining it, and sometimes following. After this survey perhaps a certain consistency will become apparent. This method will permit also of the treatment of other playwrights of importance who did their best work in association with Mr. Belasco, and of whom pressure of space will forbid separate discussion.

David Belasco was born in San Francisco, July 25, 1853, both his parents being English Jews, although the family seems to have been originally Portuguese. In 1858 they moved to the trading post, Victoria, and here he was educated, partly in a monastery under the guidance of a Catholic priest, whose influence remained for many years upon Belasco, even in the severity and uniformity of his dress. The theatre, however, was in his blood, for his father had been connected with the London playhouses as a harlequin and his parents associated with the people of the stage. He was used indeed for children's parts, in all probability as early as 1858, but he certainly acted as the Duke of York in Charles Kean's performance of *Richard III* at the Victoria Theatre in 1864. Returning to San Francisco about 1865, he entered the Lincoln Grammar School, where he remained until 1871. His education was, however, quite as much derived from extensive reading and his observation of life, and his indomitable energy, spurred on by the very moderate circumstances of the family, led him to such engagements as he could obtain in the minor offices of the theatre. In 1869 he played a newsboy in Augustin Daly's *Under the Gaslight* at Maguire's Opera House in San Francisco, and he may be said to have definitely adopted the stage as a profession when he took part in F. G. Marsden's *Help* in 1871 at the Metropolitan Theatre.

He began, too, his dramatic efforts, his first play, *Jim Black, or the Regulator's Revenge*, being written when he was but twelve years of age, and being produced on the road. In the official list of his productions, fifteen titles are recorded prior to 1872. The names[1] will indicate the nature of the plays sufficiently, their significance lying simply in the precocity of the boy and the unmistakable impulse toward romance. His life was a precarious one, and his early plays, all of which have disappeared, consisted probably of the re-shaping of fiction, poetry or other plays for an immediate market. Thus he seems to have produced and acted in a version of the Enoch Arden story, made for Annie Pixley about 1876, which is of interest on account of the later use of a similar situation in *Chums.*

During an engagement at Piper's Opera House in Virginia City, Nevada, in 1873, Belasco came under the influence of Dion Boucicault, and the lessons he learned from that master of technique have remained with the pupil in the keen sense of what is theatrically effective and in that combination of romantic material and realistic treatment which is one of the reasons for Belasco's success.

In 1874 began his association with James A. Herne at Maguire's New Theatre, where he acted a dwarf in Herne's production of *Rip Van Winkle.* He was employed as actor, as-

[1] See List of Plays.

sistant stage manager, and even prompter with Bartley Campbell and the Hooley Comedy Company, during their visit to
California, never scorning to take even the humbler positions if
thereby he could learn something of value. His own list of
productions, the list given by Winter in his *Life of Belasco*,
and the accounts in *My Life's Story* are contradictory, but
out of all the bewildering mass of material there emerges the
figure of a hard-working actor and playwright, learning his
profession in a school which developed Herne, Harrigan and
other dramatists, the highly colored life and theatre of California in the seventies. Of all who worked in that atmosphere,
Belasco seems to have been most deeply affected by it, as was
perhaps natural since it was his native soil, and while the others
saw it from the point of view of the theatre, it had been part
of his education. He continued apparently to adapt plays,
especially from the novels of Dickens and Wilkie Collins, but
does not even claim these in his own list.

His second association with Herne began at Baldwin's Academy of Music in 1876, but it was intermittent. Meanwhile he
adapted *Article 47*, under the title of *The Creole*, for Eleanor
Carey, and this was produced at the Union Square Theatre in
New York in 1881. During the spring of 1877 he wrote and
directed eight plays, nearly all in one act, which were performed at Egyptian Hall in San Francisco, and in which he
acted as well. To judge from the casts that have survived, they
were either moral melodrama, like *The Prodigal's Return*, or
else were built up upon a stage device known as "Gardner's
Egyptian Mystery," a variant of the once-famous "Pepper's
Ghost"—an optical illusion again appealing to Belasco's love
of the bizarre. Even before this time he had been experimenting with new effects in stage lighting. By use of colored silks
he had anticipated his own gelatine slides, and there can be no
doubt that Belasco in his theatres in California was developing
that remarkable sense of the part played by lighting in the
illusion of the stage, in which he anticipated more widely known

efforts of foreign directors and which led eventually to the marvelous construction of the Belasco Theatre in New York.

His wanderings took him to Oregon, but he was soon back at the Baldwin Theatre to direct such plays as *Saratoga* and *The Danites*, a connection which took him on tour in the spring of 1878, and culminated in a deserved tribute to his skill.[1] His position at the Baldwin led him to the dramatization of novels such as *The Vicar of Wakefield*, and the quick imitation of Eastern successes, such as *The Banker's Daughter*, under the title of *The Millionaire's Daughter*. The delightful confusion of such adaptations is indicated by the fact that a character by the name of Adam Trueman, the farmer in *Fashion*, was inserted in the play and that Belasco defended himself from the charge of plagiarism on the ground that his most effective scene, that of the duel, was taken from *The Corsican Brothers*!

His association with Herne in *The Moonlight Marriage* and in *Chums* and *Hearts of Oak* has been analyzed sufficiently.[2] The separation was inevitable, for dramatic rather than personal causes. Herne went on developing a form of drama with which Belasco was really not in sympathy, and the latter returned to the Baldwin Theatre, in April, 1880, as actor and dramatist. Here he produced such melodrama as *Paul Arniff*, laid in Russia, or *The Eviction*, in which he seized the current interest in the difficulties between landlord and tenant in Ireland.

Meanwhile he was nursing his ambition to gain a footing in the East. Believing that if he could attract Wallack's attention the way would be opened, he secured Osmond Tearle and Gerald Eyre from Wallack's company for a summer engagement at Baldwin's Theatre, and also persuaded Maguire to engage Mary Jeffreys-Lewis, who was in San Francisco, for the leading part in a play to be written by him. *La Belle Russe* was first presented at the Baldwin Theatre on July 18,

[1] Winter. *Life of Belasco*, I, 106.
[2] Pp. 133-6.

1881. It is based on two plays, *Forget Me Not*, by Herman Merivale and Charles Groves, and *The New Magdalen*, by Wilkie Collins, both of which had been acted under Belasco's management.[1] It is a sensational melodrama of English social life, in which an adventuress attempts to impersonate her twin sister, even carrying her efforts to the point of taking that sister's place as the wife of her long-lost and re-found husband. The play was announced as "from the French," as San Francisco shared with the other American cities a distrust of home talent, and only when it proved a success was Belasco's name attached to it. He went to New York with Maguire to place the play, but through the latter's insistence upon dealing with other managers, he was prevented from selling it directly to Wallack, though the latter eventually secured it. It was produced at Wallack's Theatre on May 8, 1882, with Rose Coghlan as Beatrice, and scored a popular success, being put on at the Pavilion Theatre, London, April 17, 1886. Nearly forty years later, at a dinner given to Belasco, Rose Coghlan paid her tribute to the possibilities which the part afforded an actress in a strong emotional rôle.

Back in San Francisco, he continued his work at the Baldwin Theatre until a meeting with Gustave Frohman not only occasioned the last production of a play by Belasco in San Francisco—the melodrama, *American Born*—but led also to his final departure for New York. In the fall of 1882, through the Frohmans, he became stage manager at the Madison Square Theatre, succeeding Steele MacKaye, who had broken relations with the owners, the Mallory brothers, after making the Madison Square Theatre well-known through his plays and his stage devices. Belasco signalized his advent in the East by the production of Bronson Howard's *Young Mrs. Winthrop*, and he showed his ability at the direction of a different kind of play from that which he had been writing and directing in San Francisco. It was a potent organization to which he had come. The Mallorys had a policy of encourag-

---

[1] Winter, I, 231.

ing American playwrights, like Howard and Gillette; they had in Daniel Frohman one of the shrewdest business managers in America, and the company headed by George Clarke, Mr. and Mrs. Thomas Whiffen, Agnes Booth and W. J. Le Moyne was a splendid one.

Belasco's first effort as a playwright under his new conditions was produced on April 12, 1884, and ran until September 27. *May Blossom*, which was an alteration of an earlier play by Belasco, *Sylvia's Lovers*, produced in 1875 in Virginia City, is a variant of the story of *Hearts of Oak*, with the returned wanderer a lover instead of a husband. Richard Ashcroft and Steve Harland are both in love with May Blossom, and she accepts the former. Ashcroft, who is a Confederate sympathizer, very naturally, since the play is laid in Virginia during and after the Civil War, is arrested by the Federal authorities and begs Harland to tell his *fiancée*. Harland, hoping to marry May, allows her to believe that Ashcroft is dead, and they are married after a year. Ashcroft returns in about two years and demands that May elope with him. She refuses, partly on account of her child and partly since she has apparently begun to love Harland. Ashcroft departs. Of course May upbraids her husband and Steve joins the Confederate army, returning in about six years, having gone on a whaling trip after the war is over. May becomes reconciled to him. This play, which for many years was the only published example of Belasco's work, can hardly be looked upon as one of his best. The characters are inconsistent, especially that of Harland, who is represented as being an honorable man and yet is capable of unspeakable treachery. In feminine psychology, however, Belasco made no mistake, for it is extremely likely that a wife would forgive a crime prompted by her husband's overpowering love for her. The one-thousandth performance of this play was made the occasion for a tribute to the author.

Belasco remained in association with the Madison Square Theatre for only two years, then resigned. After various

DAVID BELASCO

experiences, including an association with Lester Wallack, for whom he adapted Sardou's *Fernande*, a brief return to San Francisco, in 1886, to direct a stock company at the Baldwin Theatre, which numbered among it such actors as Mantell, Henry Miller, and Maurice Barrymore, he became stage manager of the Lyceum Theatre, in 1886, then under the direction of Daniel Frohman.

This position led to the second important period of Belasco's playwriting, that in which he was associated with Henry C. DeMille (1850-93). DeMille, who had been a school-teacher and a play reader at the Madison Square Theatre before he became a playwright, had written a social comedy, *John Delmer's Daughters*, which had been produced at the Madison Square Theatre in 1883 and had failed. His frontier play, *The Main Line or Rawson's Y*, had been no more successful when put on at the Lyceum Theatre in 1886, and the description of it implies that it was of no especial significance.[1]

The combination of Belasco and DeMille produced four of the most successful plays of their day. *The Wife*, which was produced November 1, 1887, at the Lyceum Theatre, was written definitely with the stock company led by Herbert Kelcey and Georgia Cayvan in mind. The central idea was an old one. Robert Grey and Helen Freeman, though lovers, have parted because Lucile Ferrant, who had been jilted by Robert, tells Helen of their earlier relation. Helen marries, out of pique, the Hon. John Rutherford, who in due time becomes aware of the situation. Here Belasco, under the inspiration of Howard's *The Banker's Daughter*, suggested that Rutherford, instead of behaving as the stage husband usually did under those circumstances, should endeavor to win his wife's love, having too much pride to acknowledge that an early girlish passion must necessarily be more powerful than her reaction to his own love and confidence. Rutherford finally succeeds, not without some inner struggles. The play is significant in studying Belasco's development, for it is the least effective

[1] *Theatre Magazine*, II, 24-5.

of this series. It is artificial, and the early motives and actions are quite obvious in their relations to later scenes. The main theme is so padded out with comedy at the beginning of each act that it seems as though material were lacking. The audience, too, has to be told everything, and "asides" are plentiful. In short, it belongs to the fashion of that day.

The relative shares of Belasco and DeMille are best indicated by a description of their methods of collaboration. According to Daniel Frohman,[1] DeMille wrote most of the play. After it had been developed to a certain point, they brought it to the Lyceum Theatre. DeMille sat at a desk near the empty stage and Belasco acted upon the stage the scenes of the drama. If the result was not satisfactory to Belasco, DeMille changed lines, cut out or added scenes and otherwise modified the play, always with a view to stage effectiveness. If the heroine had been introduced upon the left side of the stage when her entrance would have been more telling upon the right, and the script forbade the change of position, then the script had to be altered. When the authors handed over the manuscript, the labor was only half done. Every scene had to be adjusted to the stock company, whose very excellences in some cases proved embarrassing. Grace Henderson, who played Lucile Ferrant, the adventuress, had a peculiarly sympathetic voice. According to the play she was to indicate by her intonation that she was lying to Helen in her revelation of the earlier relation between Robert Grey and herself. But her voice was so appealing that the audience refused to sympathize with anyone but her. So the melodramatic line, "Robert Grey, I'll bring you back to me, no matter what was the cost," was inserted, and she said this to the audience as an aside.

This incident is illuminating in its revelation of the difficulty of appraising justly the work of playwrights of this period. The line in question was added at the instigation of Daniel Frohman, and he was probably justified from the point of view of stage effect. Read in manuscript, it is a blot on the play.

[1] Statement to the present writer.

There can be no question that this was only one of hundreds of cases where the necessities of a stock company rather than the will of a playwright determined the final form of a drama. Such incidents may well have been contributing causes to the decline of the stock companies. Weak and at times commonplace as it was, *The Wife* proved a financial success, receiving two hundred and thirty-nine consecutive performances and leading to the production of other plays by the two playwrights.

Lord Chumley, their second effort, was produced at the Lyceum Theatre, August 21, 1888. It was written for E. H. Sothern, and the hero is not without a certain resemblance to Lord Dundreary, his father's successful part. *Lord Chumley*, like many interesting and successful plays, is made up of situations and characters that are not strictly original. But the central character, that of a young English nobleman who, apparently stupid, vapid and inane, is really brave, acute and above all loyal in love and friendship and willing to sacrifice himself for the sake of friend and lover, remains after nearly forty years, a vivid and delightful memory. The part was just suited to Sothern, and he was provided with lines which are a decided improvement upon those in *The Wife*.

During the interval between *Lord Chumley* and *The Charity Ball*, Belasco directed a production of the *Electra* of Sophocles, in which, as has been pointed out,[1] "the much admired and highly extolled 'modern novelties' of simplicity in stage settings and lighting displayed by Mr. Granville Barker, in 1915, were used by Belasco—twenty-eight years earlier." *The Charity Ball* was produced at the Lyceum Theatre, November 19, 1889. It is a strong play, of intense feeling at times, in which a successful attempt is made to bring sin and suffering into vivid contrast with the brighter phases of social enjoyment. The Reverend John van Buren, a fine type of clergyman, is contrasted with his weak and selfish brother, Dick, who has seduced Phyllis Lee and abandoned her on account of his

[1] Winter, I, 355.

desire to marry Ann Cruger, an heiress, who is really in love with John. The relations of Dick and Phyllis become known to John and Ann during the Charity Ball, and that night Phyllis comes to appeal to John for comfort. He has become fascinated by her physical beauty, but he crushes this feeling, and on Dick's return home demands that he immediately marry Phyllis, offering to perform the ceremony. The quarrel between the brothers, intense yet subdued, was heightened by the entrance of their mother, who, blind but watchful, has heard a disturbance and enters at the height of the scene. Her simple words of gentle reproof, "My boys, my boys," which quiet them, spoken by Mrs. Thomas Whiffen in the original cast, were an example of the use of the family relation as a theme for drama which it would be hard to excel. The marriage is performed, and later John and Ann discover that their love, if a bit placid, is sufficient for happiness.[1]

The last play in which DeMille and Belasco collaborated was *Men and Women*, produced at Proctor's Theatre, October 21, 1890. The germ of the play was furnished to Belasco by a recent banking scandal, in which the father of a young man who had speculated with the funds of his bank is said to have exclaimed, "I'll save the bank, if it costs me a million a day." *Men and Women* is a compound of the themes of banking, speculation, love and family affection. The partners recognized that in the intense moments of anxiety which come to those who are carrying on financial operations which bring them within the shadow of the law, there are fine opportunities for drama. William Prescott, a bank cashier, has taken bonds belonging to the bank and loaned them to Arnold Kirke, a broker, who fails. Suspicion falls on Edward Seabury, the assistant cashier, who is engaged to Dora Prescott, William's sister. At a midnight meeting of the directors of the bank, Seabury is accused of theft. He denies the charge but is

[1] I wondered at the reason which had led to the insertion of the proposal scene with its involved reference to the love story of David Copperfield and Agnes Wickfield, to find at last, from Daniel Frohman, it was inserted to give Georgia Cayvan, the leading lady, an opportunity to resume the stage, from which she had been absent too long!

arrested. Agnes Rodman, the *fiancée* of Prescott, who has been told by Mrs. Kirke that William is the culprit, begs her father, Governor Rodman of Arizona, to save the bank, if Seabury is released. But Calvin Stedman, counsel of the bank, declines to let Seabury go, for he loves Dora and wishes to disgrace his rival. Rodman's offer is accepted, however, by the directors, and then Stedman denounces Rodman as a former convict and therefore untrustworthy. Pendleton, one of the directors, saves the bank, using the phrase which had inspired the play, but he is not interested in Seabury. Then comes a daring but successful climax when Prescott, finding that Agnes knows his guilt, confesses by putting on himself the handcuffs which are waiting for Seabury. The last Act falls decidedly in interest: Prescott is looking for a position, which Pendleton eventually gives him.

What held the audience was the vivid picture of moral and emotional conflict, especially in the characters of Prescott and Agnes. The language when read in the manuscript seems at times stilted and overwrought, but in the fine performance of the original company, which included Sydney Armstrong as Agnes, Maude Adams as Dora, Frederic de Belleville as Cohen, William Morris as Prescott and Orrin Johnson as Seabury, these defects were not noticeable. What remains most clearly is a picture of the normal life of people with real standards without much stress being laid upon them. The peace and comfort of such life makes the tragedy, when it comes, more striking, and the ball given while the bank is under its strain was well conceived and executed.

Belasco had withdrawn from his association with the Lyceum Theatre in March, 1890, in order to secure his independence. He had succeeded as a playwright and as an actor, but he knew that his greatest strength lay in the field of production and direction. DeMille, before his death in 1893, adapted *Das Verlorene Paradies* of Ludwig Fulda which as *The Lost Paradise* was successful. Those who saw *Men and Women* and *The Lost Paradise* recognized that they belong to the same species—the domestic drama which was eminently "satisfactory" to the audience, which had progressed quite far from the sickly sentimentality of *The Stranger*, and whose limitations it is quite possible to overstress. A comparison of the two plays indicates also the large share which DeMille must have had in the verbal expression of the plays in which he collaborated with Belasco.

Though Belasco's efforts to establish Mrs. Leslie Carter as a star led ultimately to success, they engrossed his attention at this time with financial loss and anxiety, and they led at first to no important drama. *Miss Helyett* (1891), a comic opera, is negligible, and *The Girl I Left Behind Me* was produced, not for her, but for the opening of the Empire Theatre in 1893. In collaboration with Franklyn Fyles, then dramatic critic of the New York *Sun*, he constructed one of the most vivid plays of Indian and army life which our drama contains. The time was ripe, for the death of Sitting Bull and the successful operations of General Miles were in the public memory. The scenes were laid in an army post near Fort Assinniboine, in the Sioux Country. General Kennion, who is in command, is visited by his daughter Kate, and a ball is given in her honor. Throughout the gayety there is suggested an impending danger of Indian uprising, under the leadership of Scarbrow or John Ladru, the chieftain of the Blackfoot Sioux. This is accomplished by the constant receipt of telegrams from Fort Assinniboine. Inside the post, the personal relations are also strained. Kate is engaged to be married to Lieutenant Parlow, and finds too late that she loves his colleague, Lieutenant Hawksworth. Parlow had some time before seduced and abandoned the wife of Major Burleigh, one of the officers, who is ignorant of the name of her betrayer. The first crisis occurs when the telegrams which have been coming from the fort suddenly cease, and the savage whoops outside indicate the approach of the Indians. Hawksworth volunteers to go to the fort and bring succor.

In the third Act occurs a striking episode, expressed briefly but forcibly. The situation grows desperate and General Kennion stoops to treat with Ladru. The audience sees the stockade, with the whites behind it, and Ladru rides up, unseen, his voice alone being heard. Some time previous, his daughter, Fawn Afraid, who is in love with Hawksworth, had come into the stockade to bring water to the whites, and has been shot, although this is not known to those within the post, who believe she is living. Then follows this scene:

Kennion: (*His eyes fall on Fawn. With an inspiration.*)
    Ladru, your child is here. What shall I do with her?
Ladru: Fawn is with her own people. (*Fawn kneels.*)
Kennion: (*Pointing toward Fawn*) She is with us. I will be more
    merciful than you. (*Deliberately*) The first shot you fire
    on this Post, I will give the order to—kill her.
Ladru: (*With a cry of intense feeling.*)
    Ah!
Burleigh: That reached his heart.
                    (*A pause*)
Ladru: If Fawn is with you, show her to me.
    (*Kennion turns to Burleigh. As Burleigh starts to bring
    Fawn to the parapet, she sinks to the ground. Dr. Pennick
    goes quickly to her, opens her blanket and examines her.*)
Dr. Pennick: She is dead.
    (*All stand aghast. Kennion remains motionless on the parapet, not daring to show his despair to Ladru. A pause.*)
Ladru: My soft-eyed Fawn is not there to protect you.
Kennion: I give you my solemn word—she is here.
Ladru: Then let me hear her voice.
    (*The sun by this time has fully risen and the sky is illumined, the light falling on the hopeless faces of the group.*)
    She cannot stay my hand again!

The constant anxiety of an army officer for the safety of his wife and daughter which Belasco had suggested to him by the description of Mrs. George Crook, widow of General Crook, a veteran of Indian warfare, was dramatized in the scene in which General Kennion, when hope has been abandoned, is about to kill Kate to save her from worse than death. According to one school of criticism, he should have discarded this

idea, because Sheridan Knowles had in *Virginius* taken a similar motive from Roman history. The playwrights should
probably have silenced also the clear bugle notes of the rescu-
ing cavalry which Kate, with her attentive faculties keyed to
the highest pitch, naturally hears first, because Boucicault had
written *Jessie Brown*. But our drama would have missed one
of its best portrayals of deep but repressed emotion, when
civilized men and women are brought into peril from a foe
whose savage standards make desperate resistance the only cause
of action.[1] *The Girl I Left Behind Me* ran from January to
June, 1893, a second company remaining at the Empire Theatre while the first company went to Chicago during the Colum-
bian Exposition.

Belasco, in his autobiography, speaks of the principle of
suggestion employed in this play, through which the audience
hear the Indians chanting and the soldiers galloping, but are
unable to tell whether there are ten or ten thousand at hand.
He states also that such scenes were new in the East. Leaving
aside the question of novelty, there is no doubt about the effect,
for it is due to a principle greater than that embodied in any
one play, the principle of suspense.

After a dismal failure in his effort to adapt *Schlimme Saat*
under the title of *The Younger Son*, Belasco produced *The
Heart of Maryland*, with Mrs. Leslie Carter as Maryland
Calvert, in October, 1895. His adventures before he succeeded in finding and retaining financial backing read like a
romance, but at last he secured an established position as dramatist and producer, for the play proved an abounding success. It is a melodrama of the Civil War, not as significant as
Shenandoah (1888) or *Secret Service* (1895), but it moves
quickly despite a complicated plot. Belasco had visited Maryland to study the situation and the Southern atmosphere is
well portrayed. The liking of the audience is caught at first

---

[1] See Winter, I, 403–21 for an exhaustive and enthusiastic analysis of the play. His
one criticism, that it is impossible that Kate, "though she loves Hawksworth, has
promised to marry Parlow," is a curious error, since Kate was engaged to be married
to Parlow before meeting Hawksworth.

by the Northern officer, Alan Kendrick, and since his success means the salvation also of Maryland Calvert, who has risked her life and forsaken her own cause to save him, the audience is led cleverly to transfer its sympathy from the Southern side to the side that must win. The play is marred, however, from the point of view of permanent worth, by the situation in which Maryland swings out from a tower holding on to the clapper of a bell which was to have been the signal for the lover's doom.

Neither Belasco's adaptation of *Zaza* (1899), nor his farce, *Naughty Anthony* (1899), is of significance to us. Yet, the latter, being too slight to fill the requirements of an evening's entertainment, led to the production of one of his finest plays. Looking for material with which to construct a one-act play, he read the story of *Madame Butterfly* by John Luther Long and saw its great dramatic possibilities. The resulting collaboration which produced the play of *Madame Butterfly*, ushered in the period of Belasco's career when his most permanent contributions to dramatic art were made. His instinct had always been for the romantic, and in Long he found a collaborator whose creative power far surpassed that of any other playwright with whom Belasco had been associated, with the exception of Herne. But Herne's best work was done with the material of familiar life; Long's taste was for the exotic, and to the exotic every instinct of Belasco, even his Oriental extraction, responded. It was one of those singularly happy combinations that are rare in dramatic history, and it gave to dramatic literature three masterpieces.

Madame Butterfly, first performed at the Herald Square Theatre, March 5, 1900, is a tragedy of Japan, but the motive is a universal one. Cho-Cho-San, a Japanese girl of good stock, is an orphan, whose father, an officer in the Imperial army, has committed suicide on account of his inability to carry out the commands of his Emperor. Her relatives have persuaded her to form an alliance with an American naval officer, Lieutenant B. F. Pinkerton, who looks upon the matter as a temporary affair, as indeed it is considered by everyone but

Madame Butterfly, as Pinkerton calls her. The very choice of the name is an inspiration on Long's part. It strikes the note of tragedy, for upon this careless lover, who has been away for two years, who has told her he will come back "when the robins nest again," and who has in reality married legally an American wife, Madame Butterfly has lavished a love so strong, so enduring that it lifts her into greatness. To others the form of marriage through which they had gone was an idle tribute to custom—to her it was the symbol of her devotion. Long caught well the spirit of Bushido, the Japanese noblesse oblige. Madame Butterfly preserves the dignity due not only to her blood but to her assumed position as "Mrs. Leftenant B. F. Pinkerton," and hides under her habit of courtesy her breaking heart. Sharpless, the consul, cannot bear to tell her all the truth and so Butterfly believes that Pinkerton, whose ship has arrived in port, is to come home to her the next day. It was necessary, therefore, to show the passage of time, and here Belasco's art intervened and in a striking scene he showed the approach of night, the circuit of the stars and the stealing in of the morning, with the servant, Susuki, and the little child asleep, but with Madame Butterfly standing by the window, in the chill terror of the gray dawn. Pinkerton returns, but they do not meet, for she has gone to the "liddle lookout place" to see him sooner, and as he stands gazing at the playthings on the floor we hear her voice singing the song he had taught her, in his arms:

> "Rog'-a-bye-bebby,
> Off in Japan,
> You just a picture
> Off of a fan."

He cannot face her and he leaves Sharpless with money for her, to tell her of his marriage. She takes the blow bravely but is hardly conscious when Kate, his wife, enters and the air becomes electric with the brief interchange of words:

Kate: Is this? (*Sharpless nods and goes. There is a short pause, while the two women look at each other; then Madame*

Butterfly, still seated, slowly bows her head.) Why, you poor little thing—who in the world could blame you—or call you responsible—you pretty little plaything.
(*She takes Madame Butterfly in her arms.*)
Madame Butterfly: (Softly) No playthin'—I am Mrs. Leftenant B. F.—No—no—now I am only—Cho-Cho-San, but no playthin'. . . .

Madame Butterfly gives up her child that he may be brought up in his father's country and she kills herself with her father's sword. Pinkerton enters just in time for her to die in his arms; plucky to the last.

The play follows the story quite closely, almost completely so far as the language is concerned. In the story, Pinkerton does not return to the house but leaves money with Sharpless, which she refuses. Kate and she meet in the consul's office and Madame Butterfly, after attempting suicide, decides to live for the child's sake. The changes make far more striking situations, and here Belasco's hand is evident. But the conception of character and the central situation belong to John Luther Long and these are the two qualities of *Madame Butterfly* which have given it a place in the literature of the world. The part of Madame Butterfly was created in America by Blanche Bates, and the rôle was assumed at the Duke of York's Theatre in London, April 28, 1900, by Evelyn Millard. In both cases it was recognized as a distinguished work of art. Giacomo Puccini was present at the first night in London, and though he was unable to understand the words, he saw its dramatic value and at once requested permission to compose an opera on the basis of the play. *Madama Butterfly* was first performed in New York in English, November 12, 1906. But its greatest production was in Italian, at the Metropolitan Opera House, February 11, 1907, when Geraldine Farrar sang Cio-Cio-San; Louise Homer, Susuki, and Enrico Caruso, Pinkerton. The opera is naturally enlarged, but follows the lines of the play in general. It has now taken its assured place among operas of the first rank.

From the point of view of dramatic history it will be best to treat together the plays in which Long and Belasco collaborated, omitting for the moment the theatrical history which intervened. Belasco, on looking for a play with which to fill his new theatre, naturally turned to Long for assistance. The partners proceeded logically. Certain themes, they reasoned, had been successful on the stage. What were they? Long made a study of those dramas which had become classic, and he found that the three themes, heroism, patriotism and love, seemed to be the widest in their appeal. So it was decided that all three should be put into the new play. The result was *The Darling of the Gods*, produced first at Washington, November 17, 1902, and brought to the Belasco Theatre in New York, December 3, 1902.

The story of *The Darling of the Gods* centers again about a woman. The Princess Yo-San, played by Blanche Bates, is betrothed to a courtier whom she does not love, and to postpone the evil day she makes a provision that before she marries him he will capture a notorious outlaw, Prince Kara.[1] Kara is but a name to her, but in reality she had been saved from danger by him and he had promised to come to her father's palace. When he appears, he has been wounded in his attempt to break through the cordon of the war minister, Zakkuri, a remarkable character whose fiendish nature was represented brilliantly by George Arliss. Yo-San conceals him in her apartments. She is suspected by her father, the Prince of Tosan, and Migaku, a spy of Zakkuri has traced Kara to his sanctuary. Inu, a mute giant, who guards her, takes care of Migaku effectively and the scene proceeds to the climax of the second act.

---

[1] The statement in Winter's *Life of Belasco*, II, 71, that *The Darling of the Gods* is based on an old play, *The Carbineer*, the manuscript of which was "turned over to Long" is without foundation. Long never saw such a play. *The Darling of the Gods* is entirely original. In Long's study of Japanese history, he was attracted by the heroic defense of Saigo, a leader in the rebellion of 1868, against the Imperial army in its attack on Satsuma. Saigo and thirty of his followers committed suicide. At Belasco's suggestion, the "two-sword men" were reduced to ten in the play to make the struggle more tragic.

Yo-San: Father!

Prince of Tosan: (*Horrified*) Yo-San!

(*Kugo crosses the bridge, but lingers beyond the center half, turning—his head and the lantern just showing.*)

Yo-San: Forgive my appearing here. No Kimono (*She modestly draws her robe about her as a veil.*) —no veil—but I am much frightened . . . while I slept a man looked through my shoji. . . . Inu killed him—there! (*She points down the steps. Inu holds up the body of Migaku from the lotus by the moat—as though it had drifted nearer shore.*)

Inu: Ugh!

(*The water drips from Migaku's face—as Kugo, reaching over the bridge, holds up his lantern to throw the light in Migaku's face—All look*)

Prince of Tosan: (*To Zakkuri*) Is this one of your spies?

Zakkuri: (*Puzzled—but with craft*) He deserved his miserable death—if he were not killed for what he saw!

(*Inu drops Migaku's body into the water.*)

Prince of Tosan: The zealous Zakkuri dared to say that an outlaw—Kara—sought shelter behind your shoji. . . . Answer. . . .

Zakkuri: Upon oath . . . before Shaka!

(*All kowtowing, save the Prince, who resents the insult.*)

Prince of Tosan: Zakkuri!

Zakkuri: (*Craftily*) I am but a servant of the Emperor, who must have the truth—

Prince of Tosan: (*To Yo-San*) Before Shaka! (*All kowtow.*)

Yo-San: (*Holding up the incense*) Before Shaka, God of Life and Death—to whom my word goes up on this incense—I swear, hanging my life on the answer—I have not seen this Kara! (*Simply*) With much shame, I ask you, how could I? Since I am dressed for sleep?

(*Setsu at a look from Yo-San appears—takes the lantern and exits into the house.*)

Prince of Tosan: (*Stands looking at Zakkuri*) You hear!

Zakkuri: Lord of Tosan, I was too zealous for the Emperor! (*Fawning to Yo-San*) May the Gods give you good sleep! (*He crosses up to the bridge—turns, looks at Yo-San—then snaps his fingers for his spies to precede him. Zakkuri and Tonda-Tanji and Kugo disappear from bridge. The Prince of Tosan has ignored his kowtowing.*)

Prince of Tosan: (*Raising his hand*) My daughter! The goddess of good dreams visit you! (*He goes off.*)
Yo-San: (*Without moving, wiping the tears from her impassive face with her fingers*) It is better to lie a little than to be unhappy much.

For forty days Kara stays with her; then he hears from his band and must go. The scene of parting is memorable for its expression:

Kara: Answer . . . how long since the night I was brought in behind this shoji?
Yo-San: (*Monotonously*) Say but two days.
Kara: Oh!
Yo-San: (*Quickly*) Four days . . . then. . . .
Kara: Setsu! (*She does not come from behind the screen.*) Setsu! (*Setsu comes down timidly.*) How long?
Setsu: August Prince, I think to-day is Friday.
Yo-San: (*Kneeling*) You think too rapidly . . . it is earlier . . . Monday.
Kara: Yo-San, answer!
Yo-San: (*Frightened*) It is set out on the tablet of time, my Lord and Master.
Kara: (*Demanding it*) The tablet! (*Setsu stands a moment, then takes the calendar from the table and comes slowly down*)
Kara: (*Angrily*) Ah! (*He starts to take it.*)
Yo-San: (*Still on her knees, throws herself between him and Setsu.*) Aie, aie! He takes such beautiful moments as we have had . . . and calls them days . . . hours. . . . Aie! They will look longer than they were.
Kara: (*After taking the tablet from Setsu . . . counting*) . . . Forty days . . . Shaka!
Yo-San: Ah no, belovèd, it is still the night you came!

They are, however, discovered. She is an outcast and he is doomed to torment, unless she betrays the hiding place of his followers. At first she refuses; then when she is made to see through the trapdoor what awaits him, she gives the information. But both are tricked by Zakkuri, and when she finds her way to Kara's citadel, it is only to watch him die with honor, surrounded by the dead bodies of his Samurai. It is an exquisite scene, as she begs him, "Let me slip by the judgment gods with you . . . in the dark." He forgives her and she is left, to follow him after she has been purged by a thousand years of her punishment in hell for the betrayal—because she loved much. The production was made on a lavish scale, and the impression was one of continuous beauty. It ran for two years, was produced by Beerbohm Tree in London, December 28, 1903; at the Theater des Westens in Berlin in May, 1903, and also in Italy and Australia.

On December 26, 1904, in Washington, D. C., Belasco produced the tragedy of *Adrea*, the third play written in collaboration with John Luther Long. The theatre was built especially for this purpose as Belasco was shut out of the theatres controlled by the Trust. On January 11, 1905, it was produced at his theatre in New York and continued until May 4, 1905. It was played the next season also, alternating with *DuBarry* and *Zaza*.

Adrea is a romantic tragedy laid in the fifth century A.D. on an island in the Adriatic Sea. Long invented the situation, which is based upon the condition of disorder that prevailed in the Roman Empire after the fall of Rome in 476. Adrea is a princess, the oldest daughter of the late King Menethus. It is a law in that kingdom that no one shall succeed to the throne unless he or she is physically perfect. Adrea is blind, so she cannot rule and her younger sister, Julia, is about to be crowned. She is unpopular on account of her character and Adrea is greatly beloved by the people. Kaeso, a neighboring prince, is to marry Julia in order to rule the kingdom. Adrea had met him some years before in Arcady and he had promised to marry her, but he forgets his love in his ambition and Julia demands that he shall tell Adrea all is over. He tries to do so but is carried away by his memories and Adrea believes that he is going to marry her. Julia, with the hatred of the woman who possesses the lover for the woman who keeps the love, takes a terrible revenge upon her sister by betraying her into the arms of the court jester, Mimus, who puts on Kaeso's armor

and who has long lusted for Adrea. They are married, and
Mimus, who can imitate Kaeso's voice, does not allow her to
suspect the truth until the morning. Shortly after the opening
of the second scene, she comes down the steps of the palace,
calling:

Adrea: O Father! O Father! What is this monstrous thing I
dare not name? . . . Father! Awake! I am Adrea! Alone
. . . afraid in the dark! I . . . I have been kissed by lips
I do not know . . . horrible lips . . . horrible lips that blis-
tered mine . . . and held my arms that . . . Ah! Father!
Give me sight . . . give me sight . . . give me sight, and
lead me to one man . . . that I may know who . . . I am
numbed . . . I dare not think . . . I dare not think . . .
no, no, no, no, . . . God, give me sight! God, give me sight
. . . give me sight!

Mimus: (*Who has come down stealthily from the palace and is
now at the bargeman's side. The bargeman has stepped out
from the darkness. Apart to him*) We are the two who go
forth . . . she and I. (*He points to her with a finger and
motions to the bargeman, who passes off.*)

Adrea: God! God! Give me sight! (*As though she would tear
the veil from her eyes.*)

Mimus: (*Taking a step forward, no longer speaking in Kaeso's
voice, but softly, persuasively, to Adrea*) Dawn breaks.
. . . The time decreed for us to go . . .

Adrea: (*Turning at the altar. In a voice frozen with terror . . .
almost in a whisper*) Ah! Who speaks . . . who is this man
they gave me to? Answer! Answer!

Mimus: (*Taking her outstretched hand*) Come. . . .

Adrea: (*As though breaking away from the very thought*) No
. . . No . . . (*She starts to stagger back from him, then
turns as though to run.*)

Mimus: (*Who has picked up the leading strings which trail across
the scene, speaking savagely, and attaching the strings to
Adrea's wrist, then winding them tightly about his own several times*) Come! Come! Thou art mine . . . come . . .
(*He drags Adrea toward him by the strings. She totters,
staggers forward, calling out, No! No! No! grasps the
altar as she is being dragged past it, and clings to it, calling
Father! and as Mimus would go toward Adrea, a stream of
lightning, accompanied by a sudden roar of thunder, darts*

from the dark sky and strikes down Mimus. He lies flat on the floor at a little distance from Adrea, the guiding strings still wound about his wrist. The altar is overturned; Adrea totters, still clinging to it, and falls lying on it. The fallen brazier's light still shines. The rumble of thunder dies away, but the stage is still dark; a storm cloud seems to hang over the city, surrounding it. Adrea, stunned, her eyes closed, puts her hands to her head, dazed, then opens her eyes, then opens and shuts them, looks about and vaguely comprehending that she sees, passes one hand before her face, staring at it.)

Adrea: I see! I see! *(Then she looks again, seeing something she had never known before, then stares about at all the strange scene and the mystery of it. Suddenly finding on looking down that her guiding strings are still held, the memory of the past night comes over her. With terrible anticipation, she tracks the strings until they lead her to the figure on the floor)* You! . . . *(On her hands and knees she stares at Mimus. Then still on her knees, with a mad impulse lifting up the unconscious body until her face peers into his, the brazier light shining past her, falling on his face. In a whisper)* God! God! *(She lets him drop. Then with a low cry of horror, shuddering, her eyes staring, her outstretched fingers stiffened, she draws in a long breath of terrible realization, swaying where she kneels.)*

Adrea goes to die in the Tower of Forgetfulness, but hearing the cries of the wedding procession, especially Kaeso's laugh of triumph, and being warned by the shadow of her father that she is to reign, she decides to take the throne in order to revenge herself upon Kaeso. She is crowned and Kaeso is brought before her and acknowledges his wrong but pleads only his ambition to rule the world. She condemns him to be whipped publicly through the city. At the end of the coronation festivals three days later, the Queen sends for Kaeso again, to condemn him to death—then begins to relent. She finds, however, that Mimus is still alive and at sight of him all her rage breaks forth and she condemns Kaeso to be torn to pieces by wild horses. The senators at first object to this so that she tells them the story of his wrong to her. "I shall not bear

a child to sit this throne—for I should fear to see its face—
lest it be red and white—I bring none after me—this lost ac-
cursed thing he made—this wanton of a fool is Queen of
Adrea!"

In witnessing Kaeso's remorse she begins to relent, but the
senators hold her to her word and she finally stabs Kaeso to
save him from the wild horses.

In the Epilogue fourteen years later, she sends for the son
of Kaeso and Julia, a boy, Vasha, who is to reign in her place.

Adrea: (*Looking back at the boy*) Ay? To-day thou goest to my
 dear land. Nay! Nay! 'Tis in the playing. . . . Think
 of me often here in Arcady.

Vasha: I go to—Adrea?

Adrea: Yea . . . and think of me as one who dwells here, happy
 . . . and if, when thou dost weary of thy ruling, thou
 wouldst play again . . . steal back—Nay—nay—'tis in the
 playing still—steal back and kiss me . . . so. (*She kisses
 him. He looks at her warily, half converted.*) And lead me
 with thy gentle hands along the ways of old . . . perchance
 one day thou wilt not come alone, sweet Prince . . . Oh,
 build thy throne upon love . . . for only love endures. . . .
 Garda!
 (*Enter Garda and the Herald of the Senate. Garda carries the robe, the Herald of the Senate follows with the crown
 and the scepter on a gold cushion. Adrea takes the robe
 from Garda and wraps Vasha in it. He lays his little shield
 at the foot of the throne steps.*)

Vasha: But why dost thou wrap me in this robe?

Adrea: It is a little . . . a little game we play. We play at being King. (*The Herald of the Senate and Garda exeunt.*)
 Thou the Prince, and I, the Queen, who being blinded may not
 rule. (*She offers the crown.*)

Vasha: (*Rejecting it*) But I would not have a throne for which
 a queen must give her eyes.

Adrea: 'Tis in the playing . . .

Vasha: Oh . . . then! (*He allows her to put on the crown.
 Adrea leads Vasha to the throne. As Vasha sits, his little
 legs are not long enough to reach the platform.*)

Adrea: Come . . . come . . . now turn thy head . . . (*She turns
 his face from the window*) so . . . thou mayst not look . . .

until I speak the word . . . that makes thee King . . . and makes me (*Falters*) only happy Adrea again. . . . (*She puts the scepter in his hand. He kisses her in childish fashion, puts his arms about her, happy because he is having his own way.*)

Vasha: Ha! I love this playing! (*He is tempted to look.*)

Adrea: Dost thou? (*Puts his hands over his eyes.*) Put thy hands so . . . look not. . . . wait the word . . . I wish thee joy, dear little Prince. (*She retreats to the window, facing the child, who sits on the throne, crowned and robed.*) Think of me in the Spring when all is green in Arcady . . . happy, peaceful, wishing thee well . . . and do not forget me. (*Vasha turns.*) Nay . . . Nay . . . 'Tis in the playing . . . look not. Live long, love long, and see dear children at thy feet. May the gods keep thy heart young, thy faith pure, thy soul at peace, O child of Kaeso! (*As he tries to peep*) Nay . . . nay . . . look not! (*Adrea, at the casement, takes her last look at Vasha, peering at him, smiling.*) So let me see thee last . . . so let me see thee last . . . at play. Nay . . . look not. (*She pulls down the covering of skin at the window.*) O Sun, who took my sight at birth . . . I give thee back . . . I give thee back thine own! (*She turns and opens the window. She stands, a golden figure in the flood of dazzling sunlight. After a pause during which she has been looking into the sunlight, she turns, blinded, and comes down, groping her way to the throne.*) Long live the King! (*She kneels at the feet of Vasha on the throne, the sun pouring in.*)

Adrea is the finest of the plays written by Belasco and Long and it has so far not been excelled in its own species, the romantic tragedy, by any play acted in English in the Twentieth Century. The spirit of the age is caught wonderfully—whether it is accurate or not does not matter—it satisfies the auditor as a fit background for great, unrestrained passions and emotions. The character drawing of Adrea is magnificent. All through the play she is dominated by her great love for Kaeso. She hates terribly because she loves greatly. The crown is merely a means to her to be revenged on him for his betrayal. Julia she forgets—because Julia was not loved by

187

her, but in a speech in the fourth Act she utters the cry of the woman who has lost her belief in the love of the man she loves, as well as it has been put in modern drama.

In contrast with her, Kaeso's main passion is ambition. He sacrifices her to it, and when he has been beaten and is facing death he loses our sympathy by his apparent weakness. She keeps the sympathy, always. Fate has played her evil tricks, and she has met them with the patrician spirit that came from her Roman ancestors. Life to her and to her age was cheap in comparison with the satisfaction of the passions of love and revenge. The sense of patriotism was local, but she could feel also responsibility for her country; and something of the royal sense of the fitness of things attributed to Elizabeth is indicated in her relinquishing the scepter to a man-child who above all is Kaeso's son.

After *Adrea*, Belasco and Long produced no plays under their joint authorship. Long made several essays alone, the most successful being his dramatization of his own short story, *Dolce*, produced by Mrs. Fiske in 1906. It is the story of an artist who has painted the picture of a little Italian girl in New Orleans, then loses sight of her until some years later she comes, a countess, to his studio in Florence and demands that he sell her picture, which, of course, he refuses to do. Their recognition and reunion made an appealing climax to a play based upon the fragrance of youthful memories. *Kassa*, written for Mrs. Carter (1909), was a rather turgid drama laid in Austro-Hungary and was not successful, though it provided Mrs. Carter with a mad scene at the end of the play.

Crowns, which was produced at the Provincetown Theatre in November, 1923, is a romantic tragedy, laid about the time of Christ, somewhere in Palestine. But, as in *Adrea*, locality is not important. The theme is the contest of love and ambition. Ardan and Yolan are left at their respective fathers' deaths contesting heirs to a kingdom which is conquered by Sargon. They are spared and live in an olive garden shut in from the outside world till they are grown to young manhood and

Photo by Wm. Shewell Ellis

John Luther Long

womanhood. But the leaders of their factions will not let them be and, after murdering Sargon, the captains plant the seeds of ambition in their minds, separate them, and by lies and stratagems bring on a war between them. Long draws in a highly poetic way the lust of power and the passion for war in all their tragic meaning. Ardan and Yolan still love each other, but through misunderstanding believe themselves enemies. Yolan's troops win, for Ardan goes mad after he kills Elfer, the loyal servant who had reared them, and the moment of her crowning is to be the signal for his death. But because her love is the greater, she kills herself, and he is brought in shackles to her chamber of death, his mind cleared of its madness. As he is led to the throne, he presses to his brow the crown of thorns she had made for herself. *Crowns* is perhaps too subtle for popular approval, and it did not succeed on the stage. But it is the product of imaginative power, and the tragedy is poignant with the agony of frustrated love.

Belasco's energies had been divided during this period between his work with Long and his establishment as an independent producer. He had devoted himself also to the training of Mrs. Leslie Carter, who achieved in the character of Adrea the summit of her artistic career, and to the development of David Warfield from a variety actor to a leading part in melodrama like *The Auctioneer*. The struggles of Belasco against the "Theatrical Syndicate" belong to the history of the theatre rather than to that of the drama, although they have profoundly affected the methods and the opportunities of production. It was the growth of the "Theatrical Syndicate," which brought under its own control the main theatres throughout the country, and hence was able to dictate terms to any producer of a play, which spurred on Belasco to have a theatre of his own. In 1900 he secured a lease of the Republic Theatre and began to alter it to suit his purposes. The possession of the theatre made him secure so far as New York was concerned, but his fight against dictation continued.

Meanwhile, he was revising a play upon the courtesan,

Madame DuBarry, the mistress of Louis XV, which had been written by Jean Richepin, and which Belasco found unsuitable for his purposes. After *DuBarry* was produced, on December 12, 1901, at Washington, suit was brought by agents of Richepin to compel Belasco to share the receipts of the play. Belasco had already paid the French dramatist $3,500 for the manuscript which he stated before the court he had not used. The suit was allowed to lapse and while Richepin's play was produced in London in 1905 it has not been possible for me to compare the versions. *DuBarry* was a gorgeous dramatic spectacle, in which Belasco indulged his fancy in conceiving of situations in which violent passions rose, triumphed and fell. The most striking scenes were those in which DuBarry conceals her lover in her own bed while her master, the King, and also her enemies, are searching for him, and the final passage of DuBarry through the dirty streets to the guillotine, howled at by the mob. Contrasts are plentiful, and Mrs. Carter made good use of them. The skill of the playwright was shown most clearly in the way by which he secured the sympathy of the audience, not so much for the courtesan, as for the woman the courtesan might have been. This was done by painting her, in cheerful disregard of history, as a woman who really regretted the life of peace and honor she might have lived with the lover of her youth. Yet she was not made so heroic or so virtuous that the same audience might not be completely reconciled to her doom.

Belasco next made out of a novel, *The Bath Comedy*, by Agnes and Egerton Castle, a charming light comedy, *Sweet Kitty Bellairs*, which was produced on November 23, 1903, at Washington. It was a very different Eighteenth Century from that of *DuBarry*. The effect was one of charm rather than of splendor and the central character, a coquette with a warm heart, with a gift for intrigue, but with a soul a bit above her heartless companions, was well portrayed by Henrietta Crosman. The original story was artificial and so was the play, but it proved a success and was played in 1907 in London.

For the next period of his playwriting, Belasco turned from the gorgeous spectacles of history to the vivid panorama of Western life in America. In both he selected incidents and characters that were out of the ordinary. *The Girl of the Golden West* was prepared with the capabilities of Blanche Bates in view and a heroine who is at once pure, courageous, loyal and passionate, who keeps a saloon and is able to cope with any situation which presents itself, appears to a modern auditor so utterly impossible that he ceases to criticize her from that point of view at all, which is of course what the artful dramatist who produced the play foresaw would happen. The climax of the drama is an illustration of Belasco's skill. "The Girl" having resisted the advances of all comers, falls in love with Dick Johnson, a picturesque, if overclean, outlaw. He is pursued by the sheriff, Jack Rance, who traces him to her cabin, where, unchaperoned, she has retained the respect of the neighborhood. Johnson has been wounded by Rance before reaching the cabin and is concealed by the girl in a loft. Rance enters, looks everywhere but in the obvious place of concealment, and then the girl challenges him to play a game of poker with her, on the understanding that if he wins, she is the stake and if she wins, he will discontinue his efforts to find her lover. She cheats him by an old card trick, and he is about to leave when a drop of blood falls from the wounded man upon his handkerchief. The drama hardly seems to be capable of going further in the direction of improbability. Yet Belasco has told us in detail in his autobiography how he based this scene upon an incident which was witnessed by his father.

Belasco has also recorded the fact that the character of Jake Wallace, "a traveling camp minstrel," was an exact photograph of a Jake Wallace whom he knew and that when negotiations were under way between Puccini and himself preliminary to the writing of *La Fanciulla del West*, it was this singer of camp songs who provided the theme upon which the

Italian composer based his opera. Belasco is too experienced a dramatist, of course, not to know that the mere fact that a certain event happened is no presumptive evidence of its probability. But perhaps after all both Harte and Belasco realized the probabilities of the West better than those who know that life only at second hand. He was justified in one sense, by the popularity of the play, which ran three years after its performance at the new Belasco Theatre in Pittsburgh, October 3, 1905. The opera by Puccini was produced at the Metropolitan Opera House, December 10, 1910, with Emmy Destinn as Minnie, the girl, Enrico Caruso as Dick Johnson and Pasquale Amato as Jack Rance. It was the first grand opera to be written on an American theme.

The Rose of the Rancho (1906) in which Belasco continued his presentation of Western life, was based on an earlier play, *Juanita*, by Richard Walton Tully, which Belasco revised. It is an interesting study of an important if disgraceful period in American history, that of the occupation of California by the settlers from the United States. The Spanish owners, who had occupied the land for centuries, were dispossessed by land jumpers, because they were either too proud or too ignorant of the situation to file claims in the American land offices. The play is concerned with the love of Robert Kearney, who has been sent by the government to investigate the land cases, and Juanita Kenton, the "Rose," whose grandmother, Doña Petrona Castro, is owner of the Rancho. Kearney is endeavoring to block the movements of Kincaid, who with a band of ruffians is forcibly taking possession of the estates. Juanita's mother announces her engagement to Don Luis de la Torre, a wealthy young man from Monterey, but Juanita declines him. She is then horrified to find Kearney apparently in Kincaid's band, which he has joined in order to protect her. She repudiates him, but of course all ends happily. The character of Juanita is more consistent than that of Minnie, and the Spanish race pride and the way in which they react to an appeal to their courtesy was well portrayed. The production, like that of *The Girl of the Golden West*, was sumptuous. The pictures of the scenery of southern Califorania were marvelous, and every device which could represent that region as it was known to Belasco was lavished by him upon the stage production. If there is really Portuguese blood in him, it showed in the sympathy with which he entered into the interpretation of Latin-American civilization. This play introduced Frances Starr as a leading woman.

In December, 1906, he laid the corner stone of his new theatre, first called the Stuyvesant and now the Belasco Theatre. In it are contained the results of years of experiment, and it is not exaggeration to say that from the point of view of stage mechanism, it is complete. Probably the devices for lighting are the most remarkable. Belasco has had as his associate in this field Louis Hartman, who has installed and remodeled a system of lighting which is exactly fitted to its purpose, the concealment of the means and the securing of the effect. Belasco has been a student of lighting since the early seventies. He was present at what was probably the first attempt to use electric light for stage illumination, at the California Theatre, February 21, 1879,[1] and he has labored constantly to bring light as it is brought in nature, from above rather than below. As early as 1879, when he directed the Passion Play in San Francisco, he had experimented with the abolition of footlights and in 1917 he did away with them entirely. Light comes from various sources, especially from a great iron hood, which hangs behind the proscenium, and from lights attached to each sliding scene. In the balcony, light streams from a panel which is apparently ornamental, but which consists of small doors, which are controlled by the great switchboard that stands on the stage. These doors open and shut so gradually that to the audience the light is fading or increasing in brilliancy, from an unknown source. Belasco spares nothing in his desire to reach perfection in this regard. For each play, new "dimmers" by which the light is shaded, are provided, and one glance at the

[1] Winter, II, 245.

collection of lamps, used once and once only, in his stage settings, illustrates the prodigality of Belasco's methods.[1]

The Stuyvesant Theatre was opened October 16, 1907, with *The Grand Army Man*, the joint product of Belasco, Pauline Phelps and Marion Short. The central character of this play, which is not especially significant, is that of Wes' Bigelow, who has brought up the son of a former sweetheart and who finds the boy dishonest. Nor need Belasco's adaptation of *Le Lys* by Pierre Wolf and Gaston Leroux, produced in December, 1909, detain us. It has to do with the revolt of a daughter against parental tyranny for the sake of her younger sister.

The Return of Peter Grimm, first produced at the Hollis Street Theatre in Boston, January 2, 1911, while it owes its inception to Cecil DeMille, the son of Belasco's former collaborator, deals with just the kind of theme which the romantic fancy of Belasco would find congenial. Peter Grimm is an old bachelor, a practical botanist, gentle but stubborn. He expects to be succeeded in the business by his nephew, Frederik, a selfish and immoral person, whose real nature has been concealed from his uncle, for Peter extracts from Kathrien, a girl he has brought up and loves dearly, a promise that she shall marry Frederik. She is in love, however, with James Hartman, one of Peter's employees. Peter has also taken charge of a little boy, William, who is the grandson of old Marta, the cook, and is really the illegitimate son of Frederik by a woman who does not appear. Peter has joked with an old friend, Dr. MacPherson, about the possibility of the dead returning but has taken a sceptical attitude toward such reappearances. At the end of the first Act, Peter dies suddenly.

The remainder of the play consists of Peter Grimm's efforts to undo the wrong he has done to Kathrien. He appears not as a wraith but exactly as he had looked in real life, and he

---

[1] The subject of stage lighting cannot be adequately treated here. The above statements are based on my inspection of the Belasco Theatre under the guidance of Mr. Hartman.

makes fervent attempts to communicate with his friends. None of them see him, though Frederik, to whom he makes one of his strongest appeals, believes for a moment that he sees his uncle's ghost. But he is present as an influence upon Kathrien and Frederik and, most potently, upon William, who speaks to him and who goes willingly when Peter Grimm carries him off to the other world at the end of the play. Peter Grimm reaches the child most easily because he loves him and because William, through his illness, is already nearing the other world. In William's feverish condition his reactions are most probable, also, from the human point of view. It is this careful avoidance of the spectacular in dealing with the supernatural which makes the play so artistic. The occult and the real are blended with so skillful a hand that the line which separates the known and the unknown presents no difficulties for the auditor to cross. One can believe that William simply remembered, under the sharpening influence of fever, that the man who had come to see his mother was Frederik, and thereby showed Kathrien that her promise need not be kept. Or if he prefers, he can believe that Peter Grimm spoke to the boy through the invincible power of love. But the dramatist who called back the soul of Peter Grimm had no thesis to prove except the quotation which begins the play: "Only one thing counts—only one thing—love." Skillfully, too, does he avoid any description of the future life. Peter Grimm is happy there evidently so that the death of the child is felt to be a release for him. As Peter puts it:

Before your playing time is over—you're going to know the great secret. No coarsening of your child's heart, until you stand before the world like Frederik; no sweat and toil such as dear old James is facing; no dimming of the eye and trembling of the head such as the poor old Doctor shall know in time to come; no hot tears to blister your eyes; tears such as Katie is shedding now; but in all your youth, your faith—your innocence, you'll fall asleep.

One of the most effective bits of stage management was the creation of the bridge of light which seemed to connect Peter to the living. Very little light was thrown on him, but there was a distinct rose color in the light on the living characters, which made him seem less vivid in contrast, without making him spectral.

Interest in the occult probably led to the production of *The Case of Becky* written by Edward Locke and revised by Belasco, which dealt with a girl of double personality. The staging of this play, especially those scenes in which Dorothy or Becky, the heroine, is so conscious of the unseen presence of her stepfather who exercises an evil control over her that it throws her into hypnosis, excited the admiration of the medical profession.[1]

Since *Peter Grimm*, Belasco the dramatist has become secondary to Belasco the producer. *The Governor's Lady*, the joint product of Belasco and Alice Bradley, on the theme of a woman who does not advance in mental growth with her husband and who is supplanted in his affections by a younger woman, is a melodrama with one strong situation in which the younger woman calls on Mrs. Slade, to persuade her to agree to a divorce. But in his desire to provide reality of stage setting, Belasco placed an utterly absurd last Act in a restaurant which was scrupulously photographic to the last spoon and fork.

Van der Decken, which was based on the myth of the "Flying Dutchman," was tried out at Wilmington in 1915 but has not yet been produced in New York and cannot be said to be in a finished state. *The Son Daughter* (1919), written with George Scarborough, is a Chinese melodrama laid in New York City, with an absurd plot, on which Belasco wasted some striking lighting effects, especially in the scene of the death of the patriot leader who poisons himself in order to avoid being tor-

---

[1] See Reichert, Edward Tyson, M. D.: "'Dr. Jekyll and Mr. Hyde,' and 'The Case of Becky,' as staged by Mr. David Belasco, together with actual instances of Dual Personalities." *Lectures of the University of Pennsylvania.* Vol. for 1914-5.

tured for his secrets. Since 1920, Belasco has with one exception contented himself with adaptations of foreign plays. *Kiki*, from the French of André Picard, gave Lenore Ulric an opportunity to represent a coquette who became, with a wrench, a "good girl" at the end of the play. *Laugh, Clown, Laugh*, from Fausto Martini's *Ridi, Pagliaccio* was a more significant production, with some scenes of real sincerity, as was also *The Comedian* of Sacha Guitry. In these plays, Belasco translated successfully foreign aspects of the theatre. The sense of the responsibility of the actor to his audience was especially well carried over from the French original in *The Comedian*.

Belasco's production of *The Merchant of Venice* in 1922 belongs to our theatrical rather than our dramatic history, yet it was in a sense the crowning achievement of his career. For admirable as was Warfield's representation of racial revenge, it was the production which was of most significance. Belasco translated to a modern audience the beauty with which the imagination of the Elizabethans endowed the performances of Shakespeare, and which our flabbier fancies do not create.

No final judgment upon Belasco as a playwright is possible. So intangible is that contribution which takes an idea from experience, from observation, from the fiction, the poetry, even the plays of others and by a process explainable only in terms of genius, translates them into successful drama, that it would be idle to pretend to finality in critical judgment. But in viewing his work historically, over a period of sixty years, certain general facts emerge. He began with a predilection for what was unusual, intense and even bizarre, and his consistency in this preference has been remarkable. To him the drama is not the representation of familiar life. Incidents are selected, even in domestic drama like *May Blossom*, from among the unusual episodes of an ordinary life. His characters are not those with which we are normally familiar, and if his collaborators, like Herne or DeMille, lead him into the placing of such characters upon the stage, one of two things happens. If like Herne, the other playwright is his equal, there is an inevitable separation. If Belasco is the dominant force, as was the case with DeMille, the plays show the definite trend away from the calmer scenes of *The Wife* to the intense, almost melodramatic climaxes of *The Charity Ball* and *Men and Women*. If his collaborator is himself predisposed to romantic situation, Belasco's love for the colorful and the sensational runs unchecked, and the result is *The Rose of the Rancho* and *The Girl of the Golden West*. Once only among his many associations, did he meet with a collaborator whose imagination was more powerful than his own, who provided him with great characters, not normal and not familiar. It was to Belasco's credit that he recognized the genius of John Luther Long, and that he treated the material provided him in *Madame Butterfly*, *The Darling of the Gods*, and *Adrea* with the respect which a creator of one kind feels for a creator of another. The result is romance which scorns restriction, which has the high courage that soars beyond the provincial, to deal with universal passions and emotions, which rides right at the five-barred gate of probability, knowing that if it fails, it falls into the ditch of nonsense, but if it rises triumphant, it outlines against the sky the imperishable figures of literature. It is a grim commentary on our artistic recklessness, that two of the noblest creations of our romantic drama live still only in the memories of the audiences who saw them and the few who have read them in manuscript.

It is not necessary to deal here with the discussions that have raged over the questions of plagiarism in Belasco's acknowledged plays. Frequently these disputes have led to lawsuits which have invariably ended in his favor. Dealing only with those plays which are available in print or manuscript, this apparent paradox appears. Leaving aside *The Return of Peter Grimm*, his most important work was the acknowledged result of collaboration with James A. Herne, William C. DeMille, Franklyn Fyles, and John Luther Long. This work exceeds in value *May Blossom*, *The Heart of Maryland*, and *The Girl of the Golden West*.

Yet with the exception of Herne, none of these four collaborators has been able to write a successful play. Long has written imaginative and interesting dramas, but they have not held the stage. To the historian who has met the term "derivative" till he is weary of it, the conclusion is obvious.

If Belasco has no great invention, as seems probable, he has what is of more importance in drama, a keen sense of the instinctive motor and emotional reactions of an audience. To him a play is a living thing; it is a compound of playwright, actor, director, and auditor. With every instinct tingling with the love of romance, he has sought to make that necessary compound tangible by lavishing upon his productions every known device by which stage realism is secured. He conducted for many years a struggle, at first against overwhelming odds, for the right to his artistic independence, and his position as the foremost director of the United States was recognized by the spontaneous tributes tendered him in 1921 by the dinners given in his honor by the Society of American Dramatists and Composers and by the Society of Arts and Sciences. No one who was present can forget the sincerity of the appreciation of those he had directed. If more emphasis was laid upon his achievement as producer and director than as a playwright, his failure to print his plays is perhaps responsible.

CHAPTER VIII

The Indian Summer of Romance

WHILE the general tendency toward the treatment of actual American life upon the stage was being established, the heroic play based upon universal themes was not by any means neglected. The Drama of the Frontier and the work of Belasco and his associates were not the only evidences of the ever-present desire for romance. Romantic tragedy had seemed, indeed, to pass from favor during the sixties, but it rose again into a flowering in the seventies, largely under the inspiration of Lawrence Barrett. The heroic or romantic play has usually depended upon the interest of an actor to whom the character of a hero, defying fate or his enemies, has strongly appealed. This romantic tradition of the stage, while it had its great period from the thirties to the sixties, nevertheless has persisted in the succession of which Barrett, Mansfield, Sothern and Skinner are perhaps for us the foremost examples. These actors turned frequently to Shakespeare or to other English and even to continental drama, but their biographies reveal their constant search for American playwrights who could furnish them with material. The result was sometimes achieved by the excursion of a realist into an alien field. We have seen how Howells furnished Pope and Barrett and Salvini with successful adaptations of Spanish and Italian drama.[1] It was Barrett who revived Boker's *Francesca da Rimini* in 1882 and showed for the first time the possibilities of that masterpiece. He inspired Boker, too, to write *Nydia* and *Glaucus*, although he did not produce them.

William Young (1847-1920), whose plays with two exceptions remain in manuscript, provided Barrett with two of his

[1] See pp. 68-72.

leading parts. *Pendragon,* produced first at Chicago, in 1881, is a blank-verse play in five acts dealing with the Arthurian story. Barrett played King Arthur, and Young made of him a man less frigid than the traditional figure. Launcelot, played first by Louis James and later by Otis Skinner, is more human, too, than is usual, and Guinevere is a strong figure. Modred drives the tragedy on through Vivien, his tool, and brings it to a high point in the Queen's chamber when Arthur, after Launcelot has been condemned for his treachery, shows how death is easy compared with his living fate of knowing how his best friend has betrayed him. The climax of Barrett's acting, however, came in the fourth Act at Almesbury, when Arthur takes leave of Guinevere:

Arthur: Woman—for thou art woman—I am man.
Never again, upon this brink of time,
Shall we two meet—hear then my last confession!
Yea, though I know that every wanton drop
That makes thee smooth and fair hath played me false—
That thou hast sold me for a lecher's kiss,
To endless shame—still—still, despite it all,
I love thee—love thee! Dost thou hear? I love thee!
Let men hereafter gibe at me, and say:
"This is that Arthur, who once thought to match
His puny strength against the bulk of Rome,—
Yet could not win and keep one woman's heart!"
Despite it all, I care not, still I love thee—
And in that word take thou thy full revenge!
Slight, though thou art, yet art thou conqueror!
And, O, should'st thou not well be satisfied?
'Tis I, at last, who burn, whilst thou art cold,
'Tis I, at last, who plead, whilst thou art voiceless!
Self-signed and sealed, a madman, or a knave,
I quit this world, in which I hoped so much,
Without a hope. And thou for whom I suffer—
Now—even now—at this last hour thou wilt not
So much as say "God bless thee!" Then, will I!
God bless thee, and forgive thee! Yea, forgive,
As I forgive. God make thy pillow soft,
As thou hast made mine hard—thine end as sweet,

As thou hast made mine bitter!—shield—protect thee
From every harm—from shame, from pain, from sorrow!
Give thee love, fortune, friendship, length of days—
And at the last receive thee to that Heaven,
Whose gate this hand hath shut against my soul!

Ganelon, written in 1888 and produced in New York in
1891, has apparently perished, but according to Winter it
gave Barrett one of the finest opportunities of his career. Certainly the conception was a truly tragic one. Ganelon is the
son of the traitor who betrayed Roland at Roncesvalles, and
Young portrayed the burning desire of the knight to redeem
his name. After saving a Corsican city from the Saracens, he
is defrauded of his reward and when his attempted suicide
places him in their hands, he, maddened by a sense of injustice,
repeats the treachery of his father and betrays the town to the
enemy. Death comes after his repentance, fighting again for
his own people. The impression made by Barrett's imperson-
ation of a proud spirit, stung by injustice to madness, and
passing from one emotional state to another, was apparently
tremendous. Young published only two plays, *The Rajah* and
Ben Hur. *The Rajah,* produced at the Madison Square Theatre, June 5, 1883, ran for two hundred and fifty performances. It is a romantic comedy, laid at an English country house, with a conventional plot, but with extremely clever
conversation and well-established characters, especially Harold Wyncot, the "Rajah," who has been a captain in the East
India Service and who inherits the estate. Young's most popular play was his dramatization of Lew Wallace's novel of *Ben
Hur,* which was first given at the Broadway Theatre on November 29, 1899, and after running through three seasons in
New York, Philadelphia and Boston, became a perennial of the
theatre. Young had good material with which to work and
used it to distinct advantage. He was a skilful artist, working
sincerely and capable of writing a blank verse flexible and at
times distinguished. His plays, with the exception of *Young*

America (1896), seem to have been upon foreign themes, but twice at least he touched the universal note of tragedy.

Barrett constantly made changes in the texts of the plays he controlled, and in the case of Richard Mansfield this dictation of the actor-manager went much further.[1] Mansfield as will be seen, wrote plays himself. His first real success as an actor came in the part of Baron de Mersac in Henry Guy Carleton's (1856-1910) *Victor Durand* (1884), a romantic melodrama of artificial quality, in which he impersonated a villain who imperils his own safety by bringing about the recapture of the husband of the woman he loves. Carleton began his play writing with a tragedy, *Memnon* (1881), partly in verse, which Booth and McCullough seem to have considered producing. It is the only one of his plays deserving the name of dramatic literature, and at times it rises to a considerable height. It is laid in Thebes, and in the character of Memnon, the arch-prophet of Egypt, Carleton drew a heroic figure, surrounded by the jealousy of conspirators at home and the pressure of Persian ambitions. Discouraged apparently by his failure to secure an audience for his sincere attempt at romantic tragedy, Carleton turned to the production of *A Gilded Fool* (1892) for Goodwin, an absurd play; *The Butterflies* (1894), a more adroit farce comedy, in which John Drew and Maude Adams made a stage success; and *Colinette* (1899), an adaptation from the French of Lenôtre and Martin, which was skilfully made for Julia Marlowe.

Mansfield was himself driven to writing *Monsieur*, his first play (1887), by the paucity of material to suit his special talent. It is a romantic drama, laid in New York City, with a central character of André de Jadot, or "Monsieur," a French gentleman, who endeavors to live by the teaching of music. Contrasts are provided by his appearance at the house of a wealthy patron, and his collapse on account of hunger. In its plot, which provided a happy ending tinged with the sentiment of love triumphant, it is reminiscent of an older school, but

---

[1] See account of the composition of *Beau Brummell*, pp. 266-9.

Mansfield's performance of André de Jadot was gallant an‹
was comparatively successful. Upon *Don Juan* (1891) h
lavished a great deal of effort, but the public did not respond
He kept it in his répertoire, however, for some time. His con
ception of the eternal lover, brought up with the most rigorou
care, and breaking into life with a zest for adventure that car
ries him finally to his death, has some reality and power. It i
built, however, upon Byron, Dumas and Molière, and does no
deserve the extravagant praise Winter gives it. The bes
scene is that in the oratory of the Duchess, in which Donn‹
Julia, Lucia and Geralda reveal their love for Don Juan i‹
various ways. There is also some sharp satire upon the atti
tude of the public toward actors. Mansfield's part in the pro
duction of *Beau Brummell* (1891) belongs more properl‹
under the discussion of the plays of Clyde Fitch.

Thomas Russell Sullivan, who had made the adaptation o
Dr. Jekyll and Mr. Hyde (1887) for Mansfield, wrote a‹
original play for him upon the life of Nero (1891) which wa
a failure, but which seems to have provided a powerful tragi
climax in the Emperor's death. In 1896, Mansfield was agai‹
the inspiration for a play called *Napoleon Bonaparte*, b
Lorimer Stoddard, which is really a series of scenes represent
ing the Emperor at various points in his career, the first ac
being laid in his tent at Tilsit and later acts including a pre
lude to Waterloo, and his death at St. Helena. The scenes, fo
it is hardly a play, are written to make Napoleon the cente
of attention, and Kings and Queens, ministers and corporals
confide to the audience their private and public affairs in th
orthodox manner of one form of the romantic drama.

Mansfield was sensitive to a mistaken criticism which ob
jected to his joint work as playwright and actor, so when h
and J. I. C. Clarke dramatized *The First Violin* (1898) b
Jessie Fothergill, he assumed the name of Meridan Phelp‹
The play, which is itself of no great importance, marks hi
passage into that phase of the romantic movement whic‹
brought upon the stage the dramatization of novels, and whic‹

led to his production of *Beaucaire* in 1901. But while other interests claimed his attention, it must be remembered to his credit that he encouraged American playwrights in his own way, if that way was not always to their liking.

It is an illuminating exercise in the discrimination between what is permanent and what is passing in dramatic literature to compare such plays as Carleton's stage successes with the work of Thomas Bailey Aldrich (1856-1907). Aldrich had a real dramatic sense and also a keen desire to write for the theatre. His early correspondence records his rueful regret when his plays were returned unopened by the actors to whom he sent them, and this may have caused his hesitation in allowing *Mercedes* to be produced, when A. M. Palmer urged him to permit it. But while much of the romantic work of the period seems hopelessly old-fashioned, Aldrich's dramas are to-day as fresh and vital as when they were written and produced. *Mercedes*, published in 1884 and produced with Julia Arthur, selected by Aldrich himself, for the title rôle, at Palmer's Theatre, May 1, 1893, is a prose tragedy in two acts laid in Spain in 1810 during the Napoleonic campaign. In the dialogue between Captain Louvois and his lieutenant Laboissière, we learn that they have orders to massacre the inhabitants of the village of Arguano, where Louvois had been nursed back to life by Mercedes, and had grown to love her. In the second Act, laid in a stone hut in Arguano, Mercedes has stayed to protect her old grandmother and her child, Chiquita, at the risk of her own life, when the rest have fled. Before going they have poisoned some wine and hidden it. Laboissière enters the hut and while Mercedes is quietly defying him, the soldiers appear with the wine. Then Aldrich showed his power to write telling dialogue:

Laboissière: Open it, some one, and fetch me a glass.
    (*To Mercedes*) You will drink this.
Mercedes: (*Coldly*) When I am thirsty I drink.
Laboissière: Pardieu! this time you shall drink because *I* am thirsty.

Mercedes: As you will. (*Empties the glass*) To the King!

Laboissière: That was an impudent toast. I would have preferred the Emperor or even Godoy; but no matter—each after his kind. To whom will the small-bones drink?

Mercedes: The child, señor?

Laboissière: Yes, the child; she is pale and sickly-looking; a draught will do her no harm. All the same, she will grow up and make some man wretched.

Mercedes: But, señor ——

Laboissière: Do you hear?

Mercedes: But Chiquita, señor—she is so little, only thirteen months old, and the wine is strong!

Laboissière: She shall drink!

Mercedes: No, no!

Laboissière: I have said it, sacré nom ——

Mercedes: Give it me, then. (*Takes the glass and holds it to the child's lip.*)

Laboissière: (*Watching her closely*) Woman! your hand trembles.

Mercedes: Nay, it is Chiquita swallows so fast. See! she has taken it all. Ah, señor, it is a sad thing to have no milk for the little one. Are you content?

Laboissière: Yes; I now see that the men may quench their thirst without fear. One cannot be too cautious in this hospitable country! Fall to, my children; but first, a glass for your lieutenant. (*Drinks.*)

The child dies and Laboissière draws his sabre just as Louvois enters and there follows a deeply moving scene of recognition under the shadow of approaching death for both of them as the wine slowly does its work. In this drama, intense and swift in movement, there is the quality of reticence, which made Aldrich's lyrics so exquisite. Only one brief gesture of Padre Josef in Act I hints at Louvois' fatherhood of the child; it deepens the tragedy but Mercedes does not tell him in the few moments they face certain death together. Although his dramatic dialogues date from *The Set of Turquoise* in 1858, Aldrich's work crossed the new century. In 1865 he had published his narrative poem, *Judith,* which he revised in 1896 as *Judith and Holofernes.*

Out of this he made a tragedy in four acts, acted by Nance O'Neill at the Tremont Theatre in Boston in 1904, and later on tour. Aldrich made a loving human woman out of the Biblical heroine, whom he describes as "a beautiful cold-blooded abstraction." In the camp of Holofernes she is saved not only by the power of her undaunted soul triumphing over the natural weakness of a woman, but also over the attraction which the royal attributes of Holofernes have for her own lofty nature. Her cry is from her heart:

> Oh, save me, Lord, from that dark cruel prince,
> And from mine own self save me! for this man,
> A worshipper of senseless carven gods,
> Slayer of babes upon the mother-breast,
> He, even he, hath by some conjurer's trick,
> Or by his heathen beauty, in me stirred
> Such pity as unnerves the lifted hand.
> Oh, let not my hand fail me, in Thy name!

It is to be noted, however, that the blank verse is end-stopped, and suffers from the lack of flexibility which was a characteristic of the Victorians, and which partially accounts for the failure of some of the verse plays of the Nineteenth Century. Their authors wrote about romantic subjects but their form was affected by the restraint which the period bred in them. No one who is familiar with Aldrich's poetry, especially the dialogues like *Pauline Palovna*, can fail to realize his sense of the dramatic. His mastery over the art of suspense is shown in his short stories, of which *Marjorie Daw* is only one brilliant example. The stage lost a playwright through the existence of conditions against which a man of letters like Aldrich did not care to struggle.

The heroic tradition was handed on by many actors, for during the nineties there rose a wave of interest in romance which revealed itself in the novel and in poetry as well as in drama. Julia Marlowe was one of those whose talent lay in this field and while she acted usually in plays of foreign authorship, she was seeking, like all the stars, for native plays that suited her. In *Chatterton* by Ernest Lacy (1863-1916), a Philadelphian, she found a one-act tragedy of exquisite pathos and of telling dramatic effect. Lacy had made a long study of the life of the poet, and he presented a picture of Chatterton in his garret, burnt out by a flame of aspiration too great for his mind and body to support, until in the terror of approaching madness, he takes his life. Lacy afterward elaborated the theme into a five-act tragedy, *The Bard of Mary Redcliffe*, for E. H. Sothern, but the combination of Sothern and Marlowe in a program of Shakespearean plays prevented its production. Lacy's second play, *Rinaldo, the Doctor of Florence*, was produced by Joseph Haworth in 1895, first in Boston and later in Montreal and on tour. It is a five-act tragedy in blank verse, with some real poetry but with constant interruption of the dramatic action by comments upon life and self-introspection. The last scene, in which Rinaldo dies of remorse, in the presence of the body of the woman who has loved him, brought in to be a subject of his knife, represents the virtues and defects of the romantic tragedy.

Owing its inception to the same desire for romance, but with an appeal to a different audience, the dramatization of novels progressed throughout our entire period and rose to a climax toward the end of the century. This phenomenon was much less important in the history of drama than in that of fiction, but even if only for its unfortunate effect upon the opportunities of playwrights, it must have its place in our record. Daly's work in this field has already been mentioned and the share of Frances Hodgson Burnett (1849-1924) in providing material for the early plays of Thomas and Gillette, calls attention to the dramatic quality of many of her novels. She dramatized her story, *Little Lord Fauntleroy* (1887), and made a success of it, though the play does not skirt the edge of the sentimental so successfully as does the novel. Mrs. Burnett was, of course, international rather than American, and *Little Lord Fauntleroy* had its first production in England, where a lawsuit consequent upon an attempted piracy established the right of a novelist to protect himself against an unauthorized dramatization of his book.[1] Mrs. Burnett's later plays are nearly all upon English subjects. She was more successful than another novelist, also international in scope, who made persistent efforts to write for the stage. Francis Marion Crawford (1854-1909) attempted to dramatize *Dr. Claudius* in 1897, but it was a failure. Later he tried to invert the usual process and planned *In the Palace of the King* (1900) first as a play, consulting Viola Allen, whom he had selected as the heroine, in its construction. He then wrote the story and the final dramatization was put in shape by Lorimer Stoddard. Certain changes were made, and additional characters like the Cardinal Luis de Torres were added. The English version of *Francesca da Rimini* (1902), written originally for Sarah Bernhardt, reveals Crawford's real skill as a dramatist. It is the simplest and the most direct of all the dramatic treatments of the story, and while it has not the great sweep of Boker's play, it follows the historical facts more closely. It is laid fourteen years after the marriage between Giovanni and Francesca, and their daughter, Concordia, is an unconscious instrument in bringing on the tragedy. Crawford's understanding of the Italian patrician is shown in his use of Paolo's neglected wife as a dramatic motive, which brings about the climax of the second Act. Francesca at first thinks she is a woman of the people, and she is revolted at the thought that Paolo has been unfaithful to her with such a rival. But when Paolo confesses that it is his wife, a noblewoman, to whom he has been unfaithful, and in whose death he is an accessory, Francesca's love is restored. The last scene is swift and powerful. Giovanni, who has been led to suspicion by Concordia's artless prattle and by a spy he has employed, comes into Francesca's room and finds the lovers together. Francesca throws herself between Paolo and his sword and is mortally wounded

---

[1] See William Archer's "Review of the Season of 1887-8" in *The Dramatic Year.* Ed. by Edward Fuller, Boston, 1889, pp. 28-31.

before Paolo is killed. Then after her cry to Paolo—"Wait for me one little moment!"—she turns to Giovanni and strikes at him with her weapon as he has struck her with his: "I would not kill you if I could, lest I should see your face in hell. It is not large enough to hold your soul and ours." And she mocks him as she kisses Paolo passionately. "This is what you have asked for in vain and I have refused—what you shall never have of me!" Francesca is at all times the central character. She is the passionate medieval Italian, as are all the characters, and they proceed with that simplicity and singleness of purpose which Crawford and Boker alone, among the writers of English versions of the story, have understood and interpreted.

The work of industrious playwrights like Paul M. Potter, Edward E. Rose, Paul Kester and others, who arranged for the stage the most popular of the romantic historical novels that swarmed during the close of the Nineteenth and beginning of the Twentieth Centuries, needs no analysis. Some of the novelists whose work they dramatized tried to share in their rewards. For example, Winston Churchill, whose *Richard Carvel* had been adapted by Rose, himself wrote a stage version of *The Crisis* for James K. Hackett. But none of this work is of permanent value.

It is difficult to limit this romantic impulse to any definite period for not only Belasco, but also Gillette, Thomas, and Fitch were affected by it to some extent. There is, however, a certain homogeneity in the work of the playwrights discussed in this chapter, if only in their treatment of universal rather than native themes, and in their frequent choice of verse as a medium. In one sense it was a survival of an older impulse, and its relative lack of popular success was partly due to this quality, while the romances of American life like *Secret Service, Arizona, Nathan Hale,* and *The Heart of Maryland* were packing the theatres. But in view of the popularity of *Ben Hur* even this explanation falters. Perhaps, after all, the distinction, more clear then than to-day, between the professional and the amateur offers the best explanation. Yet from the point of view of its permanent place in our dramatic literature some of the products of this late flowering of romance, like *Mercedes* and *Chatterton*, rank with the best of the products of the Nineteenth Century.

CHAPTER IX

WILLIAM GILLETTE AND THE REALISM OF ACTION

IN CONSIDERING the drama as a living thing, one of the most insistent problems is the proper estimation of the relative values of words and action. The student of the drama as literature is naturally prone to lay greater stress upon the former, for to him the word is the permanent factor and he is so conscious of the temporary quality of the history of the theatre as compared with the history of the drama, that his constant danger lies in underestimating the significance of those accompaniments of the verbal expression which have in many cases been responsible for its survival.

In a letter accompanying a revision of *Secret Service*, which he was good enough to make for a volume of plays I was editing, William Gillette expressed a point of view worthy of the attention of those who are willing to accept the word of a creative artist as of more significance than that of the critic:

I thank you for incorporating the Acting Directions with the actual words spoken, in the case of *Secret Service*, notwithstanding your evident opinion that the words constitute the play. We differ there in a marked degree—for even in book form,—to be read only, I would much prefer that people read what my characters *do*—how they *behave*—and what is in their minds—than to merely get the words they utter.

It is to be noted that Gillette is speaking of the action which springs from the playwright as creative artist, not the interpretation which an actor may put upon both words and action. He allies himself here with the position of Herne, which led to the striking scenes in *Margaret Fleming* and *Shore Acres*, already discussed, in which no words are spoken. But while

With highest regard
and best of wishes for the work
William Gillette

GILLETTE AND THE REALISM OF ACTION

Gillette stands in our dramatic history for the development of action, it is for action which reveals character as well as action which develops striking situations.

William Gillette was born in Hartford, Connecticut, July 24, 1855, his father, Francis Gillette, being at one time Senator of the United States. As early as 1875 he acted professionally in *Across the Continent* in New Orleans, and appeared as Guzman in *Faint Heart Never Won Fair Lady*, at the Globe Theatre in Boston. His first appearance in New York was at the Park Theatre in 1877 in *The Gilded Age*, where he acted as Foreman of the Jury, and his "entire vocal effort," as he expresses it, was "We have!" and "Not guilty." He was, in other words, learning his profession gradually. Gillette differs, however, from his contemporaries who were equipping themselves, during the seventies, for their dramatic careers. While acting at the Park Theatre, he was attending classes at the College of the City of New York, and later, when playing small parts in Boston, he made arrangements for special classes at Harvard and the Massachusetts Institute of Technology, and was a regular student at Boston University. None of these courses led to a degree, but they probably helped in that development of the sense of form which Gillette so markedly possesses. The fact that Gillette's taste led him in such a direction is of more significance perhaps than the results of his labors, for it reveals a desire for a broader outlook than the theatre alone can give. It was a natural result from the cultivated surroundings in which he had grown up in Hartford.

His first striking success as an actor came at the Boston Museum as Prince Florian in Gilbert's *Broken Hearts*, and he progressed so steadily in critical approval and popular favor that his reputation as a playwright has been somewhat obscured by his success in the interpretative field.

His first play, *The Professor*, produced at the Madison Square Theatre, June 1, 1881, is a character study of Professor Hopkins, who is a middle-aged teacher, admired by a bevy

of girls and in consequence badgered by the younger lovers
of his pupils. Gillette acted in the leading part and it was
a distinct success, running for one hundred and fifty-one consecutive performances, and later being taken on tour as far
west as St. Louis, where Augustus Thomas records his impression of its charm.[1]

In his first published play, *Esmeralda*, Gillette collaborated
with Mrs. Frances Hodgson Burnett, whose story of *Esmeralda* had appeared in *Scribner's Monthly* for May, 1877.
Mrs. Burnett, who was born in England but who was profoundly interested in certain phases of American life, discovered in the mountaineers of North Carolina dramatic
material which has recently been rediscovered. Only one act,
however, of the play is laid in North Carolina. The Rogers
family, headed by Mrs. Lydia Ann, who has dominated both
her husband and her daughter, Esmeralda, is determined to sell
the farm and is unwittingly about to close the bargain for five
hundred dollars with Drew, a speculator, when Dave Hardy,
a young neighbor, prevents the sale. Dave loves Esmeralda
and suspects that Drew has discovered ore on the land. Lydia
Ann is shrewd and when she sees the opportunity of wealth
she wastes no time in resentment but drives a good bargain
with Drew and just as relentlessly tells Dave they are through
with him. Dave at first defies her, but again she presents the
one argument that could win him, the appeal to his generosity
to let Esmeralda have a chance of comparing him with other
men before she marries him. There was of course in 1881 a
sentimental flavor to the family discussion, but even yet there
is a vivid contrast between the dominant woman who has been
a school-teacher at the county town and the man whom she
had married "for a whim," a gentle lovable soul, inarticulate
in his joy or sorrow.

Esmeralda is taken abroad and in Paris Mrs. Rogers arranges a marriage between her and the Marquis de Montessin.
Dave comes over, of course, and it turns out that the ore is

---

[1] *Print of My Remembrance*, 137.

really on his land. The sub-plot is unimportant but the scenes in the third Act, in which Esmeralda defies her mother, are quite vigorous. Even better is the "old man's" assertion of his right to be the head of the house, trembling all the while, but nerving himself to "go through with it."

The original story had been laid in Paris and was told by a French teacher of languages, who helps Esmeralda and her father in their loneliness and struggle against Mrs. Rogers, the latter appearing only in the background. To Mrs. Burnett is due the creation of the four main characters, but in the play they become active rather than passive figures. Gillette laid out the plan, Mrs. Burnett wrote the dialogue and then Gillette revised it, so that the drama may be looked upon in a real sense as a collaboration.

Esmeralda ran continuously from October 29, 1881, until October 7, 1882, and held the stage as long as 1900. Annie Russell and later Viola Allen played Esmeralda, and John E. Owens made the part of Elbert Rogers memorable. When it was played as *Young Folks' Ways* in London, John Hare took the part of Rogers, and Mr. and Mrs. Kendal were in the cast. Gillette's first two plays helped to establish the fortunes of the Madison Square Theatre as a place in which American dramatists would have an opportunity, and the Mallorys reaped a large reward for their sagacity.

The stage history of *The Private Secretary*, in which Gillette turned to the comedy of *Der Bibliothekar* (1878), by Gustav von Moser, illustrates the difficulties of passing critical judgment upon the drama of that period. *Der Bibliothekar* was adapted by both Gillette and Charles Hawtrey, an English playwright. On September 29, 1884, Gillette opened at the Comedy Theatre, New York, with his version, called *Digby's Secretary*. On the same evening, A. M. Palmer produced Hawtrey's version, under the title of *The Private Secretary*, at the Madison Square Theatre. Palmer tried to prevent Gillette from performing his play, but as Gillette had obtained von Moser's permission and was paying him a royalty while

Hawtrey was not, Palmer proposed a compromise. After playing his own version for a few months, Gillette continued under Palmer's management, making a new adaptation, founded upon his own, but using certain features of Hawtrey's play. It was in that composite production that Gillette appeared for five seasons.[1]

Gillette kept the plot of *Der Bibliothekar* in its main outlines, but there are many changes in details, owing to the increased importance given to the part of the Rev. Robert Spaulding, played by Gillette. In the German he is a minor character, does not appear in the second Act, and in the last Act is brought on just at the end. The comedy is broad farce in both cases. Robert Spaulding has been engaged as a private secretary by Turner Marsland, a country gentleman at Edgington, in England. Marsland's nephew, Harry, persuades his friend Douglas Cattermole, who is beset with duns, to go down to Marsland Manor with him, and represent himself as the private secretary. They persuade Spaulding, who is a guileless creature in rubbers, to stay in Cattermole's rooms for a time, but of course he follows them down to the Manor and a series of very comic situations develop. Gillette added to the low comedy by the addition of a wife and children for the clergyman, who are at first accredited to Douglas Cattermole, with a consequent misunderstanding between Edith Marsland and himself. Gillette amplified the slight references to spiritualism in the original by making the Reverend Mr. Spaulding appear as a medium. In this amplification there is reflected the current interest in spiritualism, in 1884.

In his next play Gillette wrote the first important drama of the Civil War. It was indicated in an earlier chapter that the writing of plays laid in the Civil War was practically continuous. Most of them were, however, of a hopeless quality. Boucicault's *Belle Lamar* (1874) has already been discussed. There are some vigorous moments in *Allatoona*, by Major General Judson Kilpatrick and J. Owen Moore, especially dur-

---

[1] Letter from Mr. Gillette, January 7, 1916.

ing the "battle in the clouds." It is truly a chronicle play, beginning at West Point, where the hero, Harry Estes, and his classmate, Charles Dunbar, take opposite sides, and proceeding to General Sherman's headquarters at Atlanta and General Corse's stubborn defence of his position. The latter is made one of the characters in the play, and Moore, who probably wrote nearly all of it, claims in the introduction historical accuracy.

But it is not accuracy which spells success in historical drama. There must be no flagrant distortion of well-known facts, but the audience is primarily interested in the personal relations of the characters and the conflict between the North and the South must be symbolized in a hero and heroine who represent the dramatic struggle in such a way that our sympathy is secured for them both. Boucicault had attempted this in *Belle Lamar*, but he had not recognized the greater appeal of the war play if it presents the tense moments when the imminence of tragedy is set against a background of domestic life. The characters must have courage and decision and the danger of the hero is intensified if it is reflected to the audience by the love and anxiety of the heroine.

These qualities were all present in *Held by the Enemy*, which began its career at the Criterion Theatre, Brooklyn, February 22, 1886, and came into the Madison Square Theatre in August. The action takes place in "a Southern city which has been captured and occupied by Northern forces," and in the first act Gillette established the atmosphere of refinement and comfort in the home of the McCreerys, aunt and nieces, while outside the war is raging. Eunice is betrothed, by a family arrangement, to her cousin, Lieutenant Gordon Hayne, who is in the Confederate army. But Colonel Harvey Brant, and Brigade Surgeon Fielding, of the Union army, are also in love with her, and the play centers on the efforts of Fielding to win her, by force, if necessary. The attempt of Hayne to enter the city as a spy, to make plans of the fortifications, and Brant's capture of him, give Fielding his opportunity. At

Hayne's court-martial, Fielding is judge advocate and cleverly directs the evidence to prove that Brant is animated by his rivalry with Hayne to convict the Confederate spy. Eunice plays into his hands by bursting out, in forgetfulness of all save her desire to protect her cousin, that no one but Brant has seen the incriminating paper which has been taken from Hayne. Brant when questioned, declines for her sake to testify against Hayne, and then Hayne to save him from the charge of dishonor acknowledges he is a spy and is proud of it. It is a conflict of honor between two men who love the same woman, and through Hayne, Gillette expressed in vigorous language the pride of the spy in his secret mission.[1]

Gillette here expressed the idea he was to bring to more complete development in *Secret Service*—the heroism of the spy. Hayne almost escapes from his prison in the next Act through the destruction of the walls by a timely shell, but is shot. In the fourth Act, laid in a military hospital, Gillette produced a scene which for sheer intensity of emotional appeal has rarely been exceeded. The McCreerys have secured from the commanding general a permit to bring Hayne's body through the lines. He is not really dead, and how the examining surgeon was deceived is never made clear, but in the whirl of incident that is forgotten. The sense of danger of discovery, of the great pressure of time, is well expressed, and largely through clever comedy, which prevents the situation from becoming too tense. Thomas Beene, a Northern war correspondent, and Susan McCreery, a younger sister, provide the comedy. Beene, a part later played by Gillette, is a preliminary sketch of the cool, quick-thinking and acting man, which is the playwright's favorite character. Fielding, returning, suspects that Hayne is not dead, and the efforts of Eunice and of Brant, who is unaware of the deception, to prevent the body from being examined, build up a skillful piece of stage arrangement. It is one of those situations which, under analysis, fall into

---

[1] See *Theatre*, II, 178, for the effect made upon the audience by this scene as acted by J. E. Kellerd in the part of Hayne.

pieces, and read coldly in type, seem almost absurd, and yet in action appear probable. For as a matter of fact, Gillette had studied the psychology of military discipline. To a civilian, it may seem impossible that Brant should order Fielding to desist from having the body examined, yet the soldier knows that the possession of an order from the commanding general made even the brigade surgeon's interference an intrusion. The soldier is accustomed to obey orders and ask no questions, and also to allow no one else to ask questions. Then when General Stamburg comes on the scene, Brant, in order to justify himself, asks the General to order the body to be examined. Eunice glides near him and whispers that Hayne is alive. From this point until the curtain there is an opportunity to study a series of rapid changes of action dictated by conflicts of emotion.

Fielding: (*Dashing across the stage*) D'you see that! D'you see that! She's just told him the man's alive— And now he can't speak!

Gen. Stamburg: Colonel, is that what Miss McCreery said?

Brant: (*Without hesitation*) Nothing of the kind, sir—he's a contemptible liar!
(*Fielding strikes Brant in the face almost on the word. Brant seizes Fielding's arm before he can get it away and holds it.*)

Gen. Stamburg: (*Quickly on the blow*) Halt!—You forget yourselves! (*Brant instantly releases Fielding's arm.*) That man on the stretcher alive? Why the thing is impossible. . . .

Fielding: (*As he swings around*) Impossible—Ah—(*pointing to the stretcher*) Look at that!—look for yourself, General! Unless I'm greatly mistaken the man is *breathing!*

Gen. Stamburg: Surgeon—examine the body at once!
(*Fielding strides to the stretcher near c. and throws the covering from Hayne's head and breast and at once stoops over making hurried examination. Eunice, almost as Fielding throws back the blanket, glides quickly to the stretcher from up r. c. where she had been moving during last speeches, and stands on Fielding's right, very near to him, but bending over Hayne as if to see.*)

Eunice: (*In a sharp breathless whisper to Fielding as she is ap-*

parently looking at Hayne and as Fielding bends down with his hand at Hayne's heart) Oh, save us! Save us and I'll marry you! I will, I will! *(Fielding stops in his examination of Hayne—and listens)* I promise!—On my sacred word—whenever you say!—On my sacred word—that I'll never break! I will! *(She rises and stands back a few steps motionless—her eyes lowered—waiting)*
(Fielding who has listened motionless while Eunice was whispering does not stir for an instant after she ceases.—Then he goes on with the examination for a moment, but his hand shakes as he puts it to Hayne's throat. He bends down and puts his ear to Hayne's body over the heart. Then he rises erect, and turns toward General Stamburg.)
Fielding: *(Speaking with an effort)* General—I owe Colonel Brant—and this young lady—an apology. My suspicions were groundless. The man is dead.
(Brant, whose eyes were lowered, slowly raises them and looks off front—realizing what has happened.)

The last Act, in which Brant forces Fielding to release Eunice from her promise, is hardly up to the earlier ones. It has some charming love-making, however, between Susan and Beene.

Gillette's dramatization of *She,* the novel by Rider Haggard, need not detain us. No play based on such a novel could be important, and the play was apparently no better than its source.[1] *A Legal Wreck,* which began at the Madison Square Theatre, August 14, 1888, is laid mainly in a New England fishing village. It exists now in published form as a novelette, written by Gillette and based upon the play. In 1888 dramatizations of popular novels were plentiful, and it occurred to the management of the play that it would be helped by the publication of the book. Gillette wrote it in five and one-half weeks, and it appeared about one week before the production. Considering the circumstances, the novel is remarkably well done. The opening chapter, in which Gillette calls attention to the effects of the sea upon those who live near it, shows his power of observation. "Gap Harbor took gossip . . . with a chill-

[1] See Winter, *Life of Belasco,* I, 337–40.

ing calmness. And it was because the people, instead of being shut into a place where they were forced, for the excitement which the human system craves, to prey upon themselves, were neighbors with the ocean." The style is vivid, and while the conversations are brisk, as would naturally be the case, it is interesting to see how the plot is carried on by the revelation of the thoughts of the characters and by the descriptions furnished by their creator. Several stand out clearly. Captain Smith, a fine portrait of the retired seaman, has brought up tenderly the little girl Olive, left to him by her father, who in a fit of depression had cast himself into the sea. His son, "Ed," is a hulking, dissipated lout, whose passion for Olive leads him to attempt to secure her by having her abducted from a railroad train by the supposed agents of an insane asylum. Her salvation by Leverett, the hero; Ed Smith's attempts at revenge, and the recovery of Olive by her mother and sister, who has been, all unknowing, Olive's friend at college, are more in the conventional tone of melodrama. Yet a rereading of the novel, when the plot is fully known, shows that it is the manner of the telling which is its main attraction.

Gillette did not act in *A Legal Wreck*, in his dramatization of *Robert Elsmere* (1889) or in his farce comedy, *All the Comforts of Home* (1890), adapted from *Ein Toller Einfall*. This play deals with the adventures of Alfred Hastings, a young man whose uncle, Mr. Pettibone, leaves his residence in London in order to take his wife away from a supposed lover, Smythe, who is really in love with his daughter, Emily. Alfred is in financial difficulties and, together with the assistance of his man, Tom McDow, "who gits half," starts a lodging house in his uncle's handsome home. To this lodging house come various people, among them the Bender family, and Alfred falls in love with Evangeline Bender. The Pettibones come home unexpectedly and complicate matters, but, of course, everything ends satisfactorily. The play is clever but of no great significance. Alfred, however, is another example of the cool young man who meets circumstances adroitly.

A clever farce which went extremely well on the stage was *Mr. Wilkinson's Widows*, adapted by Gillette from *Feu Toupinel* by Alexandre Bisson. After a try-out at Washington, it opened at Proctor's Theatre, March 30, 1891.[1] The scene of the play is changed from Paris to Edinburgh. The central motive is that of the complications which arise from the bigamy of the late Mr. Wilkinson, who married two women, both of whom have remarried. His relicts, Mrs. Percival Perrin and Mrs. Henry F. Dickerson, meet, and on comparing notes, each believes that she is the legal wife, since they were both apparently married to Mr. Wilkinson on the same day. In Bisson's play, a wife and a mistress furnish the complications with more probability if less propriety. Another play of Bisson, *La Famille Pont-Biquet*, was the source of *Settled Out of Court*, a farce in three acts, produced at the Fifth Avenue Theatre, August 8, 1892.

After this period of adaptation, Gillette wrote a play with more original elements, *Too Much Johnson*, which was one of the most popular of his efforts, and in which he took the leading part of Augustus Billings. This character, the cool, unabashed center of overwhelming complications, was his own invention, and much of the plot was his. From *La Plantation Thomassin* of Maurice Ordonneau, a species of musical comedy, he took the idea of a tropical plantation, to which the characters go, and the confusion as to its ownership. Billings, who has been deceiving his wife by representing to her that his frequent absences have been due to his visits to his sugar plantation in Cuba, finds that she and her mother have decided to accompany him. He has barely time to secure staterooms when they arrive at the dock. On the same boat appears Mr. Leon Dathis, with whose wife Billings has been enjoying New York, and who is looking, with half a torn photograph, for his rival. There are also Mr. Francis Faddish, and his daughter, Leonora, whom he has contracted to marry Joseph Johnson,

---

[1] An English version, by Fred Hunter, under the title of *The Late Lamented*, was produced at the Court Theatre, London, May 6, 1891.

WILLIAM GILLETTE AS "CAPTAIN THORNE" IN *SECRET SERVICE*

the owner of the Columbia plantation in Cuba. Billings has been conducting his love affairs under the name of Johnson, because there are "about fifteen thousand in the directory," and the consequent complications when they arrive in Cuba and Johnson mistakes Mrs. Billings for the *fiancée* he is expecting, can be imagined. Johnson is so irascible that the confusion becomes hilarious and through it all Billings stalks unperturbed, finally escaping with his wife and mother-in-law, without their suspecting the real situation. Pure farce as the play is, that character remains in the memory as a real person.

Secret Service, Gillette's most significant play, was first produced as *The Secret Service* at the Broad Street Theatre in Philadelphia, May 13, 1895. While the usual statements concerning its original lack of success are exaggerated, it was in a revised form that it appeared in October, 1896, at the Garrick Theatre in New York, where it remained until March, 1897. Of even more importance, Gillette instead of Maurice Barrymore played the leading part. He has now so completely identified the rôle of Captain Thorne with his own personality that it is hard for those who have seen him play, to imagine anyone else in it. On May 15, 1897, Gillette began an engagement at the Adelphi Theatre in London, which terminated at the Comedy Theatre in August. After his return to America, William Terriss, Herbert Waring and other actors appeared in London and in the provincial theatres in the part of Captain Thorne. *Secret Service* was also produced in a version by Pierre Decourcelle at the Théâtre de la Renaissance in Paris, October 2, 1897.[1]

Secret Service is an admirably constructed play. Every action proceeds naturally without apparent effort on the part of the playwright. Unity is preserved, even that of time, for the first Act begins at eight o'clock, the second at nine, the third at ten and the fourth at eleven o'clock at night in Richmond, while the Union forces are attacking the city. Gillette has placed the scene well, for some of the incidents, which might

---

[1] *Plays of the Present*, 244-5.

otherwise seem impossible, are to be accounted for by the confusion natural to such a time. As in *Held by the Enemy*, he strikes a note of personal devotion to the Confederacy through the Varney family—Mrs. Varney with her cool, quiet repose of manner; Edith Varney, more intense and swayed by her love for "Captain Thorne"; and Wilfred Varney, the sixteen-year-old boy who is longing to go to the front where his father is fighting, while the older son, Howard, is lying wounded upstairs. They are all spirited people, and the sympathy of the audience goes out to them at once. It is not so keen, however, as the reaction when Lewis Dumont, the Northern spy, who has secured entrance to the city as "Captain Thorne" of the Confederate army, enters, for we feel instinctively that in addition to the personal liking we have for them all, his continued danger appeals to our interest in the preservation of the hero. Not a word is wasted and not an action. Edith has secured a commission for him as Major, attached to the Telegraph Service of the Confederate army, and the whole situation between them is revealed in their brief conversation, when after a few words in which he tells her he must leave Richmond that night, she begs him to stay and he bursts out with a passionate exclamation, "Ah, my dear one—how can I?" and then suddenly stops and recovering control of himself says, "No! You shan't have this against me, too." She tells him of the commission and he says quickly, decisively, "I won't take it, I couldn't take it, Miss Varney. . . . If you ever think of me again remember that I refused it." She leaves the room to get it, however, and he is about to avoid temptation by flight when he is stopped by the entrance of Caroline Mitford, a girl of sixteen, one of the most charming of all the creations of our stage. She and Wilfred Varney provide in their love affair the lighter side of the shield, and her efforts to help him so that she won't be "the only girl on Franklin Street that didn't have a—some one she was engaged to at the front," are so closely interwoven in the plot that she becomes a potent factor in it. But above all else, it is the absolute reality of the characters which is impressive. Without a bit of heroics, they all move under the shadow of danger, playing the game; even Benton Arrelsford, of the War Office, who is trying to prove Captain Thorne's real mission, is not overstressed. By the end of the first Act we seem to have known these people always, because in this play Gillette represented the indomitable spirit of the American gentleman and gentlewoman, intelligible to North and South alike, and the audience recognized that whatever happened to them, they were worth while. There is a dramatic heresy now current that "little souls" are just as well suited for the stage as great ones, but those who hold it will be burnt at the stake of oblivion. Edith Varney, forced by fate to submit her lover to the test of his fidelity to the Confederacy, and bound by her promise to Arrelsford to keep Thorne in her house until his brother, Henry Dumont, can be brought from Libby Prison to confront and expose him, goes to her task with the light words of apparent careless gaiety on her lips while her heart is almost breaking. A woman's frustrated love is sometimes tragic, sometimes merely pitiful, but love shot through with the agony of doubt in the truth of the lover, while the woman must use her power to bring the lover to the test that may prove him a traitor, is one of the most truly dramatic motives that can be conceived.

This motive is carried out in the second Act. Henry Dumont has allowed himself to be captured and has sent a message to his brother Lewis through old Jonas, the negro servant. This has been taken by Arrelsford from Jonas. It reads, "Attack to-night—Plan Three—Use Telegraph." Edith gives this to Lewis Dumont (Captain Thorne), and then Henry is brought into the room by the soldiers as though he were escaping. Arrelsford, who is concealed, hopes to convict Thorne in this way. But when the brothers meet, Thorne grapples with Henry, who shoots himself with his brother's revolver. Then as the lights flash up and everyone comes on, Thorne stands, with an easy swing of his arms replacing his revolver in his holster and saying quietly, "There's your prisoner, Corporal—look out for him."

Baffled in his efforts, Arrelsford makes one more attempt to prove to Edith that Thorne is a spy. The scene of the third Act is the War Department Telegraph Office. The atmosphere is again caught at once; the intensity of the struggle is underlined by the click of the instruments and by the rumors of imminent danger. Caroline comes to the office to send a telegram to Wilfred, who has gone to the front, and there is much pleasant comedy till Arrelsford arrives with orders to take charge. A clash between him and Caroline sends her off to bring General Randolph later, and Edith Varney and Arrelsford conceal themselves on the balcony outside the office. Then follows a scene of rapid action by which Thorne, who comes on with a forged order, clears the room of all the other operators and prepares to send the dispatch which will weaken the Confederate defense by withdrawing a division from an important point. Arrelsford, however, stops him by a shot from the balcony and calls for the guard. Then follows a sudden change of front. When the guard come, Thorne orders them instantly to arrest Arrelsford. With the instinct of the soldier to obey the man in uniform, they respond to Thorne's commands against Arrelsford's protests. Into the mêlée Caroline brings General Randolph, an irascible old officer, who combines a single-track military mind with a dislike of the secret service. With every fact and chance against him, Thorne proceeds quietly to send the order, despite Arrelsford's violent protests. Then when the men who have been sent away by his forged orders begin to come in and even General Randolph orders him to stop, Edith Varney appears with the commission which he has previously refused to accept and presents it to him.

This situation illustrates some profound laws of dramatic construction. Edith Varney has had a decision to make between her love of country and her love of Captain Thorne. She decides in favor of the human love and everyone in the audience approves her choice. As soon as the commission is given to

CHICAGO
FEBRUARY
1911

To William Gillette
with best wishes of
Charles Dana Gibson.

"CAPTAIN THORNE" SENDING THE MESSAGE IN *SECRET SERVICE*

him, the choice between patriotism and love is transferred to Thorne. He instantly glides to the telegraph instrument, to send the dispatch, and the audience follows his movements with equal approval. This apparent inconsistency is founded on the most primitive instincts of human nature. To the man, his duty to his country comes first, for he carries on the nation. To the woman, her love comes first, for she carries on the race. Then instantly a new element is introduced. Edith appeals to his honor. "I brought it," she says, "to save your life! I didn't think you'd use it—for anything else. Oh—you wouldn't!" Reinforced by this appeal, the love triumphs and he revokes the message and tears up the commission. And the audience approves, this time tumultuously.

If Gillette had ended the play here, he would have created a tragedy of uncommon power. But in the next act, by an improbable piece of clemency, Thorne is saved. The play becomes melodrama of a high order. On the stage the illusion of probability remains, because so deeply has the sympathy of the audience become involved in the success of the main motive of the play, the love of Thorne and Edith Varney, that it tolerates any device which will secure that success.

It is the fashion to classify as melodrama all plays in which the conclusions are not strictly logical and to treat them all as outside the province of art. One essential quality of melo-drama, as I have explained elsewhere,[1] lies in its freedom, but like all products of art, it has its laws, and *Secret Service* obeys these perfectly. It is possible to point out the absurdity of the awarding of the commission, or of the details of the forged signature on the dispatch, but these are on the surface. *Secret Service* is founded on a proved law of the theatre, that the motives of self-preservation, love, patriotism, loyalty, and personal honor are the most universal in appeal. Many plays have succeeded with one of them—*Secret Service* has them all, now playing against each other, now joining forces, but al-

[1] *History of the American Drama from the Beginning to the Civil War*, p. 102. See also Chapter XVII in this history.

ways expressed through concrete characters who act as well as speak.

In 1898 Gillette turned from the intensity of *Secret Service* to the light comedy of *Because She Loved Him So*, adapted from *Jalouse* by Alexandre Bisson and Adolphe Leclerq, and first produced in New Haven, October 28, 1898. The play is a study of the effects of jealousy. Gertrude West, a young wife, is insanely jealous of her husband's supposed attentions to other women. They quarrel so frightfully in consequence that her parents, Mr. and Mrs. John Weatherby, who have never had a dispute in their lives, pretend to have fallen out in order to show their children the evil effects. They do this so realistically that Gertrude believes her mother has been deceived and nearly wrecks a friendship between her parents and Señora Gonzales, a charming tenant of John Weatherby. The action is rapid and amusing, and the play was a distinct success. The acting of J. E. Dodson as John Weatherby, the bride's father, was especially noteworthy, and the adaptation was made with Gillette's usual skill, for he succeeded in preserving the light touch of the original while omitting the unnecessary indelicacy.

There can be little doubt that it was the imperturbable personality of Sherlock Holmes which attracted Gillette's attention to his possibilities as a stage character. The detective whom Conan Doyle had modeled on Poe's Monsieur Dupin was well known and exactly suited Gillette's style of acting. In constructing the play, he took three characters from Doyle's stories, Sherlock Holmes, Dr. Watson and "Professor" Moriarty, the leader of the band of criminals, but the other eighteen were of his own creation, and the episode is not found in Doyle's stories. The novelist, moreover, did not see the play until it was finished, and had no part in its construction.[1]

The plot turns upon the efforts of Sherlock Holmes to pro-

---

[1] Letter from Mr. Gillette, December 10, 1924. The publication in England of *Sherlock Holmes* as "By Arthur Conan Doyle and William Gillette" was unauthorized by the playwright.

cure certain letters and photographs which had been sent by a mysterious royal personage in Germany to a girl who had died some time before the play opened. Her sister, Alice Faulkner, is determined to punish the offender for his treatment of the dead woman. Alice Faulkner has fallen into the hands of a pair of precious rascals, James and Madge Larrabee, and Holmes, who visits their house and secures the papers by a clever trick, is so much impressed by Alice that he returns the papers to her and proceeds on a new tack, that of persuading her to deliver the papers herself to the representatives of his royal employer. The Larrabees call in Moriarty, who is anxious to circumvent Holmes, and then the audience is treated to a series of scenes in Holmes's own rooms, in Moriarty's "Gas Chamber" and in Dr. Watson's office, in which the detective balks with skill all the efforts of craft and violence, until he secures his purpose. Incidentally he wins Alice Faulkner, who gives up her scheme of revenge under the more alluring prospects of love. Naturally the play is not in the same category as *Secret Service*, for while the plot is skilfully constructed, Gillette was dealing with characters who are not and cannot be made real. Sherlock Holmes and Dr. Watson are faint copies of the brilliant creations of Poe, and it was only the superb acting of Gillette which carried the play into favor here and abroad.

In 1903 he departed from his policy of appearing in his own plays by taking the leading part in Barrie's *The Admirable Crichton*, but in 1905 reassumed his joint function of playwright and actor in *Clarice*. In this play, first produced at the Duke of York's Theatre, London, September 13, 1905, and during the season of 1906-7 in this country, Gillette probably made use of atmosphere and material which were the result of his earlier stay in North Carolina. At his home at Thousand Pines, in the western part of the state, he had regained his health and had written *Too Much Johnson*. *Clarice* is laid in a village in South Carolina in 1904, and most of the action takes place in the living room of Dr. Carrington. The atmosphere of refined comfort without ostentation is at once established by the furnishings of the room, and the characters, few in number, are woven into the background with his usual skill. Gillette took the old story of a man who has brought up a young girl, Clarice, only to find that he loves her, while he feels that he must hide his passion. The relations between Clarice and her guardian are delicately expressed, and the half-maternal care she takes of him is contrasted with the tender solicitude he feels for her. Over this idyllic situation hovers the guardian spirit of Clancy, the cook, who is as fine a picture of old-fashioned negro loyalty as Thomas Nelson Page or Hopkinson Smith ever drew. The close identification of Clarice with the doctor's life is revealed not only in the way she prescribes for one of his patients, but more definitely in her sketches that she is making for his book on plants, which is to be his great accomplishment.

But into this happy situation there comes the disturbing element that is inevitable in drama. There is a rival, of course, a younger man, Dr. Denbeigh, but he is not the moving force of what is almost a tragedy. To direct the countermotive Gillette provided one of the best-drawn characters in his gallery, Mrs. Trent, Clarice's aunt. Years before the play opens she had cared for Carrington and he had not responded, and while no word is said by her to indicate her continued resentment, the audience realizes that he is dealing with an implacable enemy, who will hesitate at nothing to injure him. Under the guise of fostering the love affair between Denbeigh and Clarice, she plays skillfully upon Carrington's dread of the incipient tuberculosis whose menace had broken up his early career and sent him to South Carolina. She is the feminine prototype of his favorite male character, the calm, clear-headed person who moves quietly and quickly among circumstances to her end. Her first plan, to persuade Clarice that Dr. Carrington approves of the match between her and Denbeigh, almost succeeds, for Carrington's generosity makes him an apparent party to it. But at the end of the first Act occurs one of those situations which Gillette has built up on the basis of his theory that action is more eloquent than words. Clarice has told him she will accept Denbeigh if he desires her to do so. But a natural circumstance leads her to leave the stage for a moment, and on her return she discovers him tenderly kissing the rose she had given him, and then plucking it to pieces. Without a word she glides from the stage to give Denbeigh his refusal, and returns to pledge her life to Carrington. This is the kind of scene which can either be sickening in its sentimentality or exquisite in its sentiment. In Gillette's hands it was the latter, but it also revealed the power of an action which could change the whole current of three people's lives.

Mrs. Trent is not daunted by apparent failure. She deftly insinuates into Denbeigh's mind the suggestion that he deceive Carrington into a belief that his condition is hopeless and she writes Carrington a note telling him that Clarice can remain with him only at the peril of her life. This note is brought to him at the end of the second Act, after a love scene between him and Clarice which is charming in its whimsical quality. The ending of this Act is a remarkable example of the sudden striking of terror into happiness. He begins to read it aloud under the impression that it is a letter of congratulation. The audience knows its contents and hears him falter, then sees him brace himself to turn the deadly missive into a harmless note of approval.

Car.: (*Calling out after her*) Nonsense, Clancy! (*He turns and looks down smiling at Clarice—who looks up in his face.*) Why, I know what it is!
(*He has the open letter and the envelope in his left hand, having just succeeded in getting the letter out. Clarice is silent, her head down again against his breast.*)
It's the answer to the note I sent her this afternoon telling her about you and me. (*She looks up into his face and he down into her eyes for a moment.*) You and me!—My dear, my dear— (*He turns again to the letter.*)
Listen, sweet—you'll like to hear this! Why, she's got to send us good wishes—whether she wishes 'em or not! Oh

yes, she has! There's nothing else to do! Let's come a little nearer the light! (*He moves up a little with her so that the lamp is near his left shoulder.*) There we are! Now listen! (*He holds the letter up in his left hand and reads it*) "Dear Dr. Carrington:—I'm afraid from what I hear that you changed your mind after I saw you this morning." (*He stops and looks down at her smiling. She looks up at him.*)

Changed my mind! Well, I should think I did! (*He continues to look at her tenderly for a moment—then turns to the letter again.*) "Now, sorry as I am to—" (*He stops suddenly and stands motionless looking at the letter. There is a slight pause and then he speaks*)

Wait a minute—I can't quite make out— (*Reads*) "Sorry as I am to—" Ha ha—this is odd, isn't it? (*Turning to her*) Of course she's sorry about something—we can understand that!

(*His eyes have glanced quickly down the sheet during the foregoing pauses.*)

Clarice: Why don't you read me the rest?

Car.: (*Quickly*) Yes—yes—as soon as I—I was trying to—to get at it from the context. (*He turns back to the letter in his left hand.*) How far had I—

Clarice: She said she was sorry about something.

Car.: Oh yes—here we are! (*A fleeting glance toward her and back to letter again.*)

I told you she'd have to do it! (*Rather rapidly and as if reading from the letter*) "Sorry as I am that you were unable to see the wisdom of my plans, I have no doubt it will turn out for the best! I certainly hope so, and send my good wishes and congratulations . . . to you—you both!" (*He crumples the letter and envelope quickly in his left hand on the last word or close after it and crowds them hastily into the left hand pocket of his coat.*) There—you see! (*He holds her close in both arms.*)

Your Aunt Max is all right! (*Gently pressing her head down on his breast*) Your Aunt Max is all right!

(*He turns his head away to left front—his eyes down, and his face showing his dreadful anguish—while still holding her pressed close to him, and repeating mechanically—not knowing what he says*) Your Aunt Max is all right!

Powerful, too, is the climax of the third Act. Believing after Denbeigh's examination that his days are numbered, he declines to give Clarice that reason, for he knows she would pay no attention to it. He determines to make it impossible for her to remain with him, so he changes from the lover to the guardian and brusquely, almost violently, tells her that he has made a mistake; that she is interfering with his life work, even her amateurish sketches are a hindrance, and he harshly bids her prepare to go to Washington that night with her aunt. As he leaves the stage he calls Clancy to come help her mistress pack and then the scene closes.

> (*He turns and goes off unsteadily. Clarice makes an involuntary move toward him as he goes out but stops near the table and stands still. After a time she turns very slowly and goes toward the foot of the stairs. She stops there a moment without looking around. Then she slowly goes up the two or three steps to the landing, steadying herself by holding to the stair post with her right hand. She raises this hand to the post above her as she is starting at the first step. She goes up the stairway. When part way up she stops and turns her head a little, speaking to the front.*)
> Come, Clancy.
> (*She turns and goes up the stairway. Clancy, who has stood motionless, not looking at Clarice during the scene, turns and follows her up the stairs.*)

Judged by one standard, the play might have ended here in tragedy, and the last Act, containing his attempted suicide, his salvation by the unexpected return of Denbeigh and later of Clarice, can be conveniently called melodrama. But in reality it was quite probable that Carrington, facing the slow wasting of his life in utter loneliness, should decide to end it. It is equally probable that Denbeigh, who returns to inform Carrington that Clarice has refused to go with her aunt, should react to his discovery of Carrington's condition and, with a physician's instinct, save his life. It is also probable that Clarice should return, and that she times her arrival at the moment when her knowledge of the location of the antidote is essential, may be forgiven any dramatist. For the action in each case is determined by the character, and the characters in this play are among the most real that Gillette has drawn.

Gillette experimented in the next few years in the writing of one-act plays, among them *The Painful Predicament of Sherlock Holmes*, in which he appeared in 1905, and a rather vivid if improbable vaudeville sketch, *The Red Owl*, in 1907, laid at midnight in a house in the suburbs of New York. Better than the last is *Among Thieves*, a skillfully planned drama of situation, laid in Arizona. Gillette represents in this one-act play the lengths to which a criminal will go in loyalty to a man who has befriended him and also the eternal suspicion and watchfulness which are his only security.

In 1908 Gillette produced his translation of Henri Bernstein's *Samson*, which followed the original more closely than his other adaptations. He took the part of Maurice Brachard, who in order to revenge himself upon his wife's lover, pulls down in a day the great financial structure he has built up through years of effort, satisfied that he has wrecked his enemy. The part was created by Lucien Guitry in 1907 at the Théâtre de la Renaissance.

Gillette made an effort to employ new sources for his material in *Electricity*, which opened at the Park Theatre, Boston, September 26, 1910. It is a three-act comedy laid in New York City, and is concerned with the love affair between James Hollenden and Emeline Twimbly, the daughter of Duncan Twimbly, who is "at the head of a corrupt corporation." Emeline is a modern girl who declines to accept her lot in life as an idler and who is gently satirized by Gillette in her rather feeble efforts to secure employment. Hollenden, who belongs also to the inheritors of wealth, has fallen in love with her photographs which her brother Samuel has had in their joint rooms at college, and being warned by Sam that she will not be attracted to him unless he is a worker, Hollenden bribes Bill Brockway, who is wiring the Twimbly house, to let him take his place. The situation rapidly becomes farcical, and by 1910 the denunciation of corporate greed was no longer a fresh note. Yet there is some rather good characterization, especially of the Brockway family, and Emeline's call of ceremony on them when she believes herself to be engaged to Bill Brockway, is amusing comedy. *Electricity* in its published form is interesting reading even if its success on the stage was not great.

In his latest plays Gillette has returned to his favorite sphere, that of the character who is playing a difficult hand against a number of opponents, who are usually lawbreakers. *The Dream Maker*, produced in 1921 at the Empire Theatre, was founded on a short story by Howard E. Merton. The scene is laid in the cottage of well-to-do people in a summer resort near New York City, and the central character, Dr. Paul Clement, baffles a set of blackmailers who are preying upon a young matron, the daughter of a woman he had once loved. At times there was a flash of the earlier fire, but it was rather in the actor than in the playwright, for the pivotal situation, in which young Mrs. Bruce puts herself in their power through her midnight appointment with Geoffrey Cliffe, is unbelievable. In *Winnie and the Wolves*, based on short stories by Bertram Akey, and tried out at Philadelphia in May, 1923, the material was no more worthy and there was no such personality as Gillette to make the stage presentation significant.

Gillette's dramas may be classified most appropriately in three groups: the original plays, the dramatizations of fiction, and the adaptations from foreign sources.

Among his six dramatizations of fiction, *Esmeralda* and *Sherlock Holmes* were deservedly successful and in each he contributed his full share. Both his adaptations from the German, *The Private Secretary* and *All the Comforts of Home*, and his four plays taken from French sources, *Mr. Wilkinson's Widows*, *Settled Out of Court*, *Because She Loved Him So*, and *Samson*, were also distinctly well received. Like Augustin Daly and Belasco, Gillette worked from translations made by others, and, except in the case of *Samson*, he reshaped the material extensively. In *Samson* he kept the scene in Paris, in *Settled Out of Court* he transferred it to America, in *Mr. Wilkinson's Widows* he laid it in Edinburgh and in the others he placed it in England. In only two of the foreign adaptations did he play himself, *The Private Secretary* and *Samson.* Indeed, Gillette acted in only nine of his twenty full-length plays, *The Professor, The Private Secretary, Held by the Enemy, Too Much Johnson, Secret Service, Sherlock Holmes, Clarice, Samson* and *The Dream Maker.*

If Gillette has confined himself in his acting to the expression of a limited number of characters, it must not be forgotten that he has done so consciously and in accordance with his own theory of art.[1] Criticism is too prone to require an artist to accord with a preconceived standard to which he never attempted to suit his methods, and its real function is to ascertain what the playwright and actor have endeavored to accomplish. According to Gillette, "actors of recent times who have been universally acknowledged to be great have invariably been so because of their successful use of their own strong and compelling personalities in the rôles which they made famous. And when they undertook parts, as they occasionally did, unsuited to their personalities, they were great no longer and frequently quite the reverse."

The personality of William Gillette is so definite that it shines through every part in which the present writer has seen him. But he is not a one-part actor. It is not because Thomas Beene in *Held by the Enemy*, Augustus Billings in *Too Much Johnson*, Captain Thorne in *Secret Service*, and Sherlock Holmes are the same character that his performances are successful. They are quite different, as a matter of fact, and it is only because the compelling personality of the dramatist actor has so successfully infused them with his own nature that he has made of the group a dramatic unit. As characters the

---

[1] See his "The Illusion of the First Time in Acting," *Publications of Dramatic Museum of Columbia University*, 1915; also "Mr. William Gillette Surveys the Field," Supplement to *Harper's Weekly*, February 2, 1889.

Gen R. ~~Send it~~ Go on and send it!

[Thorne at once drops into seat at telegraph
instrument and begins to send rapidly]

Arrelsford [seeing what is going on ~~to Sarrel~~] No no!! – It's a —

Gen R. ~~to Sarrel~~ Silence!!

[Pause] [Rapid click of telegraph instru-
ment as Thorne sends. ~~This holds barely four~~ seconds.]

Arrelsford [Breaking in wildly] Do you know what he's
telling them.

Gen. R. ~~Certainly that~~ No! – Do you?

Arrelsford. ~~Yes I do~~ Yes! – It's a damnable plot! He —

Gen. R. [To Thorne] Wait! [Takes copy of despatch from which
Thorne was sending]
[Thorne stops telegraphing and stands waiting]

Gen. R. [Turns to Arrelsford] What was it?

~~as~~ What did he send just now?

Arrelsford [Repeating] ~~We told them to withdraw~~ Marston's Division
from present position. ~~as at it still~~

Gen. R. That is perfectly correct!

Arrelsford ~~That may be correct~~ Correct – by that despatch – but that
despatch is a forgery!

[music swells slightly and down again]

General R [looks at despatch] Nothing of the kind! – This is the Secretary's
signature!

Arrelsford He cut it off from a genuine order
— I saw him do it!... See if
the sheet isn't pasted on!

Thorne. It is, General — they often ~~cut the~~ come that
way.

Arrelsford [instant retort] He's a liar —
They never do!

[Thorne quick angry turn to
Arrelsford. Arrelsford glaring savagely
at him. Gen. R. eyeing them sharply.]
[Instant's Tableau as above]

A PAGE FROM THE ORIGINAL MANUSCRIPT OF *SECRET SERVICE*

playwright gave them variety; as an actor he gave them unity. These two qualities, the most essential in any product of art, have endowed them with a vitality in his hands which may set a limit to their stage life. For it would be a daring actor who would challenge Gillette's performance in *Secret Service* while the memory of stage generations is awake. Yet notwithstanding its creator's own words, it is a play to read as well as to see, for the spirit of a great epoch in our history is there set glowing against a background of heroic acts and impulses.

What makes this unity of accomplishment all the more significant is that it is based on a long experience during which Gillette saw the decline of the older school of acting, and the rise of the more repressed and delicate art of the theatre. He recognizes that an actor cannot be absolutely true to nature, but that he must constantly study, not simply to reproduce the words of the text, but rather to place himself in the mental and emotional position of the character, who is really only becoming aware of what he is to say, while the actor who represents him knows already just exactly what his lines are to be. Not only in what he says, but also in his actions, the actor must simulate that gradual or sudden birth of motor impulses whose handling or mishandling draws the line between success and failure.

Knowing how deeply their creator has pondered on these and other problems of the actor's art, the characters of Gillette the playwright take on an added significance. For the final judgment upon his position must rest, of course, upon the eight original plays, *The Professor, Held by the Enemy, Secret Service, A Legal Wreck, Ninety Days, Clarice, Electricity,* and *Too Much Johnson,* the last being so largely his creation that it must be included in this category. In these the types are by no means limited. The charm of naturalness not only in the characters he plays, but in the others he has created, like Caroline Mitford, Wilfred Varney, Mrs. Varney, Susan McCreery, Captain Smith, Gordon Hayne, Clarice, Judith Clancy, is that of intelligence. Intelligence, too, is the basis of the distinct impression of restrained power for evil made by Mrs. Trent. They are not puppets: they do their own thinking and acting; and their thoughts and actions proceed as though Gillette, once having created them, allowed them to proceed on their own initiative. Of course this is only another way of saying that they are dramatic creations.

They are not parochial, and yet they are American. They are the embodiments of courage, chivalry, loyalty, self-sacrifice, patriotism—these are not the peculiar property of Americans—and yet they represent them in a way that is our own. For the European noblesse oblige they substitute that impelling motive of the responsibility which comes with the very disappearance of permanent caste, and they possess that poise which it is a cherished delusion of European criticism that we fail to possess. Perhaps it was this note of poise, of restraint and self-control, which accounted for Gillette's success in England. For while the British playwrights and British critics have never been overhospitable to our artistic products, everywhere the gentleman recognizes the gentleman.

CHAPTER X

WHILE the seventies saw the early struggles of Howard and Harrigan in the East, of Herne and Belasco in the Far West, there was growing up in St. Louis, Missouri, a playwright who stands even more definitely than any of these for the drama of American life. It was the Middle West which produced Augustus Thomas, and the place and the period of his boyhood are similar to those out of which Mark Twain evolved. But while Mark Twain's instincts took him West, Thomas's broader interests made him at home in Alabama, in Arizona, in New York and in Washington. There can be no one play in which all the many facets of our national life may be reflected, but in his work there is the nearest approach to it. Lowell once said, "It is not enough to love one's country, one must be in love with it," and the pages of Thomas's fascinating autobiography reveal an American whose roots are deep in the soil, whose experiences have been native, and who combines a proper sense of patriotism with a broad toleration of all the elements of our national life. He has been a student of the best of the foreign drama, but he has imitated none of it, and his work has been singularly free from mannerisms or methods. He has simply depicted certain forms of native life, certain phases of modern American thought, with a sympathy and an art that have won him wide recognition.

Augustus Thomas was born in St. Louis, January 8, 1857. His father, Dr. Elihu B. Thomas, had served during the Mexican War on General Taylor's staff and raised a company of volunteers on the outbreak of the Civil War. But an old injury prevented his seeing active service, and in 1863 he reopened the St. Charles Theatre in New Orleans to provide amusement for the Federal troops. Thomas grew up in democratic surroundings. The family fortunes were not ample, and his education was mainly a series of contacts with life. At the age of eleven, he became a page in the Missouri House of Representatives, and in 1870 went to Washington in a similar capacity. He was a keen, observant boy, and the regular education which circumstances interrupted was well replaced by a broadening intercourse with men and affairs. Here he met, at his uncle's table, E. L. Davenport, James E. Murdoch, and other actors of that generation, and his predilection for drama was strengthened.

In the fall of 1871 he was once more in St. Louis at high school, and at the age of fourteen he began his seven years' experience in the business of transportation with the St. Louis Transfer Company. Later he joined the St. Louis, Kansas City and Northern Railroad. He was also educating himself by wide reading, especially in English poetry.

In his *Print of My Remembrance* Thomas tells of his dramatic beginnings. His first full-length play, *Alone* (1875), was written for the Marion Place Dramatic Club of St. Louis. That Thomas is still a hearty advocate of the amateur dramatic society and of the Little Theatre is proved by these significant lines in his autobiography:

They [his readers] may infer that the money side of the return is of the lesser worth; that the big value is the self-expression obtained; that the debating society, the dramatic club, the singing school, the art class, the pursuits that invite brain to the finger tips, and to become articulate, are the interests that make life eloquent. They may even come to have opinions and to believe that the amount of self-expression encouraged and protected in any country is the measure of liberty in that country.

He was being trained as an actor, too, with this club, which was almost semi-professional. It was the transition period, when the traveling company was coming in, and he had opportunities to fill in as substitute professionally. He became, for

the moment, juvenile lead in the company of John W. Norton
and he saw the greatest actors of the day: Booth, Barrett,
Fechter and McCullough.

He gave up at this time, for family reasons, an opportunity
to study painting in Paris, and while it was a keen disappointment at that time, he now believes that the "rough and tumble
education" which he received from the world was of greater
value for the dramatist. He became a master workman in
the Knights of Labor and in 1876 was studying law in the
office of John P. Colby, father of Bainbridge Colby, now his
brother-in-law. But the lure of the theatre was stronger than
that of the law. He had joined the McCullough Club, an
amateur organization of St. Louis, of which he soon became
stage-manager and leading man. His performance of Rogers
in *Esmeralda* links him to the drama of Gillette and he also
was to make use of the dramatic quality of the fiction of Mrs.
Burnett. The story of *Editha's Burglar* in *St. Nicholas*
attracted the attention of Thomas and he dramatized it for
the club. Later it became his first play to be performed professionally. To the central idea, that of a little girl so charming a burglar that he failed to accomplish his purpose, Thomas
added the motive of paternal love by making the burglar the
father of the girl. Her stepfather, who has brought her up
after her mother's death, is devoted to her, and she believes
him to be her father. The anxiety of the child to save her supposed father from the dangers with which the name of burglar
is associated are very naturally expressed. The dramatic climax, in which Bill, her real father, tells her that his little girl
is dead, is also quite simply and effectively done. It is the
moral contrast, which has its perennial appeal on the stage.
But the progress of Thomas's art from *Editha's Burglar* to
The Witching Hour is apparent to any critic who turns the
pages of the manuscript of his first play, with its obvious introduction, its asides and the stilted language of Paul, the father,
much of which was altered during the extensive revisions which
the play underwent. Yet the secret of Thomas's art was

already expressed: the knowledge of what will appeal to human sympathies.

About 1880 he definitely abandoned the study of law and became the box-office man for Pope's Theatre in St. Louis. With *Editha's Burglar* and other attractions he organized the Dickson Sketch Club in 1883 and toured Minnesota, Iowa and Missouri towns, going as far south as New Orleans. During this New Orleans engagement Charles Frohman saw the performance of *Editha's Burglar* and arranged for its production by E. H. Sothern. This was the beginning of Thomas's relation to New York. It also led him to rewrite the play as a four-act drama called *The Burglar*, in which the past and future of the robber are woven around the one-act sketch.

Thomas advises would-be playwrights to do three things— read many and good plays, act professionally for a time, and report for a metropolitan newspaper. In 1885 he joined the staff of the St. Louis *Post-Dispatch*, and in his account of his experiences he pays eloquent tribute to the value of that training. During this time he wrote *A Man of the World*, as a newspaper sketch, a one-act play afterward produced at the Madison Square Theatre in 1889. The dialogue is refreshingly real; and very convincing is the way in which Captain Bradley saves a young woman from wrecking her happiness by the application of common sense to the solution of the eternal problem of readjustment to the conditions of early married life. Feeling that the newspaper work was only temporary, he refused flattering offers in Leavenworth, Kansas, and hoped for a New York opening. Yet when Sothern offered to put on *The Burglar* if Thomas would make changes which the playwright felt were inartistic, he refused.

Thomas came East in 1888 to act as manager for Julia Marlowe. He had in his trunk two full-length plays and five or six short ones, and he had a knowledge of theatrical business. He had produced four plays that he had written. But his managerial experience was short and it brought him back to St. Louis to act as advance agent for a mind reader, Washington Irving Bishop. Some experiences gained in this position led later to the writing of *The Witching Hour*. In June, 1889, his play, *The Burglar*, was produced in Boston with Maurice Barrymore in the lead. It was successful there and in New York, and was played for ten years. This led to a long association with Barrymore, for whom he wrote *Reckless Temple* (1890), a play based on a newspaper clipping which told about two men who drew lots from a hat with the understanding that the man who drew the marked card was to commit suicide.

Thomas has told us how inspiring to a young dramatist was the association between playwrights and actors at the Lambs Club and at other meeting places in New York. The American playwright was coming into his own with the success of *Held by the Enemy, Shenandoah, The Midnight Bell* and *Lord Chumley*. The Madison Square Theatre was becoming the theatrical center, rivaling the Union Square and the Star Theatre as fashion was moving north.

In May, 1890, A. M. Palmer, the manager of the Madison Square Theatre, offered Thomas the position as adaptor or revisor of foreign plays, which had been occupied by Dion Boucicault, thus again linking Thomas with the history of the stage. At Palmer's request, he wrote a one-act play called *A Constitutional Point*, for Agnes Booth, but it was not produced until seventeen years later, when it became the germ of *The Witching Hour*. Instead he produced a one-act play for Agnes Booth, *Afterthoughts*, in which Thomas himself acted during its Boston engagement. This may be considered his period of probation. His next play established his reputation.

Alabama was written first as a one-act play, but realizing the strength of the characters, Thomas developed a series of situations which have as their central motive the reunited country. Colonel Preston represents the irreconcilable South, the man who has driven his son away from him because of Harry Preston's sympathy with the North. Harry, who reappears as "Captain Davenport," a railroad man, stands for the Southerner who thinks nationally. Colonel Moberly is the type who stands midway between these extremes. He is chivalric, impetuous, but still is half-reconstructed. Squire Tucker is the type of white citizen whose horizon is quite limited, but who exists in much larger numbers than fiction or drama usually represents. Mrs. Page, Colonel Preston's niece, who had been engaged to Harry Preston but had broken the match because of their close relationship, is drawn as a charming widow and "Captain Davenport" wins her hand at last. The love story of youth, without which a play in the nineties could hardly have succeeded, was also introduced, beginning in the charming garden scene of the first Act. Thomas tells how this scene came to him in a dream. He had seen the city of Talladega some years before, and the picture of an old man and a young girl passing through the half-ruined gateposts of the old estate presented themselves to him.

The keynote of the play is struck in a speech of Captain Davenport:

I respect your feeling in the matter, Colonel Preston, but I can't help thinking that it is your personal view that blinds you. Things, sometimes, are too personal for a correct appreciation. The North and South were two sections when they were a fortnight's journey apart by stages and canals. But now we may see the sun rise in Pennsylvania, and can take supper the same day in Talladega. It is one country. Alabama sends its cotton to Massachusetts—some of it grown very near your graveyards. The garment you have on was woven twenty miles from Boston. Every summer Georgia puts her watermelons on the New York docks. Pennsylvania builds her furnaces at Birmingham. The North took some of your slaves away—yes—but one freight car is worth a hundred of them at transportation. Our resentment, Colonel Preston, is eighteen hundred years behind the sentiment of the day.

The difficulties which native playwrights have been required to surmount are well illustrated by the history of *Alabama*. A. M. Palmer accepted it but had no confidence in its drawing power and withdrew it from rehearsal. But after the failure of three English plays, Palmer ventured to produce *Alabama* on April 1, 1891, at the Madison Square Theatre. The play was an instant success and it not only relieved Thomas of the necessity of acting as an advance agent for Palmer's ventures but also enabled him to resign from his position as revisor of plays and proceed with his own work. *Alabama* won its critical and public approval through its directness and its human quality. Every sentence is brief, but telling, and there is a sense of form which never approaches fine writing but is definitely kept down to the proper level. When the play reached Louisville, Colonel Henry Watterson said publicly that *Alabama* had done more to reconcile the two sections of this country than his editorials had accomplished in twenty years.

Thomas, as was the custom in those days, wrote his plays with a definite actor or actress in mind. *For Money* (1891), which was begun as a serious play, became a farce because the public declined to take William H. Crane seriously. *Colonel Carter of Cartersville* (1892) was better adapted to E. M. Holland, who represented admirably Hopkinson Smith's Southern gentleman. *Surrender*, a Civil War play, although it ran for a month in Boston, beginning on November 21, 1892, was only moderately successful. *Surrender* is laid in or near Richmond during the last days of the Confederacy. The main incident, the attempt to free the Confederate prisoners at Johnson's Island in Lake Erie and attack New York, proved not to be sufficiently well known to make an instant appeal. There is a light touch which carries the play out of the category of *Shenandoah* and *Griffith Davenport*, and to the historian its chief interest lies in the real progress that was made in Thomas's art between *Surrender* and *The Copperhead*.

Thomas returned to the play of locality with *In Mizzoura*. Here he was at home and the characters are real. In his introduction to the published play Thomas tells how he built it up, beginning with the part of the sheriff for Nat Goodwin, and how his visit to the village of Bowling Green suggested the blacksmith, Jo Vernon, for the heroine's father, and the hired helper, Dave, who is one of the best-drawn characters and who, with Elizabeth, the younger daughter, makes up one of the three pairs of lovers. An express robbery gave Thomas the rival to the sheriff for Kate Vernon's affection and the incident of an older man providing the means of educating a girl until she grows above him gave the sheriff a sympathetic part. It is a well-worn motive in drama, but it usually appeals. Thomas provides the hero with a fortune through the discovery of a clay which, when fired, becomes hard as flint, and which was brought to the playwright's attention by a conductor on a Wabash train. A principle of playwriting is illustrated by Thomas's use of this clay. "If you use a property once," he says, "use it again and again if you can. It is a visual thing that binds together your stuff of speech like a dowel in a mission table." So he provided a climax for his second Act by an effective scene with a crippled dog whose wounded leg the sheriff has poulticed with his clay and to whom the sheriff turns when he has been discouraged by Kate's attitude toward him. *In Mizzoura* was first produced in Chicago on August 7, 1893, and came into New York in September. It was a success and became a stock piece.

Thomas was always interested in the relations of capital and labor and in their effect on politics. In 1894 the time seemed ripe for a dramatic treatment of the trusts and Thomas built up a play around a manufacturing company in which Courtland Crandall represented concretely the conservative and his son Van Buren represented the progressive elements in the governing board. When the play opened in Chicago on July 26, 1894, the strike of the Pullman operatives had begun, President Cleveland had interfered to keep the United States mail going, and the company rolled into Chicago between lines of burning freight cars. *New Blood* was a success in Chicago, but failed in New York. Thomas believed the failure was due to a surfeit of labor themes in the daily papers. Charles Frohman attributed it to the fact that the play was definitely a document on the side of labor, to which a New York audience would not respond.

Although it was not a popular success when produced in New York in 1895, Thomas's next play, *The Capitol*, is a masterly study of politics at Washington and financial and religious influences that are brought to bear upon them. Blake, a representative from Nebraska, has come to Washington with ambitions and a wife. Carroll, a railroad lobbyist, obtains a hold on Blake through the latter's desire to be Senator, and Carroll also makes love to Mrs. Blake, who repulses him. Garretson, a well-known author, and the Very Reverend Eustace Kennard are close friends, although holding very opposed religious views. Garretson is especially wrought up over the supposed influence of the Catholic Church on legislation. One form of this influence is represented concretely by Wetmore Boyd. He is a man of culture and of wide knowledge of European conditions who wishes to be an Ambassador. The Administration desires to have a representative at Rome who will be acceptable to the Vatican, and Boyd is offered the position. Garretson is vitally interested in helping the miners who are striking in Pennsylvania and North Carolina, and when Blake's resolution in Congress placing coal on the free list seems in danger, Garretson comes to Kennard to secure his assistance to block the railroad lobby that is trying to prevent the putting of coal on the free list. Kennard arranges through Boyd that certain financial interests shall call their loans to the railroad pool. This prevents the latter's gaining control of the road to Canada over which coal could be sent to break the monopoly. Boyd finally declines the Ambassadorship because he has been accused of obtaining it on account of his contributions to the party.

Thomas knew that economics and politics alone would not make drama. The personal motive is supplied by the relations of Father Kennard and Margaret Doane, who is the leader of the Royal Cross Society. Years before, when he was a rector of a small Episcopal church, they had been married. She was dissatisfied and had left him with her lover, Carroll, taking their daughter Agnes. Finding Carroll out, she had left him and as a penance had devoted herself to social work. Agnes had been brought up in ignorance of her parents and married Blake. The instinctive appeal of Agnes Blake to Kennard for protection without knowing him to be her father, the tragic intensity of the meeting of mother and daughter, the restraint and delicacy of the final parting of Kennard and Margaret, are characteristic of Thomas. He was dealing with forces that are real and powerful, and his knowledge of politics enabled him to portray the more subtle methods of control over legislation which in 1894 had not been revealed in drama. We are spared the usual flourish of money in large packages, and we are also spared the description of the sufferings of the strikers.

The most difficult theme in this play is the treatment of the Church. In order that his picture should be correct, the playwright submitted *The Capitol* to a prelate in Washington, and indeed no member of that Church should feel disturbed by the characterization of Father Kennard or Wetmore Boyd. Father Kennard is one of the few stage clergymen who seem real, and Wetmore Boyd is a representative of the cultivated Catholic who in this country seldom appears in general literature.

It is evident that at this period Thomas felt that he had written himself out. He was discouraged by the comparative failure of his two serious studies of American conditions, and the postponement of his carefully studied play on the youth of Washington, *Colonel George of Mount Vernon*. During the next two years he was marking time, rewriting earlier plays or dramatizing the published work of others, and it was not until he had refreshed himself with visits to new fields that he returned to significant original work.

In March, 1897, Thomas went to Arizona to collect material for a new play. How close was his observation, and how stimulating, are revealed both in his autobiography and in the play itself. For *Arizona* is reality—here is the West painted in primary colors, but with no exaggeration. From the moment the curtain rises on the courtyard of the Aravaipa Ranch, the conversation between Colonel Bonham and his father-in-law, Henry Canby, the owner of the ranch, reveals two types which govern the West of Arizona. Life has broadened Canby, who is one of the best-drawn figures in modern drama, but army tradition and discipline have narrowed Bonham. When the climax of the play arrives and Estrella, the Colonel's wife, is found in Lieutenant Denton's company late at night, and Denton's refusal to explain his presence leads to his enforced resignation from the army, the different ways in which Bonham and Canby react to the charge of theft, which Denton faces to save Estrella's honor, are in perfect keeping with their natures and their training. *Arizona* is not remarkable in its plot. The Colonel and the Colonel's lady and the two officers, one of whom is a cad and the other a gentleman, go back to *Shenandoah* and beyond it. Even a closer parallel to the climax of the play may be found in *The Galley Slave* and in Sardou's *Nos Bons Villageois*. But Thomas seems to have been inspired by real people whom he placed in well-tested dramatic situations, and he was not above substituting the Spanish War for an Indian uprising when events made it advisable. When one looks back on *Arizona*, however, it is not Estrella and her love affairs that one remembers. It is Bonita, her younger sister, Denton's sweetheart, who becomes the heroine. She was drawn from a real woman, and she has the freshness and the open-mindedness which do not prevent her from being alluring. Tony, the *vaquero*, is one of the most vivid of the characters. Captain Hodgman, whose attempted flight with Estrella has placed Denton in his false position, had seduced Lina, the daughter of Sergeant Kellar. When this fact is discovered, Kellar threatens to shoot Hodgman, but Tony, who loves Lina, wastes no time in threats. He shoots Hodgman on sight, and at the first opportunity departs on the swiftest horse on the ranch. It is the justice which the West understands, and Canby puts their standard in a few brief sentences, which Thomas took from the conversation of his prototype:

Canby: (Pause) Er—a—Captain Denton. (*Pause.*) You know I—er— (*Pause. Bonita goes to Canby, who puts an arm about her.*) We take a man on here and ask no questions. We know when he throws his saddle on his horse, whether he understands his business or not. He may be a minister backslidin', or a banker savin' his last lung, or a train robber on his vacation—we don't care. A good many of our most useful men have made their mistakes. All we care about now is, will they stand the gaff? Will they set sixty hours in the saddle, holdin' a herd that's tryin' to stampede all the time? Now, without makin' you any fine talk, you can give any-one of 'em the fifteen ball. I don't know whether it's some-thin' you learned in the school, or whether you just happened to pick the right kind of a grandfather, or what. But your equal has never been in this territory in my time.

It was a far cry from *Arizona* to *Oliver Goldsmith*, first pro-duced in Albany on November 30, 1899, and written for Stu-art Robson because he looked like Oliver Goldsmith. Thomas points out in his introduction to the printed play that the dramatist's failure in drawing a historical character is usually due to his attempt to cover "all the attractive incidents in a biography rather than to grasp formally and treat thoroughly the principal dramatic happening." The greatest event in Goldsmith's life was the production of *She Stoops to Conquer.* Thomas, therefore, made Goldsmith's conception and produc-tion of that play and the consequence of its success the mo-tives of his own drama. He placed the first Act in an English country house which Goldsmith mistakes for an inn, and he surrounded him with a group of which Samuel Johnson, Ed-mund Burke, David Garrick, James Boswell and Mary Horn-eck are the main figures. In the second Act *She Stoops to Conquer* is in rehearsal on the stage of the Covent Garden The-atre and there is a clever scene in which Garrick shows the rival company how to produce the play. In the last Act, laid in Goldsmith's garret, the struggle in his heart between his

Best wishes
Augustus Thomas

love for Mary and his feeling that he is not a fit husband provides the element of conflict, which is not indeed very convincing. Atmosphere rather than action is the salient quality of *Oliver Goldsmith*, but the picture of Eighteenth Century character and setting is thoroughly well done.

Although Thomas journeyed to the West again in search of material for his next play, *Colorado* was not a success, and he turned from the depiction of American life in its more significant phrases to the production of light comedy, bordering on farce. Indeed even before *Colorado* was produced, Thomas had built up from a real incident an amusing play, first called *Treadway of Yale*, but later rechristened *On the Quiet*. A young actor had allowed his marriage with a wealthy girl to be postponed until he had gone through college, at the stipulation of her family, who agreed to support him during his course at Harvard. When they had safely separated the lovers, they calmly notified the actor that the support was withdrawn. In *On the Quiet*, Bob Treadway and Agnes Colt are secretly married before he enters Yale, and the manner in which he meets all the complications of the situation until her brother apparently forces him into the marriage reminds one of the imperturbable heroes of Gillette.

For this type of comedy, it is essential that the circumstances should constantly threaten to engulf the hero, and Thomas showed a remarkable ability in making plausible situations which by their unusual quality render the position of the central character insecure. In *The Earl of Pawtucket* (1903), the idea of an English nobleman representing himself as an American in order to pursue a charming American woman, who is really the divorced wife of the man whose name he has taken, seems at first glance absurd. But it is just the stupidity, courage and good breeding so characteristic of the type of British gentleman the Earl represents which bring him safely through complications before which a more agile mind would have faltered. Thomas wrote the play for Lawrence D'Orsay, an English actor who had played in only minor parts, and against the judgment of a practical manager like Charles Frohman, he scored a popular success. In *The Other Girl* (1903), the attempted elopement of Catherine Fulton, a girl of refinement, with an engaging prize fighter, and the substitution of Estelle Kitteridge, who risks her own reputation and her ultimate happiness to save her friend from committing an act of folly, again seem far-fetched. But once more the art of the playwright presented a plausible series of situations, including the arrest of the prize fighter and his companion for running over the *fiancé* of Catherine Fulton. *Mrs. Leffingwell's Boots* (1905) is a clever portrayal of the havoc that may be made by an irresponsible young man who has been injured by a blow on the head and who yet remains at large. Dick Ainslie has preyed upon his friend Walter Corbin, forged his name, and by placing the boots of Mrs. Leffingwell at his door has brought upon him the jealousy of her husband and broken Corbin's engagement to Mabel Ainslie. But this serious side of the shield is kept as dark as possible while a series of amusing complications takes place at and after a dinner party during "the worst snowstorm since Conkling died." Dick is cured by osteopathy and the last sentence reveals the fact that Corbin had suffered all this obloquy patiently because his hand had accidentally struck the blow which made Dick abnormal.

Thomas knew that the essence of light comedy is relief. He therefore never let it descend into mere fooling, but there was always in the structure of the play some note of sincerity. The Earl of Pawtucket might have avoided some of his difficulties if he had not been so thoroughly a gentleman. Estelle Kitteridge could have cleared herself by a word had it not been for the gratitude she felt for benefits unforgot. Walter Corbin suffered silently until his accidental victim was restored to sanity. The central characters win over circumstances—that is comedy. But they also win and keep the sympathy of the audience. That is the reason for the response which these plays evoked at the time and which they still secure for the more permanent audience of the printed page.

Thomas has always been acutely aware of the period in which he worked. In the early nineties the clever stories of Richard Harding Davis and the equally clever illustrations of Charles Dana Gibson were establishing types of men and women which have now become conventional. Thomas dramatized *Soldiers of Fortune* (1902), a novelette out of which Davis had himself made a play, and he built up from the pictures of Gibson an entertaining comedy, *The Education of Mr. Pipp* (1905), in which the selfmade man, slight physically but with shrewd common sense, is led through England and France by his aggressive wife, accompanied by his daughters and their lovers. The best element in these adaptations was the conversation, which at least in the second case was largely of Thomas's invention. His resourcefulness is shown also by his quick turning of failure into success with *The Embassy Ball* in 1906. But his desire to work with more enduring material sent him back to a motive which had interested him for many years and which led to the writing of his most successful play.

In 1890 Thomas had written a one-act play for A. M. Palmer, called *A Constitutional Point.* It was not acted then, but after trying it out at the Lambs Club sixteen years later, Thomas was encouraged to build on it a four-act play. The first sketch dealt with telepathy, and grew of Thomas's association in 1888 with Washington Irving Bishop. He pictured an elderly judge who had in his youth been in love with a girl who was fond of the odor of mignonette. Her daughter comes to plead with the judge to save her boy who is under sentence of death for murder. She hands him an old letter, written by him to her mother, who had kept it among her papers. The odor seems to the judge a symbol of the departed girl and he believes he has been in communion with her spirit. Bret Harte's *Newport Legend,* Thomas tells us, was the primary inspiration for this motive, which animates the second Act of *The Witching Hour.* But the playwright knew that this motive was not sufficient for a full-length play and he added to it the theme of hypnotism and the responsibility a person assumes who influences the mind of another. Clay Whipple, the boy whose mother has appealed to Justice Prentice, has a great fear of a cat's-eye and strikes and accidentally kills a man who annoys him with a pin containing such a stone. This takes place at the gambling establishment, in Louisville, of Jack Brookfield, a man who is above his business, and who has lost the chance to marry Clay's mother, Helen, through her dislike of his occupation. Brookfield has hypnotic power. Clay is convicted of murder, but the case is appealed on the ground that the trial has not been public, admission having been restricted to those favored by the district attorney, Hardmuth, Clay's disappointed rival in love. Justice Prentice at Helen's appeal orders a new trial. In an interview with Brookfield he shows the danger of the use of the hypnotic power. Brookfield asks him, "You mean it's bad for the man who tries it?" and the judge replies: "I mean that it constantly opens to the investigator new mental heights, higher planes—and every man, Mr. Brookfield, is ill in some manner who lives habitually on a lower level—than the light he sees."

Brookfield determines, however, to save Clay by this power. While the jury is deliberating, he publishes in the newspaper his accusation that Hardmuth has organized the plot by which a former governor had been murdered. He believes that the thousands who read this accusation will by the combined effect of their belief in it, so influence the minds of the jury against Hardmuth that his conduct of the case will react in favor of Clay and lead to the boy's acquittal. This proves true, and Hardmuth bursts into Brookfield's rooms intending to shoot him. Brookfield flashes a large drop light into his face and with the words, "You can't shoot—that gun—you can't even hold it," hypnotizes Hardmuth so that he drops the derringer in amazement. This scene, which was put on in fear and trembling, proved successful on the stage. That it does not represent accurately the process of hypnotism is of less importance than the fact of its apparent effect upon the audience. But Thomas does not leave the matter here. In the last Act he establishes the main motive of the play through Brookfield's journey across the state line with Hardmuth to save the latter from the consequences of the accusation. Brookfield gives Helen the reason:

Long before Scovill was killed, I thought he deserved killing and I thought it could be done just as it was done. . . . I never breathed a word to a living soul, but Hardmuth planned it exactly as I dreamed it, and by God, a guilty thought is almost as criminal as a guilty deed.

The part of Jack Brookfield was taken by John Mason, who gave a remarkable interpretation of the mingled lights and shades of the gentleman gambler's character. He is an outstanding figure, as is Justice Prentice, for both represent power and chivalry. It is essentially a man's play, for the women's parts are secondary in interest, though not negligible. Its greatest significance lies in its competent adaptation to drama of the theme of the occult, handled with discrimination, and never suffered to become too abstract.

The success of *The Witching Hour* and the belief that the public were interested in themes which savored of the less obvious phases of human influence and relationship, prompted Thomas to the writing of *The Harvest Moon*, first produced in October, 1909. Its theme was the sinister effect of suggestions of evil which are planted in the mind of a young girl by her aunt, one of those women who are never happy unless they control the actions of others. Dora Fullerton desires to become an actress, and her temperament makes her susceptible to the reception of such ideas. Her mother had gone to Paris to study and had finally been divorced from Professor Marshall Fullerton and married to M. Vavin, a French playwright. They had quarreled and Vavin in a fit of pique had told his wife that they were not legally married. When Dora is born Madame Vavin does not inform him and at her mother's death

Fullerton finds the baby and brings her up as his own. His sister, Cornelia, who feels that her brother's life has been ruined, plants in Dora's mind the belief that her mother was unreliable, impulsive and vain, and that she will inherit these qualities. Consequently she almost wrecks her own life when her family's opposition to the theatre and to her lover, a young playwright, calls for courage and decision. The visit of M. Vavin to this country and his delicate handling of the situation make the play. Vavin plants countersuggestions skilfully, and brings his daughter and her lover together in his apartment, using the subtle influence of colors in the production of moods. This scene, which was first tried out as a one-act play at the Lambs Club and has been recently revived with George Nash, the original creator of the part of Vavin, is remarkably effective, considering the difficulty of portraying such abstract themes on the stage. *The Harvest Moon* was an artistic rather than a popular success. The theme is too remote perhaps for general interest, and Thomas's evident care not to overstress the emotional relations of the central characters makes them less quick in their appeal.

Thomas carried over to his next original play, *As a Man Thinks*, produced in New York March 13, 1911, the idea of mental healing, but he incorporated it in a much more vivid and compelling personality, that of the liberal Jewish doctor, Samuel Seelig. As before, he tried the effect of a one-act play at The Lambs in which this doctor should cure a patient by driving out the ideas that were making him ill. As this sketch was well received he built up a play of four acts in which he added the theme that the trust of man in his wife's fidelity is the basic fact of our civilization, and he joined these themes through the character of Dr. Seelig, into a compact and vigorous drama. In it Thomas gave the answer to the sentimental discussion of the double standard of morality which is rampant in literature. Frank Clayton, a prosperous magazine proprietor, neglects his wife, who, in a moment of exasperation, visits the rooms of Benjamin De Lota, a Jew to whom

she had been engaged before she met Clayton. Clayton orders
her to leave his house, but Dr. Seelig tells him their boy's life
is in danger and Clayton leaves himself. In the next act, Dr.
Seelig, in answer to Elinor's protest against the unfairness of
the world's judgments, replies:

Seelig: Elinor. [*Pause.*] Do you hear that rattle of the railroad?
Elinor: Yes.
Seelig: All over this great land thousands of trains run every
day starting and arriving in punctual agreement because this
is *a woman's world.* The great steamships, dependable
almost as the sun—a million factories in civilization—the
countless looms and lathes of industry—the legions of labor
that weave the riches of the world—all—all move by the
mainspring of man's faith in woman—man's *faith.*
Elinor: I want *him* to have faith in me.
Seelig: This old world hangs together by love.
Mrs. Seelig: Not man's love for woman.
Seelig: No—nor woman's love for man, but by the love of both—
for the children.
Elinor: Dick!
Seelig: Men work for the children because they believe the children are—their own—*believe.* Every mother *knows* she is
the mother of her son or daughter. Let her be however
wicked, no power on earth can shake that knowledge.
Every father believes he is a father only by his faith in
the woman. Let him be however virtuous, no power on earth
can strengthen in him a conviction greater than that faith.
There is a double standard of morality because upon the
golden basis of woman's virtue rests the welfare of the world.

Clayton, maddened by the disclosure of Elinor's engagement
to De Lota, of which he had been ignorant, doubts even that
Dick is his son. He becomes ill through brooding over the
matter and Dr. Seelig cures him of his delusion by a literal
application of the teachings of Christ. "There is nothing so
disappointing," Dr. Seelig says, "as a satisfied revenge."
Without sentimentality, with just enough but not too much
repression of emotion, Thomas reunites the family. No one

who has had a child can see or read the last Act of *As a Man Thinks* without recognizing that the playwright has placed on the stage the inexorable truth, but represented it in the spirit of the Seer who modified the justice of the Old Law by the mercy of the New. As in *The Capitol*, the liberality with which Thomas views life enabled him to treat a difficult theme without offense, and his skill brought on the stage real people, who talk in brief, natural sentences, with not a word wasted. John Mason made a deep impression as Dr. Seelig and Chrystal Herne *"was* Mrs. Clayton," to quote the playwright's phrase.

It would seem that after a remarkably productive period, a dramatist must allow his creative powers to lie fallow or else it is likely that he will not produce work that is representative of his inventive powers at their best. Several of Thomas's plays from 1911 to 1917 were done in collaboration or were rewriting of other material like *Three of Hearts*. *Indian Summer* (1913) contains a sympathetic study of an artist in his forties, who wins the love of a girl because she learns to see beauty through his eyes. But the play does not hang together although the dialogue is crisp and telling. *Rio Grande*, produced first in Chicago in 1916, was laid on our borders during the trouble with Mexico, which entered into the play very little. The plot is reminiscent of *Arizona*, for it has to do with an illicit love affair between the Colonel's wife and a young officer. The difference lies in the real guilt of the lovers and the tragic suicide of the lieutenant, off the stage. But notwithstanding an eloquent plea of the Major's wife for forgiveness on the Colonel's part, because the experience will be of spiritual value to the young wife, the audience remained cold.

In *The Copperhead*, which opened at Hartford in January, 1918, Thomas triumphed over almost insuperable difficulties in order to produce the effect he desired. He took from a story by Frederic Landis, *The Glory of His Country*, the idea of a patriot serving his cause by pretending to be a sympathizer with the Confederacy, and thereby circumventing the movements of that body of Northern men who were organized to obstruct the United States Government. Of course, a similar motive had occurred in *The Spy* and in Woodworth's *The Widow's Son,* and Thomas's treatment was free.

From the dramatic point of view, it is hard to keep an audience in ignorance of the spy's real character; indeed, Thomas does not attempt to do so. Milt Shanks, a farmer on an Illinois farm, is just a plain, apparently commonplace person. Yet Lincoln, who had been his neighbor, knows his man, and when the plays opens, Shanks is represented as a member of the "Knights of the Golden Circle" or "Copperheads," as they were called, from the insignia which they wore at the beginning of the struggle. The first two Acts are striking pictures of a little Illinois farming village at the outbreak of the war and at the fall of Vicksburg. It is a faithful portrayal of life which Thomas knew at first hand. Shanks brings upon himself the hatred of his neighbors, the intolerance which war always produces, and even his wife and son shrink from him. When Joey is killed at Vicksburg the boy leaves word with "Newt" Gillespie that his father is not to see him in his coffin, and the tragedy of the loneliness of the man is infinitely touching. Forty years later, Shanks is an old man, and under the stress of his fear that his granddaughter will lose her appointment at the school on account of his past, he breaks his silence in one of the most moving utterances of our stage. Thomas with a fine instinct represented the influence of Lincoln through the life mask of his face and hand. It seemed as though Lincoln were indeed present, so vividly did the words as spoken by Lionel Barrymore project this spirit into that commonplace room.

Shanks: Colonel, do you recollec' the time you druv me to the train in March o' sixty-one?
Hardy: Very well. You went to look at cattle.
Shanks: That's what I told you. I wuz called to Washington by Lincoln, an' two days later, at night, in his library—White House—he walked over to'erd a winder, and without turning round he says: "Milt—" Funny I remember a clock tickin'

on the mantelpiece—I sez: "Mr. President—" (*Pause.*)
"Milt, how much do you love yer country?" (*Pause.*) "I
cahilate I'd die fur it," I sez. "Thousands o' boys is a-cryin'
to do that," he sez. Then he turned round. "Would you
give up sumpin' more'n life?" "Try me," I sez. The President run his hands through his hair an' went on: "It means
to be odious in the eyes of men and women—ter eat yer heart
out—alone—fer yer can't tell yer wife—ner child—ner
friend." "Go on," I sez. "The Southern sympathizers are
organizing in our state—really worse than the soldiers. I
want you ter jine them Knights o' the Golden Circle, the
Copperheads—ter be one of them—their leader, if you kin.
I need you, Milt. Yer country needs you." (*Pause.*) Hadn't
been two minutes since he was laffin', but he lifted his hands,
and it seemed we wuz the only folks in the world—and that
clock—funny I remember that. (*Pause.*) "I'll do it," I sez.
He tuk a little flag out o' his pocket—like as not this very
one—put it on the table like I'm puttin' it. (*Pause.*) "As
Chief Magistrate of the Nation, I'll muster you inter the
Nation's service," he said. He took my hand and laid it
where the blue is and all the stars, and put his hand over
mine. Only open, of course—and said nuthin'—jes' looked
in my eyes—an' looked—(*Pause.*) Well, I jined 'em. It was
terrible, when I couldn't tell my boy—

The stress of war made the audiences more than usually
responsive, but even when read in calmer moments, *The Copperhead* stirs the sense of national feeling. It is significant
that of the five best plays of the Civil War, four should have
a spy for a leading character, but unlike *Held by the Enemy*,
Secret Service and *Griffith Davenport*, *The Copperhead* has no
chivalric figure. He is individual, but he is also a type of the
undistinguished American, the average man, who in times of
national peril shows the potential devotion to his country
which has led him to give his best without display. The patriotic hero has always been a favorite subject for drama, but as
the race becomes more self-conscious his rôle becomes more difficult to establish to a sophisticated audience. It was a difficult task, also, to preserve any unity, with such an interval,
and yet it is questionable whether the effect could have been

secured without it. For as the old man goes on in his halting utterance, the sense of the forty years of spiritual exile in his native town makes his words poignant with the dignity that memory gives to sacrifice.

Since *The Copperhead* Thomas has not produced any very significant plays. *Speak of the Devil* (1920) is a melodrama, in which the love story of a returned war worker, Mildred Hanslow, and a French marquis whom she has nursed, turns from a promising beginning into a chaotic plot. *Nemesis* (1921) was a serious attempt to show the futility of the evidence based on the impression taken from the finger tips of a supposed criminal. Louis Jovaine, a sculptor, is in love with Marcia Kallan and her husband lays a trap for him. Kallan secures an impression of Jovaine's finger prints from some clay which he takes from the studio and he has rubber stamps made from these impressions. He then forces his wife to call Jovaine to their apartment and during the interval of waiting he kills Marcia and distributes the marks of her lover's fingers over the room and on the instrument with which he has killed her. Jovaine is convicted. The weakness of the play lies in the absence of anyone with whom the audience may sympathize. Interest is first directed toward the husband, but his cold-blooded action in laying the trap chills any feeling of compassion for him, and the playwright does not succeed in transferring it to the lover or the wife, who treats her marital obligations in too casual a fashion.

Still Waters, a propaganda play directed against the prohibition of liquor, attracted wide attention when it was performed at Washington, September 7, 1925, with Thomas taking the leading part, that of a Senator who votes for prohibition because his constituents desire it, but who promises himself to vote as he believes if he is elected again. It suffers from the defect of all propaganda plays and while the conversation is direct and telling, the character drawing does not rise to that of his great moments. In the character of Senator Clayborn, Thomas represented that intense love for personal liberty of action which has been characteristic of the man as well as the playwright.

Indeed, one may question whether this love of liberty, in the truly American sense, is not the controlling motive in the selection of themes by Augustus Thomas. The most obvious characterization of his work as a whole would be that he stands first, for the description of definite sections and of distinct phases of American life, as in *Alabama, Arizona* and *The Copperhead,* and second, for the reflection in drama of modes and problems of modern interest, such as the hypnotism and telepathy of *The Witching Hour,* the moral suggestion of *The Harvest Moon* and the double standard of morality in *As a Man Thinks.* These are certainly the backgrounds and the motives in which he has been most at home, and they prove conclusively the native quality of his talent.

But back of motive and scene there is always the theme and a more searching analysis of Thomas's work reveals a basic interest in those situations in which a human being becomes the center of a struggle between the intense desire for personal liberty and the circumstances which obstruct that desire in its fulfillment. The roots of all significant drama have, of course, lain in the struggle of the individual against fate or his surroundings. But the importance of Thomas's contribution lies in the distinctly American way he has treated that theme. Liberty is desirable, but in the European drama of revolt it is so desirable that everything else, from the family to the state, must go down before it. In Thomas's plays, as in the vast majority of American lives, the individual's liberty is precious, but the conflict for its preservation is constructive, not merely destructive. The prejudice of Colonel Preston, in *Alabama,* which had crushed two lives, had to break down before the wider liberty of the reunited country. The strict discipline of the army, impersonated in Colonel Bonham in *Arizona,* is contrasted with the free life of the ranch where natural standards permit Denton to defy an artificial code. In *The Capitol,* Father Kennard represents the use through the

Church of financial pressure to save the individual liberty of the new Senator and to prevent the tyranny of monopoly. Jack Brookfield, in *The Witching Hour*, has tasted the delights of individual liberty to the full. He has lost much in doing so, and he realizes, when the knowledge of his hypnotic power comes to him, that power brings responsibility with it and that his liberty has to be merged into a wider usefulness. It has been shown in the analysis of *As a Man Thinks* how the claims of woman to share the liberty of man in sex morality have been rendered abortive not by moral standards but by the justice of nature. More privilege, more responsibility, is the universal situation. In *The Copperhead*, Milt Shanks lays on the altar of his country's need the right even to his wife's love and to his son's respect. But whatever the characters give up in relinquishing individual freedom returns in the only final reward of human conduct, the consciousness of their own self-respect.

It is not necessary to insist that this basic theme is exclusively American, but it is expressed in any case by Augustus Thomas in a native fashion. It is certainly profoundly true to human nature as represented by the normal man and woman in the United States, and it may well be that the potential liberty of a republic leads definitely to a sense of constructive responsibility, just as the potential subjection of a monarchy leads to the celebration of personal revolt.

From the purely artistic point of view, Thomas's plays are decidedly uneven in merit, and yet his construction and dialogue are not different so much in kind as in degree of excellence. The plays in which the themes are largest, and the motives most significant, are constructed with the finest skill and are provided with well-rounded characters who speak that clear straightforward language which is so economical of the hearer's attention. When Thomas became too abstract or dealt with a theme almost too subtle for the theatre, as in *The Harvest Moon*, the brilliant dialogue could not save the play. When he descended to trivialities of plot or situation, as in *Speak of the Devil,* or labored in developing a theme not really interesting, as in *Nemesis,* the charm is of course not there.   But in his best period, from *Arizona* to *The Copperhead,* he was the playwright to whom America turned with confidence for the drama that clothes significant ideas with power and restraint and the comedy that delights through kindly and adroit revelation of human frailty, and for that twenty years it did not turn in vain.

CHAPTER XI

CLYDE FITCH AND THE DEVELOPMENT OF SOCIAL COMEDY

CLYDE FITCH was the product of two very different American traditions. His father, William Goodwin Fitch, went from Hartford, Connecticut, with his regiment during the Civil War and found at Hagerstown, Maryland, his future wife, Alice Clark, whose family were loyal to the Union. The influence of his mother, who came of a race that loved beauty in costume and background, is strong in Clyde Fitch, but there is also a trace of the New England sense of ethical values in the author of *The Truth* and *The City*.

William Clyde Fitch was born at Elmira, New York, May 2, 1865, his early childhood being spent in Schenectady, where, like John Howard Payne, he organized and directed groups of children in productions of various kinds. Even in his school days at Hartford and at the Holderness School in New Hampshire, he showed that independence of public opinion which reveals character but which pays the tribute the tribe demands of those who are indifferent to the fetish of uniformity. Clyde Fitch's letters from his boarding school reveal, however, a fairly normal boy, learning Latin and Greek and French rather easily, taking part in sports when his slight physique permitted, and objecting strenuously to being considered "delicate." At Amherst College, which he entered in 1882, he pursued his self-determined course, wearing clothes which were the theme of campus comment but winning his recognized place as one of the leaders of the dramatic interests of Amherst. He not only acted such parts as Lydia Languish in *The Rivals* and Peggie Thrift in *The Country Girl*, but he directed Wycherley's play, painted scenery and designed costumes. His

265

facility in composition had already declared itself, for he composed an entire act for a college burlesque opera in an afternoon, and his letters reveal the love for the stage which was to become the great passion of his life. A constant contributor of social verse to his college magazine and the Class Poet of '86, his own taste led him toward literature as a career, but his father desired him to study architecture and disliked the stage.

Like Bronson Howard, Fitch went to New York in 1886 to conquer a position. While waiting for his opportunity, he made a living by tutoring, by readings, and by occasional short stories, and he was haunting the theatres. His first European visit came in 1888 and made a deep impression upon his instinctive love for the concretely beautiful. Here he wrote the first draft of *Frédérick Lemaître*.

At last his opportunity came. Richard Mansfield had, at the suggestion of William Winter, selected Beau Brummell, the Georgian dandy, as a fit character around whom a play could be written. Dithmar, the critic of the New York *Times*, suggested to Mansfield in November, 1889, that Clyde Fitch could write such a play and a contract was made by which Fitch was engaged to write for Mansfield on salary and royalty. To Fitch the character and the setting appealed strongly and he began work at once, reading first the play on Beau Brummell by Blanchard Jerrold, and the *Life of George Brummell*, by William Jesse, on which it had been based. Fitch received many suggestions from Mansfield, to whom naturally he deferred as to an older man and a successful actor who had himself written plays. From Jerrold's play, which is laid in Calais and Caen, he took the idea of Brummell's befriending a young *protégé* who desires to marry the daughter of a rich merchant. In *Beau Brummell* this motive is intensified by the substitution of his own nephew, and the attempt of Brummell to save himself by a rich marriage which he relinquishes for his nephew's sake. Other incidents, such as the appearance of the imaginary guests just before his death, are found in the

older play and indicated in Jesse's biography.[1] Fitch followed
the narrative less closely than Jerrold and laid the first three
Acts in England, transferring the arrest of Brummell for debt
to London, for the effective climax of the third Act.

How difficult became the task of writing a play for Mansfield is apparent in Fitch's letters, and the project was indeed
for a time abandoned. But on May 17, 1890, *Beau Brummell* was performed at the Madison Square Theatre and made
a profound impression upon the discriminating critics, even
if others were unable to see even its more obvious merits. At
the very beginning of his career Fitch was to meet that lack
of understanding on the part of those who should have com-
prehended the delicacy and distinction of his art, but also
from the outset there were minds capable of anticipating the
calmer judgment of time.[2] For *Beau Brummell* has taken its
secure place in dramatic literature. The episodic nature of its
scenes, the preference of dialogue to action which disturbed
the judgment of the early nineties, could not prevent the substantial success of this masterpiece of the comedy of manners.
Beau Brummell is essentially a play built upon a striking personality, whose wit, polish, even whose heartlessness, made
him "good theatre," while at just the right moment, Fitch lets
the essentially heroic character of his creation shine through
the mask of his personality and dominate the situation. This
heroic quality was largely the creation of the playwright, for
the real George Brummell was a gentleman who lived an apparently selfish life and died a miserable death in exile. The two
qualities the playwright took from his original were courage
and social ease. Such episodes as the cutting of Brummell by
the Prince of Wales and the retort of Brummell—"Sherry,
who's your fat friend?"—are traditional rather than historic.
The climax of the second Act, in which Brummell, after defending Vincent, the city merchant, from the consequences of

---

[1] Jesse, Captain [William], *The Life of George Brummell*, 2v. London, 1844, II, 293–4.
[2] See the appreciative and penetrating critique by "Fileur" in *The Theatre Magazine*,
VI (1890), 440–1, to which are appended reviews of a contradictory nature in the
daily press.

his folly and drawing upon himself the anger of the Prince, says to the latter, "Wales, ring the bell," was chosen from among the anecdotes which Jesse[1] states are apocryphal. But the character as shown in Jesse's account grows in stature in the play, and the loyalty of Mortimer, the valet, contrasts sharply with the treachery of Isidore, Brummell's own valet. The loyalty of the servant is a fine dramatic motive, for it implies qualities in a master which do not appear on the surface, especially in such a hero as Brummell, to whom restraint is so essential.

Into the heated controversy over the authorship of the play which raged at the time of its production it is not necessary here to go.[2] Fitch's own words sum up the situation:

The idea of a play on *Beau Brummell* is, I believe, Mr. William Winter's. The execution of that play—Mr. Winter claims it has been an execution in more senses than one—some of the business and the great bulk of the dialogue are mine. The artistic touch, some of the lines in the comedy (not the important ones), and the genius that has made it a success are Mr. Mansfield's.

To any student of Clyde Fitch's plays, his touch shows unmistakably in *Beau Brummell*. Among the talents of Fitch the three most prominent—the ability to visualize any place or period in terms of its social values, the power to incarnate virtues or vices in characters who are essentially dramatic, and the gift of writing clever dialogue—all these show in his first stage success. While no attempt was made at historical accuracy, for George IV and Sheridan were kept alive for years in order to attend Brummell's death scene, the vanity, the heartlessness, the cold calculating immorality of the age, which are typified in the person of George IV, live on the stage. Beau Brummell, who meets ruin without the flicker of an eyelid, was the first of those searching studies of men and women pos-

[1] I, 254–5.
[2] See Winter, William, *Life and Art of Richard Mansfield*, New York, 1910, I, 128–36; II, 63–88, 301–12, written with prejudice and containing obvious misstatements; *Clyde Fitch and His Letters*, esp. pp. 65–8, which contain Fitch's letter in the Boston *Evening Transcript*, April 13, 1891.

sessed by one absorbing trait, later to be joined by Becky
Warder and Jinny Austin. The language of the characters
is suited exactly to their parts, still a bit conventional, for
Beau Brummell is essentially of the theatre. "Asides" are not
infrequent and every other part was subordinated to the demands of the star. Mansfield was not an easy man to work for
and even the ending had to be changed to suit his anticipation
of popular judgment. Fitch wished to have the Beau die in his
poverty. Mansfield insisted on a happy ending and suggested
that the King be reconciled with Brummell. Fitch wrote, as a
compromise, based partially on the older play, the scene in
which the Beau's friends come back in his fancy and reappear
in the flesh only at the time of his death.

If this did not furnish a happy ending it did provide a
happy compromise, for in Mansfield's hands it was a fitting
climax to an almost perfect union of playwright and actor.
The part was exactly suited to Mansfield and he kept it in his
répertoire until he left the stage. The relation between Fitch
and Mansfield did not continue, although Mansfield more than
once made overtures to him. Clyde Fitch, however, had secured
his start.

His one-act plays, *Frédérick Lemaître* and *Betty's Finish,*
were produced in Boston in December, 1890. Of these, *Frédérick Lemaître* is of especial interest for, although it was produced after *Beau Brummell,* it had been originally written in
1888 in Paris. It is a charming character study laid in that
city in 1848. Lemaître is an actor who, in order to prove to
Madeleine Fleury, a young stage-struck milliner, that she will
never succeed, improvises a scene in which a young husband
who has been abandoned by his wife acts the rôle of a brokenhearted man. Lemaître has hoped to charm her by his conduct, but the vividness of his portrayal sends her back to her
own lover whom she thought of deserting for the stage. The
characters are well conceived and the ability of Fitch to sense
a period and portray a man who is establishing his purpose by

indirect means is clearly shown. Fitch even used the real name of a French actor who long held a foremost position on the French stage.

Recognition came quickly from abroad, for Fitch was commissioned to write a play for Mrs. John Wood, to be produced at the Royal Court Theatre in 1891. *Pamela's Prodigy* is an amusing farce comedy, laid in London and on the sands of Margate about 1830. The dialogue is bright, but the play has no very great distinction. It was the first of his plays to be published and was charmingly illustrated by Virginia Gerson. Clyde Fitch was still primarily a man of letters. His novel, *A Wave of Life*, had appeared in 1891, but he wisely abandoned the field of fiction for one in which his talent could be more adequately shown.

A Modern Match, produced March 14, 1892, at the Union Square Theatre, was his first full-length play of modern social life. It is a study of the vain and selfish woman who leaves her husband at the moment of his financial ruin, and returning twelve years later is refused admittance to her daughter's wedding. The "asides," the artificial nature of the dialogue in certain portions, cannot conceal the cleverness of the playwright who covers with deft touches the thin plot and conventional situations by a mantle of interest. But the play is of most significance through its revelation of the advance Fitch made in the art of his later period. When Mr. and Mrs. Kendal produced *A Modern Match* in London, the scene and characters were Anglicized and it was renamed *Marriage, 1892*.

This early period of Fitch's work was distinctly one of experiment. His original work like *The Harvest* was tentative, being revived later in another form. *April Weather*, written for Sol Smith Russell, while it was a success in Chicago in 1893, failed later in New York.

Much more successful was *His Grace de Grammont* (1894), a charming comedy of manners of the court of Charles II, in which Otis Skinner [1] portrayed the gallant cavalier who dares

[1] See Skinner, Otis, *Footlights and Spotlights*, Chap. XIV.

the wrath of the King to win Mistress Hamilton, whom Charles desires to make his mistress. Maud Durbin, now Mrs. Skinner, played Mistress Hamilton. The sketchy plot is sufficient to carry the dialogue, but the play depended more upon the stage pictures than upon any reality in its depiction of character. Yet Fitch considered his portrait of Lady Castlemaine an important contribution, and there is something appealing in this discarded mistress of Charles who is trying to protect her unwilling rival from her royal lover.

Mistress Betty (1895), another romantic comedy of manners, was written for Modjeska and acted for a brief period, but the illness of the great actress closed the engagement. It was revived by Viola Allen in 1905 as *The Toast of the Town.* While the drama is reminiscent of *Nance Oldfield, Peg Woffington,* and all plays in which an actress simulates a part in order to convince a man she loves of her infidelity, nevertheless it has a charm and flavor of its own. Betty Singleton, who marries the Duke of Malmsbury, does so because she idealizes him; he marries her because she appeals to his vanity. She is the admired of everyone and he wishes to possess her. The consequent disillusionment of both and the tragedy that leaves her dying,[1] half crazed, in a little garret, are logical enough, but it is not the plot that is important. The characterization of the Eighteenth Century English patrician, with his or her cold-blooded attitude toward those less fortunately situated, is well done. The situations are built up cleverly, especially the farewell of Betty to the stage at the curtain of the first Act and the scene in which she pretends to love Lord Phillips, in order that the Duke will for his own happiness leave her, although her heart is breaking. The final curtain, in which she repeats while mad the speech of farewell she had given so gallantly in the first Act, is deeply moving. The conversation at times is in Fitch's best manner. The dialogue between the old man who tends Betty at the wretched lodging house to

---

[1] *Mistress Betty* ended with the death of the heroine. *The Toast of the Town* had a happy ending.

which she has retreated is worthy of him in his shrewdest moments, and provided Ferdinand Gottschalk with a part which made a profound impression upon the audience.

Meanwhile Fitch was constantly turning to the French drama for inspiration. He made a stage success with his adaptation of *Le Veglione* of Bisson and Carré under the title of *The Masked Ball* (1892) in which John Drew and Maude Adams were the stars. Its sole interest lies in the skill with which he preserved the French atmosphere of an amusing but very light farce-comedy. In this he kept the scene in France, but in *The Social Swim* (1893), based on Sardou's *La Maison Neuve*, the scene is transferred to New York City. It is a study of the young couple who leave their home expecting social progress and who meet disaster. When Daly had adapted this play in 1874 as *Folline*, he had kept the scene in France. *An American Duchess* (1893), from the French of Henri Lavedan, a satire on the shams of society and politics, proved a failure.

In *Bohemia* (1896), an adaptation of *La Vic de Bohème*, by Murger and Barrière, Fitch sacrificed the French atmosphere by keeping Mimi alive and preserving the proprieties to a degree that is absurd when dealing with such material. He varied the source of his adaptations by turning to the German of Ludwig Fulda and producing with Leo Ditrichstein *The Superfluous Husband* (1897), a well-constructed domestic drama of the Fulda type with some Fitch touches in the dialogue. The scene is transferred to New York where the conflict of husband and wife is set against an appropriate background.

Through these adaptations Fitch was learning his art and to a certain extent they bear evidence of being potboilers, to provide Fitch with the surroundings which his inherent love of beauty craved. His frank revelation in his letters of his reasons for writing *The Moth and the Flame*, a melodrama based on the earlier one-act play *The Harvest*, explains clearly why it is not of real significance. The party in the first Act with the head of the house lying dead upstairs, a suicide, is one of those effective contrasts which Fitch loved, but the rather lurid relations which develop later hurt the play. It proved a great popular success, however, and helped to establish Fitch in a position of independence in which he could work to please himself. This position was strengthened by the success of *Nathan Hale* (1898), the first of his plays based on American history. It was, however, not the history which carried the play into popular favor, but the human relations. Fitch follows correctly the main outlines of Hale's life up to his capture by the British, but the details of the council of war at which he volunteers are absurd and probability is cheerfully set at naught in order to heighten, through the refusal of all the other officers, the effect of his own sacrifice. The last days of Hale are still a matter of dispute and Fitch took advantage of this obscurity to invent certain episodes. The unconscious reaction of the audience to the fitness of things was shown by the failure of the third Act to appeal in its first form. Hale and Alice Adams, his sweetheart who has been brought by a trick of the British officer to the place of Hale's capture, are left apparently alone. Of course the officer is watching and everyone, including the audience and except Hale, suspects the ruse. Hale insists on embracing Alice and therefore discloses his identity. The audience, feeling instinctively that the business of a spy is to keep himself from discovery, did not respond to this outburst of emotion, and a change was made by which the discovery was brought about through Alice's negro servant. It was another illustration of the psychology of the auditor, who demands that the hero should not let his personal feeling conquer his patriotism, although the heroine may be permitted to do so. Fitch used effectively in the concluding scene the one dramatic episode in Hale's career, the traditional speech, "I only regret that I have but one life to lose for my country."

Fitch next departed from the scenes he knew, to write for Goodwin a Western melodrama, *The Cowboy and the Lady*, which succeeded in Philadelphia and on tour, but failed in

London, where Bret Harte[1] records his belief that Fitch was imitating him. Midge, the central female character, is certainly a Bret Harte heroine, but in reality Fitch did not know the West except at second hand, and the play, while it has some vivid moments, is not of significance. Fitch turned next to a field of which his knowledge was more sure. His mother's family had lived in Hagerstown, Maryland, and he knew the Southern atmosphere. The play of *Barbara Frietchie* (1899) opens on a charming scene in the evening, in which the boy and girl friendships of the central characters are seen ripening into love and are intensified by separation and the shadow of war. Again it is the sense of personal and social relations of families who have known each other for generations that Fitch establishes best. The war is only the background and history is violated cheerfully by making Barbara Frietchie a young girl who loves a Union officer, Captain Trumbull, and runs off to Hagerstown to marry him. The love-making gave Julia Marlowe an opportunity of which she made the most, and the tragic scene on the balcony in which she is shot waving the Union flag while her lover lies dead in her room inside was very effective. Fitch was vigorously criticized for falsification of history, and rather feebly defended himself on the grounds that Barbara Frietchie was ninety-six years of age and bedridden when Stonewall Jackson went through Fredericksburg. But Whittier's heroine, rightly or wrongly, had become established as the real Barbara and it was a dangerous experiment, since it distracted the attention of critics from the play itself. For while false to fact and legend, it is true to the spirit of the time from the social if not from the military point of view. It has not the vigor of *Secret Service* or the profound depth of *Griffith Davenport,* but it has a charm of its own, which helped largely in the success of its adaptation into the musical comedy, *My Maryland* (1927).

Fitch's adaptation of *Sapho* for Olga Nethersole, from the French of Alphonse Daudet and Adolphe Belot, is of interest

[1] *The Letters of Bret Harte,* p. 463.

chiefly as it reflects the change in taste between 1900 and our own day. The performance was stopped by the police on account of the scene in which Jean carries Sapho upstairs, an episode mild in comparison with what passes to-day without comment. It was in any case only an episode with him, for he was engaged in writing *The Climbers,* in which he entered upon his best period.

The Climbers is usually described as a satire upon New York society. If it were merely this it would not be of permanent worth. It is more truly a social comedy, depicting character and background realistically, and in truth every realistic picture of social life tends to satirize the elements of which it is composed. For men and women moving in social relations are not entirely natural, and the degrees of their repression provide a scale of effects which are fine material for a dramatist of the skill of Fitch in distinguishing lights and shades in social values. The first Act was a bit daring in 1900, and, running true to form, all the leading managers to whom it was offered refused the play. Yet Fitch knew better than they how effective it would be. It is laid in the home of Mrs. George Hunter, after she and her three daughters have returned from the funeral of their husband and father. The utter heartlessness of Mrs. Hunter and her youngest daughter, the finer nature of Blanche Sterling, the oldest daughter, who has married Richard Sterling, a weak but attractive man, are established by their reactions not only to the death of Hunter but to the fact of his having died a bankrupt. The manner in which wife and daughters attack and defend the dead husband and father, who, in order to meet the consequences of their extravagance, has gone down to ruin, is established with that almost uncanny knowledge of feminine nature Fitch possessed. But not only does Fitch reveal these characters; he creates another contrast, Ruth Hunter, the sister of the dead man, and in a few sentences makes one feel her essential superiority in breeding to her sister-in-law. He draws also, in Edward Warden, the reliable man, who has loved Blanche Sterling for years in silence, because she is his best friend's wife, and he has added two interesting types in Miss Godesby, the disillusioned woman, and Johnny Trotter, the climber who starts from the lowest social rung of them all. So much indeed did Ferdinand Gottschalk make of this part that Fitch developed it still further. No one but Fitch would have thought of the scene in which Miss Godesby and her friend bargain with Mrs. Hunter for her new Paris dresses, which now have become useless to the widow.

The theme of the play is perverted aspiration, for social standing, for money, even for happiness that is beyond the legitimate reach of the human being striving for it. But Fitch knew that such a theme alone would not carry a play, and he provided an appealing central motive in the love of Warden for Blanche Sterling, which watches over her and even her husband and becomes articulate only when Blanche reveals her own love for Warden. Then Warden turns to pursue his aspiration, illegitimate also, and his efforts to save Mrs. Sterling from disgrace and financial ruin hasten unintentionally Sterling's suicide. While this paves the way for happiness for Blanche and Warden, it is a perfectly natural solution for Sterling, who realizes too late that it is a cowardly act to avoid his responsibilities. The dialogue is extremely well done and, while there is not the unity of construction which came later, *The Climbers* is a masterly portrayal of human strength and human weakness. The strong characters are strong just in those qualities of courage, decision and unselfishness which kindle admiration, and the weak ones are tainted by a failing which, directed into a proper channel, might become legitimate ambition. They are consequently never uninteresting to the audience, for their motives always are comprehensible. *The Climbers* was well received in London, but the fact that royalty was not permitted to go to any play in which the theatre was in total darkness prevented complete success. Thus the powerful scene at the end of the second Act hurt its chances in England.

CLYDE FITCH

Captain Jinks of the Horse Marines (1901) is another period play, laid in the early seventies in New York City. The plot is thin and the character of the opera singer, Madame Trentoni, is idealized, but Fitch painted a real picture of the time and place, and the love story carried the play into great popular favor. *Captain Jinks* became a musical comedy in 1925. More significant was *Lovers' Lane* (1901), which had been written as early as 1894 and accepted by Sir George Alexander, but was not produced by him. It is a comedy laid in a small town in New York, the main theme being a contrast between the tolerant, lovable character of the minister, Thomas Singleton, and the intolerance and pettiness of his congregation. The psychology of the women of the rural community was as well known to Fitch as that of their sisters of the city, and his creation of Simplicity Johnson, the small girl whose jealousy of the woman the minister loves almost wrecks his happiness, proved again the fertility of his inventive power. Singleton is one of the few stage clergymen who seem real.

Clyde Fitch may be said to have reached the height of his popularity with the new century. Running to packed houses at the same time in New York were *The Climbers*, *Captain Jinks of the Horse Marines*, *Lovers' Lane* and *Barbara Frietchie*, plays of a varying order of merit and with widely different scenes. In the same prolific year of 1901, Beerbohm Tree produced his *Last of the Dandies*, a comedy of manners of the mid-Nineteenth Century, laid in London and Paris, with the central character of D'Orsay, a Victorian beau. *The Way of the World*, a melodrama of social life, laid in New York, was played by Elsie de Wolfe, with some success, though with little critical approval. The play is certainly not one of his best, but his inventive facility was shown in the introduction of the automobile in Central Park, as a means of bringing the characters together. For Annie Russell he wrote a play which was a departure from his usual manner. *The Girl and the Judge* was laid in "a Western state" and was based on an actual occurrence related by his friend Judge Galloway of Ohio.[1] The original incident was serio-comic, but the play is a study of a woman who is a kleptomaniac and of the power exercised over her by her daughter, who forces her to reveal her guilt. Fitch drew very well the characters of the Stanton family, the father who has been concealing his wife's shame but has taken to drink in consequence, and the girl who has unnatural responsibility thrust upon her, portrayed against the sinister background of the mother's vice. The judge, too, who must choose between his love for Winifred Stanton and his official duty, is adequately drawn and the dramatic sense of youth struggling against fate and human law for its right to happiness remains in the memory as the chief achievement of the play. Its production on December 4, 1901, marked the opening of the last play seen at the old Lyceum Theatre.

In justice to Fitch, it must be remembered that not all of these plays were written in 1901, and indeed it was not until November, 1902, that his next production occurred. *The Stubbornness of Geraldine* is one of that group which proceeded from the vivification of an emotion, in this case confidence, intensified by love. Geraldine Lang is an American girl with poise and standards. On the voyage home from Europe she meets Count Carlos Kinsey and they love each other. Circumstances bring him into disrepute. The continental custom of multiplying "Counts" by awarding the title to all the male members of a family leads to his being discredited by his brother's actions and even those who are nearest to Geraldine prove their affection by attempting to expose him. But all circumstances break in vain against her trust in the man she instinctively feels is honest and decent. As a matter of fact, Count Kinsey's reluctance to propose marriage to her until he had made good in his financial venture is overdrawn, but on the stage the American audiences found no difficulty in permitting the Hungarian noble to possess standards which would in reality have puzzled him. The very power of Geraldine's love

[1] *Letters of Fitch,* pp. 207–8.

seemed to have endowed him for the purposes of drama with qualities foreign to his real nature.

Fitch's methods of work are well illustrated in a letter written during the composition of this play.[1] "I feel very grateful to Bingham—so I got a very splendid play for her in Paris —— . . . and I have promised to do the version—it will take me perhaps three days." This play referred to was *The Frisky Mrs. Johnson* (1903), and the relative amount of effort expended upon it and one of the original plays indicates the reason for omitting any lengthy analysis, in nearly all cases, of his adaptations. He regretted indeed that he wrote such an adaptation as *The Bird in the Cage*, from the German of von Wildenbruch, but even in this absurd drama he could not help creating some interesting characters, and the Irish labor leader, played by Edward Harrigan, almost redeemed the play.

But there was no undue haste in the composition of the original plays, which were slowly matured and wrought out from the first conception to the last detail of stage setting. Eight years before *The Girl with the Green Eyes* was produced, in 1902, Fitch conceived the character of Jinny Austin, the woman who is possessed by the demon of jealousy. Here, as later in *The Truth*, he indicated that the fault was hereditary and wisely married her to a husband who was himself so incapable of jealousy that he could not sympathize with his wife's failing. He thus obtained a contrast from the start, and the very reticence of John Austin, born of his consideration for his wife's feelings, which prompts him to conceal her brother's secret marriage with Maggie the housemaid, contributes to feed her jealous suspicions. The invention of Fitch shows in the unusual scene in the Vatican, where the drama is all the more effective because the emotions aroused have to be repressed on account of the public character of the scene. The revelation which Ruth Chester makes to Austin that she and Geoffrey Tillman have been married comes like a blow to him, for he knows then that Geoffrey has committed bigamy

[1] *Letters*, p. 212.

and yet he has to conceal the fact from her and from Jinny. The instinct of the strong capable nature like Austin's is to take command of the situation, and Jinny's re-entrance into the art gallery at the moment when Ruth breaks down in her anxiety, precipitates the jealous feelings which have been held in check. The play proceeds logically to tragedy. After John has risked everything to conceal it, the disclosure of the bigamy is brought about in a powerful scene between Ruth Chester and Jinny, and John leaves his wife with the wreck of their happiness about her. She tries to commit suicide by turning on the gas and excluding the air, and the play would have been stronger if Fitch had ended it there. But probably in deference to the supposed desire on the part of the public for a happy ending, John Austin comes home in time to prevent Jinny's death.

In *Her Own Way* (1903) the most original character was that of Sam Coast, the millionaire who ruins the Carley family in order to force Georgiana Carley to marry him. Fitch proved in this play that he could draw masculine characters as well as feminine, and he portrayed admirably the conflict of wills, for Georgiana, fortified in her purpose by the right kind of love for Dick Coleman, wins eventually, while Sam Coast, whose passion is purely selfish, is helpless even with his money to back him. The opening scene at the children's party was one of those unusual stage pictures in which Fitch delighted.

Next came *Major André*, of which Fitch said, "It all lies closer to my heart, I think, than any other play."[1] Fitch made a careful study of the scene of André's capture but took liberties, as usual, with the historical details. He made André a sympathetic figure who departs on his mission with reluctance, largely because of the refusal of Sally Perkins, a Philadelphia girl, to marry him. Fitch established well the social atmosphere of New York City in 1780, the willingness of the American girls to flirt with the British officers but their real loyalty to their country. The dream of André on the night

[1] *Letters*, p. 251.

before his execution, in which he believes he sees Sally, is charmingly conceived. *Major André*, despite its fine qualities, ran only two weeks. Since Dunlap's *André* the same fate has overtaken the efforts of playwrights to vitalize the André story, and perhaps the knowledge that after all André went into the disgraceful episode with Arnold with his eyes open has prevented the success of the many efforts to place his personally attractive character on the stage. A comparison of the plays of Dunlap and Fitch will reveal the advance in skill of construction and natural quality of dialogue that has come with a century's experience. It will also reveal a certain sturdiness of character in the older play which is absent from Fitch's charming picture.

He had no time for regrets, for he was hard at work rehearsing *Glad of It*, which was produced in December, 1903, and was also a comparative failure. Yet there was something very real in the play, which took its characters through a department store, the stage of the Savoy Theatre and a boarding house in New Jersey. Fitch described it accurately when he said, "It is full of character types and subtleties of living instead of a story." The scenes and the minor characters are as real as any he has given us, and they drew an appreciative criticism from W. D. Howells, both in print and by personal letter. Howells was quite right when he said, "this is the way things happen, one after another, with only that loose allegiance to one another, that the facts of life have had happen to themselves, but that an artist had here recognized and recorded."[1] But *Glad of It* illustrated a stern law of the drama. Fidelity to life is not enough—the department store may be photographically reproduced, the stage rehearsal may be as funny as a perfect knowledge could make it, the boarding house may be absolutely true to such life, but unless these facts are fused into a coherent story, and unless important characters dominate the situations, there is no play. It was a sincere effort, however, and it was the occasion of a letter from Maude

[1] *Letters*, p. 258.

Adams to Fitch which is a remarkable analysis of his character
and the need it had of refreshment from even more vital sources
of inspiration than were provided by his usual experience.

I wish you could do some things that you'd hate to do. I wish
you could give over for a while your beloved Italy and your admired France and go to some place where the art is dead and life
is uppermost—common life. We live so much among people of
morbid tendencies, neuresthenics (I can't spell it), and the like—
that we begin to think they are real, and they are real of their
kind but it isn't a red blood kind.—You have been through a serious illness and a man doesn't recover from an illness like that in
a year, and while he's recovering he must be careful not to let himself drop back into an old environment of mind as well as of body.
Our illnesses are our vacations and we should use them to get
new turns of mind.—Don't get in a groove. Make yourself agree
with your critics for a time until you discover their secret—it is
a secret to them as well—they can't put in words the real thing
they criticize—they can't voice it—so you must discover it, but
when you've discovered it you'll find there will no longer be need
of it. Men of temperament, if they are very successful when they
are young, are in great danger. They either go to pieces or they
get two chances—and the second chance is usually better than the
first, if they are big men. It seems to me you're getting your
second chance.[1]

Seldom has an artist been better advised. What Fitch's
serious critics failed to understand was a certain overfineness
of perception which arose out of the very sensitiveness of his
impressions, and which led him to the study of feminine nature
because he found there a more fruitful field for his intuitive
talent. It cannot be said that Fitch followed the advice so
far as his work immediately following *Glad of It* is concerned,
for neither *The Coronet of a Duchess*, nor his two adaptations
from the French, *Granny* and *Cousin Billy*, marked any advance in his art. He drew in the first, however, a skillful picture of the Duke of Sundun, an English nobleman who marries
an American heiress, continues to keep his mistress, borrows
money from his wife to support "Pussy" Hawkins, and when

[1] *Letters*, pp. 256-7.

Milly demands a divorce, sells her freedom for cash. At the same time his manners remain impeccable and his steady adherence to his own peculiar standards of conduct make him more than a caricature. But the American characters were far inferior to those he drew later in *Her Great Match*, and the play was a definite failure. *Granny* was written to provide a star part for Mrs. Gilbert, then eighty-three years old. Fitch transferred the scene of *L'Aïeule* by Georges Michel to an American small town, with no local flavor. Granny first separates the husband of her dead daughter from his only son through her jealousy, and then secures the happiness of her grandson by providing him with a wife in the daughter of the woman she had traduced. There are some appealing scenes and Mrs. Gilbert made a personal success, but died suddenly while the play was on tour. In *Cousin Billy* he preserved the foreign scene for the first two acts, but he transformed one of Labiche's most striking characters to a caricature of a traveling American, possibly because the part was written to order for Francis Wilson.

The vital note is present, however, in *The Woman in the Case* (1905), a play of intense emotion, one of the finest types of melodrama our stage has known. The theme, the love of a wife for a husband, and the lengths to which she will go to save him from a false charge of murder, is made concrete in Margaret Rolfe, one of his most skillful characterizations. When her husband, Julian Rolfe, is accused of killing his friend, Philip Long, on account of his jealousy of Long's attachment to Claire Foster, whom Long was about to marry, Margaret wastes no time in natural feminine doubts of her husband's truth. She accepts his explanation that he had tried to save Long from a worthless woman, and she is contrasted with their attorney, Tompson, who is not in the beginning wholly convinced of Julian's innocence. At first glance it seems hardly likely that Margaret should give way so completely to her emotion at the end of the first Act when Julian is arrested, even trying to keep the police inspector off by force, and then should develop into the quiet intense woman of the next Act who plans to live with Claire Foster, to endure contact that she loathes, in order to worm out of Claire the evidence she needs to save her husband. But in reality it is just that intensity of her nature which justifies the great scene at the end of the third Act. Margaret has been living in the same apartment house with Claire for weeks; she has won her confidence by descending to her level of intrigue even to the assumption of an intimacy with Jimmy O'Neill, an old friend who helps her carry on the delusion. The supper scene in which Louis Klauffsky, a rich man who is keeping Claire, makes a fourth, is a masterly picture never overdone and carried naturally to a point where the men leave Margaret and Claire alone. Concealed in the next room, Tompson and an inspector listen while Margaret bit by bit draws out of Claire the description of Philip Long's suicide. Then when all is safely told she springs at Claire like a tigress and tells her who she is. The reaction is all the more powerful because of the earlier repression and all the more true because of Margaret's apparently hysterical outburst earlier in the play. Such intensity of action is usually called unnatural and "melodramatic." One is tempted to paraphrase and reply, "If this be melodrama, make the most of it." But as Fitch pointed out in his article "The Play and the Public," "One cannot live twenty-four hours in any of our cities without seeing vivid pictures of misery and happiness, vice and virtue, crime and innocence, poverty and wealth, in sharpest, loudest contrast— a daily life which is blood and iron mixed with soul and sentiment—melodrama of the ancients pure and simple." The danger of representing such intense scenes in which a woman lets her emotion control her is that in incompetent hands the scene becomes unpleasant through the shrillness of its interpretation. When Blanche Walsh played the part it was a triumph, and the success was repeated in other hands in Italy and in London. A reading of the scene will show how economical Fitch was in his demands upon the emotional reaction of his hearers. Not an unnecessary word is spoken by Margaret from the moment of her attack upon Claire until she falls unconscious on the floor. Yet she has in a few words epitomized the entire content of the character and she carries with every word the complete sympathy of the audience.

Perhaps the lightness and charm of *Her Great Match* (1905) came as a reaction from the intensity of *The Woman in the Case*. It is an international contrast in which the character of Jo Sheldon was written for Maxine Elliott, and the result was a popular success. Fitch placed against the background of a newly rich German family, who have lived some years in England, a love story between the Crown Prince Adolph of Eastphalia and Jo Sheldon, an American girl whose father is wealthy and whose stepmother is an accomplished scoundrel. His skill is shown in the opening act at a garden fête on the Botes estate, and our interest is excited by the picture of two young people charmingly in love with each other. One refreshing feature of the play is the omission of any sense of social hopelessness on the part of the American characters. The difficulties which threaten to prevent the match are official rather than social, and their solution through the relinquishment by the Prince of his right to reign is foreshadowed as soon as Jo makes clear to him that a morganatic marriage is out of the question. The few pointed words in which she draws a contrast between the basic conception of marriage in America and Germany reveals Fitch's complete understanding of his own country and of Europe. The play is better in characterization than his earlier international contrast, *The Stubbornness of Geraldine*, for not only are Jo and the Prince well drawn, but the whole Botes family are etched in skilfully, especially in the amusing scene on the morning after the party. Finally, as if for good measure, Fitch created in the Grand Duchess of Hohenstein, who is sent to break off the match but who becomes an ally, one of the most vivid characters in his plays, which the fine acting of Mathilde Cottrelly made memorable.

It was a busy period. The crisp melodrama of Western life, *Wolfville*, was adapted from a story by Alfred Henry Lewis; the reshaping of *Mistress Betty* into *The Toast of the Town* has already been described.

It is surprising at first glance that he did not make a success of his dramatization of Mrs. Wharton's novel *The House of Mirth* (1906). The theme of that story, the tragedy of a girl too fine to follow unquestioningly the rules of a selfish heartless social code and yet not strong enough to resist the appeal of its material luxury, was one to which Fitch certainly responded. That he felt the difficulties is evident, although none of the explanations he gives in his letters seems altogether convincing. For the story is really dramatic and the second scene of Act II, in Trenor's house, in which he follows the language of the book most closely, is the best in the play. That he saw the strength of the love story between Selden and Lily is to his credit, but the transfer of their exquisite scene of parting from Selden's rooms to the milliner's shop made any artistic ending difficult. In the novel, Lily goes to Selden through an uncontrollable impulse to see him once more before she takes the step, her marriage with Rosedale, which will separate them forever. Selden has nothing to say, for he has not yet recovered his belief in her, and since it is she who has taken the initiative, it is not necessary for him to say anything as yet. But in the play he is brought to the shop and then action on his part is demanded, and we are disappointed that he merely talks generalities. Again it is perhaps to Fitch's credit that he did not force a happy ending by attributing to Selden words and actions which are not in the novel, but it is surprising that the trained playwright could not see that the whole story is meaningless without the scene in Selden's rooms, for in it Mrs. Wharton lifted the novel to the lofty regions of feeling to which satire can never aspire. It is only fair, however, to add that Fitch made the dramatization after one refusal and under pressure, and it was probably his absorp-

tion in his original work, about to rise to its climax, which prevented the successful treatment of the work of another.

The Truth, which opened in Cleveland in September, 1906, was not written hastily but grew up from the conception of the central character, Becky Warder, a woman who is a natural liar. She is marvelously drawn, never forced in her deceit, which seems instinctive rather than deliberate, and Fitch has cleverly revealed in the first Act how the ordinary prevarications of social and business intercourse have built up for her a mould of insincerity into which later her serious purposes run. She loves her husband devotedly, but she flirts with Lindon just the same, for she likes to be liked, and she indulges in philandering all the more recklessly because she feels so secure in her real love for Tom Warder. He is her opposite, and just as Fitch drew John Austin without the vice of jealousy, so Tom Warder is the sensible, true man who provides the necessary contrast to Becky. She keeps our interest better than Jinny Austin, for she is less selfish; even the deception she practices on Tom concerning the money she is sending her father springs from her generosity. All the characters, especially Eve Lindon, the jealous wife, and Lindon, her caddish husband, throw Becky into sympathetic relief, and the crowning achievement was the creation of her father. Roland explains her, for he too is a liar and yet he is not merely a repetition of her. He is as masculine in his weaknesses as she is feminine, but the selfishness of age in his character makes her own more generous impulses appealing, just as his shabby careless habits reflect her impeccable neatness and greater refinement. When Warder leaves her, broken by the discovery of her falsehoods, she flies to her father in Baltimore as her only refuge. Fitch prepares for their meeting by one of the most remarkable scenes in modern comedy, in which Roland baffles his landlady, Mrs. Crespigny, who has determined to marry him. He does this without offending her, for his material comfort is dependent upon her. Just as Becky's lies often spring from not wishing to hurt anyone's feelings, so Roland gently holds Mrs.

Crespigny at a safe distance. She is a striking picture of her type, vain, good-hearted, and longing to be a lady, just as he is the best picture of a frayed gentleman in American drama. When Becky comes to him he does not believe her, for he knows her too well, but she finally convinces him through her appeal to the memory of her mother, who had suffered from his weakness. This little scene might easily have been unbearably sentimental, but Fitch held it to utter simplicity. Nothing but the expression of Roland's face and his words to Mrs. Crespigny, "Mrs. Warder's changed her mind. She's stopping here to-night," tell the revolution in his mind between distrust and conviction.

Fitch does not force a reconciliation. Roland, true to form, wires Warder that Becky is dying and stages an elaborate deception upon his arrival, to which Becky only half agrees. Mrs. Crespigny, whose one hope of happiness depends upon their continued separation, reveals to Tom the plan and Tom, in disgust, is about to return to New York when Becky thrusts the temptation aside and tells the truth in time. Warder believes her, and when she cries out that he cannot forgive her, he replies with the elemental truth, "We don't love people because they are perfect . . . we love them because they are themselves."

The Truth marks the crest of Fitch's effort. Never before in his career did he create such vivid pictures of real people, never did he portray with such apparent simplicity the complicated motives of human conduct. Every sentence tells, every speech leads to the climax or the conclusion, yet the result is the apparently effortless product of genius. It is comedy, for it is based upon human weakness, but it is high comedy, for Tom, Becky, even Roland are spirited people and without the contrast of social values there could hardly have been a play.

This smoothness of action, the very clarity and directness of the play, misled the critics in this country who saw little of its real greatness when it opened its New York engagement on January 7, 1907, with Clara Bloodgood in the leading part. There was some belated appreciation, but it came too late to save the play, which was withdrawn after thirty-four performances. But on April 6, 1907, it was produced at the Comedy Theatre in London with Marie Tempest as Becky, who scored a notable triumph. Encouraged by this success, it was revived next season by Mrs. Bloodgood in America on tour, until in December she shot herself. In 1914, Grace George made a successful revival of the comedy.

The Truth gave Fitch an international reputation. In Italy, Germany, Russia, Hungary and Scandinavia, the success of the play was universal. As a contrast to the unsympathetic notices appearing in the American press, the appreciation of the German critics was especially pleasing.[1] Fitch was called before the curtain three times when he attended the performance at Hamburg, and he saw the play in Rome, Genoa and Stuttgart.

It is a grim commentary upon the state of criticism in New York that while *The Truth* was unappreciated, *The Straight Road*, which opened on the same evening, was warmly greeted. This is a melodrama, at times sensational, whose central character, Hester Street Moll, nearly ruins her own happiness in attempting to open the eyes of her benefactress to the real character of the latter's lover. While the play is not to be compared with *The Truth* in permanent value, the characters are very human, and if Fitch drew in high light the difficulties such a woman would experience in pursuing the "straight road," his defence might lie in the pertinent fact that such difficulties are real. And Fitch gave the language of Hester Street just as correctly as the conversation of the drawing-room. Certainly it was more convincing as a picture of life

---

[1] The criticisms of the Berlin papers, especially those in the *Börsen-Courier, Vorwärts, Lokal-Anzieger* and *Post* for September 25, 1908, reveal the appreciation of the press. A quotation from *Vorwärts* will illustrate the tone of the criticisms:

"Eine mit Verstand, Geschmack und sicherem Bühnenblick durchgeführte Komödie, die sich von der flachen Harmlosigeit des deutschen Familien Lustspieltypus, wie von der Pikanterien und ausgeklügelten Verwechselungstricks des Pariser Schwankes in gleicher weise fernheit."

than *Her Sister* (1907), a domestic drama laid partly in a clairvoyant palmist's establishment in Bond Street, London, in which he collaborated with Cosmo Gordon-Lennox. *Toddles* (1906), an adaptation from Godferneaux and Bernard, was an amusing but trifling farce-comedy in which Fitch kept the foreign scene. There was more of his own quality in *Girls* (1908), an adaptation from *Die Welt ohne Männer*, by Engel and Horst. The picture of the three girls living in a studio in New York, with the pressure of economic necessity stressed just enough and their inevitable and natural desire for admiration breaking through their avowed hatred of men, is thoroughly characteristic.

Fitch felt that his name was appearing too frequently upon playbills at this moment, so he did not acknowledge publicly his share in the revision of *The Honor of the Family*, originally translated by Paul Potter from *La Rabouilleuse*, a dramatization by Emile Fabre of Balzac's novel. This play was an interesting example of collaboration. Potter's version was not satisfactory to Charles Frohman, so he asked Fitch to rewrite it. Then William Gillette suggested that Philippe Bridau should enter not at the beginning of Act II but at the end of Act I, and this change, which brings Bridau in with a flourish, turned the character into comedy while the original play in Paris presented him as a serious man of business. This play provided Otis Skinner with one of the greatest successes of his career.[1]

Notwithstanding illness and constant nervous fatigue, Fitch continued to produce rapidly. Such a light farce comedy as *The Blue Mouse* (1908), from the German, could have caused little effort in writing, but *The Bachelor* (1909) was an original play with real characters and his usual attention to detail. *A Happy Marriage* (1909) is even better, and merits more consideration than several of the published dramas. It is unified and coherent in its structure and every character has reality. Without subplot or comic relief, it attacks the situation

---

[1] *Footlights and Spotlights*, p. 284.

in which a husband and wife find themselves faced with an ebb tide in their love. Frederick Thornton turns to business, Joan to another man. This is old, of course, but then Fitch draws with skill the other man's unwillingness to play the game except for the passing moment, and the struggle of Joan Thornton to keep her ideal of the man for whom she is willing to lose her husband's love. Thornton is no hero—but he is master of each situation as it arises, and the fine scene in the second Act when he finds his wife in Paul Mayne's rooms and pretends to be deceived by her explanations in order to protect her, is worthy of Fitch at his best. There is another scene, between Thornton and Granger, Mayne's partner, in which there is a remarkable picture of two men, the surface of whose conversation hides an effort to preserve an ideal of conduct to which neither outwardly aspires. Fitch almost spoils the scene by Thornton's offer of business to Granger as an offset to his firm's losses, but perhaps the strain was already showing.

Even while Fitch was apparently engrossed with adaptations and rehearsals, he was brooding over what he intended to be the best work of his career. *The City* was conceived in 1908 and finished in June 1909, just before he sailed on his last visit to Europe. It was not produced until after his death. Worn out by excessive labor and nervous tension, he did not rally from the operation for appendicitis which was the immediate cause of his death at Châlons-sur-Marne, August 28, 1909. But *The City* was produced by the cast he had selected, on December 21, 1909, and was received with acclaim as one of the strongest of his plays.

Its general theme is the influence of the city upon the family who come from a small town where they have been the leading people for generations. But Fitch knew that such a theme must be made concrete and he soon establishes as the central character George Rand, Jr., whose father, the "foremost citizen" dies at the end of the first Act, after confessing that Hannock, who has been blackmailing him, is really his son. George has high ambitions, political and social, wishes to be of service, but has the twisted morality which his father has bequeathed him, and it needs the terrible situation which develops to startle him into a realization of truth. The nomination for the governorship is his if his record is clear. But Cicely, his youngest sister, marries Hannock, whom George has made his private secretary, out of a feeling of responsibility for his father's sin. They return to the house and George endeavors to persuade Cicely to give Hannock up. She refuses and George has to tell Hannock that he is her brother. Hannock, who is a drug fiend, goes almost insane and when Cicely re-enters, rather than allow her to be separated from him, shoots her and then himself attempts suicide. George prevents him from killing himself, although Hannock threatens him with a revelation of some of the questionable deals which George has carried on, and with the family disgrace. Fitch has conceived probably the strongest temptation under which a man could be brought, for there is also the probability that Eleanor Voorhees, to whom George is betrothed, will give him up if his real character and actions are disclosed. But the fine qualities that are in George Rand hold fast to the one inexorable fact that he has no right to allow Hannock to escape the law. The curtain goes down on a climax of character, and the last Act, in which he declines the nomination and goes through the humiliation of confessing all his derelictions to the man who has been his model and his political sponsor, is a moral tonic. All seems to be lost to him but honor, but Eleanor remains faithful to him, an action in keeping with her nature as we have been allowed to see it.

It would seem as though the New England conscience of his father's family animated Fitch in his last play. *The City* is a grim drama, and Fitch did not allow the blame for the failure of the Rand family in winning the height of their aspirations to be laid at the city's door. He shows how the city brings out in a man or woman's nature the largest values that are there, for good or evil. If they bring to the city great qualities, they may win from her great recognition in return, but if they are weaklings, they will inevitably fail.

Fitch's adaptations from French and German were as a rule hastily done, from translations made for him, although he read French easily. Usually he treated the material freely. In his adaptations from the German the characters were made American and in *Girls* the play was largely his own. In the adaptations from the French, generalizations are not so easy. Where the original was well-known, as in *Bohemia* or *Sapho*, he preserved the French scene and characters, but in a majority of instances he made the atmosphere American, as in *Granny* or *The Social Swim*. The most lasting impression from a study of his foreign adaptations is that of the facility in imposing upon the work of other men the individuality of his own manner. His happiest results came when he treated the material with the greatest freedom.

In considering the work of Clyde Fitch as a whole, the first misconception that must be dispelled is that of excessive production. Disregarding his twenty-two adaptations of foreign plays and dramatizations of novels, there remain thirty-three original plays, for *The Moth and the Flame* and *The Toast of the Town* are revisions of earlier work. Thirty-three original plays in twenty years is not an extraordinary total; in fact it yields about the average of Shakespeare. While his adaptations took comparatively little effort, his original work was slowly developed in his mind and he came to its creation on paper with plan and even dialogue often fully conceived. It is true that he worked under pressure, but it is also true that to a man of his temperament pressure acted as a stimulant to creative effort.

A classification of Fitch's work at first seems to indicate an extensive variety in the selection of material and method of treatment. England, France and the United States in the Seventeenth, Eighteenth, Nineteenth and Twentieth Centuries; city life and rural life; the East, the Middle and the Far West, all have been treated with varying success. But as a matter of fact, with Clyde Fitch neither locality nor period was the prime inspiration, and any classification based upon them is confusing. He experimented with American history when the vogue of historical romance made it a popular motive; he ventured into unfamiliar scenes in the West, perhaps unwisely; his love of beauty made him luxuriate in the costumes and settings of an earlier day, but from *Beau Brummell* to *The City* the real inspiration of Clyde Fitch came from his unremitting study of men and women in their social and personal relations. In *Barbara Frietchie* or *Major André* the Civil War or the Revolution was the point of departure; what remains are the charming pictures of social life in Fredericksburg or in New York. George IV and Charles II are not historical figures in *Beau Brummell* or *His Grace de Grammont;* they are part of the social setting of more important characters. While Captain Jinks is redolent of the seventies, there is no historical figure; it is the force of social prejudice typified in Mrs. Jinks that almost wrecks the love story. And in *Lovers' Lane* the rural setting is only a means for satire upon the littleness of small-town life.

It was not satire, however, which makes Fitch's best work emerge more and more clearly from the plays of the period. Satire alone never keeps a play alive, and though Fitch could portray feminine weakness, selfishness and heartlessness as well as any playwright of his time, it was his steady refusal to limit his art to the satiric form which proved his essential strength.

Fitch will be finally remembered for his studies of human characters who are endowed with a shining virtue or possessed by one absorbing vice. Consciously or unconsciously, he was following the example of the writers of the medieval moralities, but his sense of the theatre clothed his abstractions with a concreteness that makes the characters living things. Beau Brummell is the incarnation of the phrase, "There are some things a gentleman cannot do." Practically all the characters in *The Climbers* are the representatives of ambition. Nathan Hale represents patriotism; Barbara Frietchie, love in conflict with patriotism; Geraldine Lang, trust; Jinny Austin, jealousy; Georgiana Carley, courage; Jo Sheldon, self-respect; Becky Warder, unreliability; Margaret Rolfe, wifely devotion; George Rand, Jr., ambition. This emotional content of the leading character gives a unity to the play which is, in some way, a measure of its merit, for *Beau Brummell*, *The Climbers*, *The Truth*, *The Girl with the Green Eyes*, and *The Woman in the Case*, in which the basic emotion stands out most clearly, are perhaps also the plays easiest to establish as permanent contributions to dramatic literature. Certainly the vividness of the emotion of the central character acts and reacts upon the others and they are brightened rather than dulled by its glow. The emotions are universal, too, recognizable to all humanity, which accounts for the international success of *The Truth* and *The Woman in the Case*.

But Clyde Fitch knew that unity is only one quality of high art. Variety is almost as essential, and his rich inventive faculty provided such delightful minor creations as Roland and Mrs. Crespigny in *The Truth*, Mortimer in *Beau Brummell*, the Grand Duchess in *Her Great Match*, or Johnny Trotter in *The Climbers*. It is to be noticed that the trained playwright never let these minor characters disturb the serenity of the star. They amplified or set off the main character for whom the play was written, and they fitted into a structure so compact that in the best plays it has taken on the inevitability of a result.

It is not necessary here to recapitulate the weaknesses which make any study of Fitch an exercise in discrimination. That such discrimination was not at his service to any large extent during his lifetime is a matter of regret, for he could have profited by it. He was keen for helpful criticism, as his letters show, but the criticism that depreciated *The Truth* and hailed *The Straight Road* as "a real play," on the same day, helped him little. For while others wrote historical plays and vivid melodrama, his contribution to our drama lies primarily in the portraiture of American men and women, prevented by their social inhibitions from frank expression of their complete natures, but presenting in the consequent struggle a drama quiet yet intense, so restrained in power that his own generation mistook its fineness for weakness. There has rarely been so complete a reversal of critical judgment, for he is now placed securely among the foremost writers of high comedy and his death at the height of his power is beginning to be looked upon as a tragedy in our dramatic history.